The Complete Book Of Counseling The Dying And The Grieving

A Book
Of
Practical Counseling Tools,
Inspiring Patient Stories,
And
Edifying Quotations

By
Douglas C. Smith, MA, MS, MDiv
Author
Of
The Tao Of Dying
Caregiving: Hospice-Proven Techniques For Healing Body And Soul
Being A Wounded Healer
Spiritual Healing

Copyright 2003 by Douglas C. Smith

All rights reserved.

Portions of this book come from Doug's previous books *Caregiving* and *Spiritual Healing*. There is also much new material. All the tools, stories, therapeutic suggestions, and quotations from Doug's seminars are contained in the book.

This book, or any parts thereof, may not be used or reproduced in any manner without the written permission of the author.

Douglas C. Smith
Psycho-Spiritual Publications
601 N. Segoe Road, Suite 305
Madison, Wisconsin 53705

Printed in the United States of America

ISBN 0-9672870-3-0

Contents

Chapter 1: Assessments

Strength Assessments (counseling tool)	13
The Preacher (patient story)	15
The Dancer (patient story)	17
Focusing On Jane's Strengths (patient story)	18
The Vaudeville Magician (patient story)	19
Assessing Personal Strength, Peace, And Security (counseling tool)	21
The Writer (patient story)	22
Focusing Upon Meaningful Symbols (counseling tool)	22
Gertrude (patient story)	23
Scott's Strength (patient story)	24
Psycho-Social Comfort Assessment Form (counseling tool)	25
A Problem Assessment Form (counseling tool)	26
Family Strength Assessment (counseling tool)	27
Assessing Someone's Grieving Style (counseling tool)	28
Wally's And Djuna's Grieving Styles (patient story)	29
Assessing For The Physical Dimensions (counseling tool)	30

Chapter 2: Care Plans

Allowing Our Roles To Be Defined (counseling tool)	33
One Question Care Plans For The Dying (counseling tool)	37
Tim's Truck (patient story)	38
The Fishing Trip (patient story)	39
Rick's Campfire (patient story)	41
One Last Christmas (patient story)	42
One Question Care Plans For The Grieving (counseling tool)	42
The Canoe Trip (patient story)	43
Self-Care Plan For A Person Who Is Grieving (counseling tool)	44
From "I Need" To "I Can Get" (counseling tool)	45
My Ideal Death (counseling tool)	46
Hawaii (patient story)	47
Guided Imagery: The Medicine Man (counseling tool)	48

Using Some Detective Work (patient story)	49
Finding Some Contained Space (patient story)	50

Chapter 3: Addressing The Emotional/Psychological Concerns Of The Terminally Ill

Last Request (counseling tool)	53
The Smell Of A Horse (patient story)	53
Werther's Candy And A Beer (patient story)	54
Just One Little Pill (patient story)	54
Get Out Of My Room (patient story)	56
The Imaginary Sledgehammer (counseling tool)	57
Here: Try Me (counseling tool)	57
Susan And Her Release Room (patient story)	58
Naughty Words (patient story)	59
Sam (patient story)	60
Glenda (patient story)	61
Vicky (patient story)	62
Willy And Clara (patient story)	63
Andy (patient story)	64
Elmer (patient story)	65
High Energy And Regular Bowels (patient story)	65
Giving Control To An "Unresponsive" Patient (counseling tool)	66
Kind Words (patient story)	67
The Radio Announcer (patient story)	68
Speedball (patient story)	69
Christopher's Father (patient story)	70
A Simple Life Review (counseling tool)	71
Amanda (patient story)	72
Linda (patient story)	73
Photographic Life Review (counseling tool)	74
Pass It On (counseling tool)	74
Recording A Message (counseling tool)	75
People's Impressions (counseling tool)	76
Candy (patient story)	77
Mabel (patient story)	78
Nelson (patient story)	79
Rosie's First Visit (patient story)	80
I Fooled You (patient story)	81
La Cucaracha (patient story)	82
Smiling And Laughing Permitted Here (counseling tool)	83
Lucy (patient story)	84

Wolfgang And Rudolf (patient story)	85
A Funny Life Review (counseling tool)	86
Funny Videos (counseling tool)	87
Affirmations (counseling tool)	87
Random Acts Of Kindness (counseling tool)	88
End-Life Crisis (counseling tool)	89
Eliminating Self-Blaming Over Illness (counseling tool)	89
The Grass Can Sometimes Be Browner (counseling tool)	91
Guided Imagery: Dialogue With Death (counseling tool)	92
Guided Imagery: My Funeral (counseling tool)	93
Bill's Choice (patient story)	95
Esther's Choice (patient story)	95
Kammy's Choice (patient story)	96
Tricia's Patient (patient story)	97
Dorreen's Brother (patient story)	98
Cathy (patient story)	99
Invasion Of Privacy (patient story)	100
Dottie's Son (patient story)	101
Manny And Nathan (patient story)	102
The Birthday Party (patient story)	103
The Wedding Anniversary (patient story)	103
Family Discussion (counseling tool)	104
Coupons (counseling tool)	104
Sharing Dreams (counseling tool)	105
Giveaway Ceremony (counseling tool)	105
Family Litany As Death Is Near (counseling tool)	106
Clyde's Wife (patient story)	107
Naomi's Husband (patient story)	108

Chapter 4: Addressing The Emotional/Psychological Concerns Of The Grieving

No Time Table (patient story)	109
Standing, Waiting (patient story)	110
Keeping A Grief Diary (counseling tool)	111
Memory Book (counseling tool)	112
Memory Collage (counseling tool)	113
Memory Quilt (counseling tool)	113
Memory Jar (counseling tool)	113
The Memorial Sculpture (patient story)	114
A "Fitting" Memorial (patient story)	115
A "Dead Denny Party" (patient story)	115

Relationship Life Review (counseling tool)	115
The Fun(ny) Times (counseling tool)	116
Guided Imagery: Dialogue With The Lost One (counseling tool)	117
Service Of Remembrance (counseling tool)	118
Litany Of Remembrance (counseling tool)	119
Seeing-Eye Dog (patient story)	120
Losing Everything (patient story)	120
No "Me" (patient story)	121
Away On A Business Trip (counseling tool)	121
A Systematic Approach	
Step One: Loss Intensity Graph (counseling tool)	122
Step Two: Relationship Complexity Graphs (counseling tool)	123
Step Three: 5, 4, 3, 2, 1 - Recovery Has Begun (counseling tool)	124
A Systematic Approach	
Step One: The Treasures (counseling tool)	125
Step Two: The Tragedies (counseling tool)	126
Step Three: The Transitory And In-Transitory (counseling tool)	127
A Systematic Approach	
Step One: Accepting The Reality Of The Loss (counseling tool)	128
Step Two: Working Through The Pain (counseling tool)	128
Step Three: Filling Some Of The Gaps (counseling tool)	129
Step Four: Moving On With Life (counseling tool)	129
A Letter To Finish The Unfinished (counseling tool)	130
Affirmations (counseling tool)	131
Guided Imagery: Experiencing Unity (counseling tool)	132
Tom Was A Gruff Man (patient story)	133
The Best Sermon (patient story)	134
My Commitment To Myself (counseling tool)	135
Becoming Pro-Active With The Re-Active (counseling tool)	136
Intentions (counseling tool)	137
Opening Up To Wonder (counseling tool)	138
Life-Giving Energy (counseling tool)	138
Creating A Buddy System (counseling tool)	139
Being My Own Best Caregiver (counseling tool)	139
The Monthly Checkup (counseling tool)	140
Todd's Wishbone (patient story)	141
Rose (patient story)	142

Chapter 5: Emotional/Psychological Tools For Use With Either The Terminally Ill Or Grieving

Conscious Breathing (counseling tool)	143
In With The Good, Out With The Bad (counseling tool)	144
Guided Imagery: Forgiveness, Love, And Peace (counseling tool)	144
Peace In My Body, Peace In Your Body (counseling tool)	146
Helping Ourselves By Helping Others (counseling tool)	147
The Joy Of Serving (counseling tool)	148
Reflections (counseling tool)	148
Crushed (patient story)	151
Body Revitalization (counseling tool)	151
"I Need A Hug" Card (counseling tool)	152
Personal Mantra (counseling tool)	152
The Bird Meditation (counseling tool)	153
Guided Imagery: Garden Of Tranquility (counseling tool)	153
Not-In-Labor Meditation (counseling tool)	155
Recipe For Comfort (counseling tool)	155
Anger Time (counseling tool)	156
Releasing Anger (counseling tool)	156
Oh, Tractor! (counseling tool)	157
Hitting, Ripping, And Stomping Anger Away (counseling tool)	157
It Is Okay To Cry (counseling tool)	158
The Truth Shall Set You Free (counseling tool)	159
Finding Relief From Stress (counseling tool)	160
Countering Irrationality (counseling tool)	161
Time For Reframing (counseling tool)	162
Desires As Realities (counseling tool)	163
Being Thankful (counseling tool)	164
Singing (counseling tool)	164
Picture This (counseling tool)	165
Positive Exchanges (counseling tool)	166
I Can Be By Own Family (counseling tool)	166
Do Not Straighten Out (counseling tool)	167

Chapter 6: Addressing The Spiritual/Religious Concerns Of The Terminally Ill

My Spiritual Travelogue (counseling tool)	170
A Dying Person's Dream Journal (counseling tool)	170
Guided Imagery: A Christian Conversation (counseling tool)	172
Guided Imagery: A Jewish Conversation (counseling tool)	173

Guided Imagery: A Buddhist Conversation (counseling tool)	174
Guided Imagery: A Naturalist Conversation (counseling tool)	175
Purpose (patient story)	176
Giving Assignments (counseling tool)	178
Letter From My Higher Self (counseling tool)	178
Leaving Nothing To Chance (patient story)	179
Carol's Grandmother (patient story)	180
God's Breath (counseling tool)	180
Object Meditation (counseling tool)	181
Hazel (patient story)	181
Andrew (patient story)	183
Jean (patient story)	184
Tanya (patient story)	185
Guided Imagery: Family Reunion (counseling tool)	186
Prayers (counseling tools)	187

Chapter 7: Addressing The Spiritual/Religious Concerns Of The Grieving

Private Service Of Remembrance (counseling tool)	193
When Not Being Present At A Funeral (counseling tool)	194
Anniversary Service Of Remembrance (counseling tool)	194
The Ancient Stone Ceremony (counseling tool)	195
Altar Of Remembrance (counseling tool)	196
Letting Go Ritual (counseling tool)	197
River Of Life (counseling tool)	197
A Bereaved Person's Spiritual Affirmations (counseling tool)	198
A Bereaved Person's Dream Journal (counseling tool)	199
Forgiving The Person Who Has Died (counseling tool)	200
Graham's Stepfather (patient story)	201
Ritual Of Self-Forgiveness (counseling tool)	201
Resolving Guilt (counseling tool)	202
Darcey (patient story)	203
Treena (patient story)	203
Alternative Holiday Rituals (counseling tool)	204
The First Christmas After A Death (counseling tool)	204
The Holiday Tablecloth (counseling tool)	205
Guided Imagery: Releasing Your Loved One (counseling tool)	205
Jennifer (patient story)	206
Donald (patient story)	207
Prayers (counseling tools)	208

Chapter 8: Spiritual/Religious Tools For Use With Either The Terminally Ill Or Grieving

A Spiritual Assessment: Word Association (counseling tool)	212
A Spiritual Assessment: Exploratory Questions (counseling tool)	212
A Spiritual Assessment: President Of The Board (counseling tool)	213
A Spiritual Assessment: Dean Of The Seminary (counseling tool)	213
Jim (patient story)	214
A Withering Faith (patient story)	216
A God Who Is In The Pain (patient story)	216
A Blossoming Faith (patient story)	216
How Can I Use This (counseling tool)	217
A Wounded Healer Resume (counseling tool)	218
Joys And Concerns Altar (counseling tool)	219
Showing Some Spiritual Muscle (counseling tool)	220
Spiritual Explorations Based On Taoist Thought (counseling tool)	221
Spiritual Explorations Based On Christian Thought (counseling tool)	222
Spiritual Explorations Based On Hindu Thought (counseling tool)	223
Spiritual Explorations Based On Buddhist Thought (counseling tool)	224
Spiritual Explorations Based On Jewish Thought (counseling tool)	225
Celebrating Life (counseling tool)	226
Giving Thanks (counseling tool)	227
Dedicating Oneself To Living A Sacred Life (counseling tool)	228
Changing Philosophy (counseling tool)	229
Guided Imagery: My Loving Companion (counseling tool)	230
Guided Imagery: On Peace (counseling tool)	231
Guided Imagery: The Holy Woman (counseling tool)	232
Guided Imagery: My Sacred Temple (counseling tool)	234
Guided Imagery: The Gift Of Holiness (counseling tool)	235
Reward Yourself (counseling tool)	236
Prayers (counseling tools)	237

Chapter 9: Additional Tools To Increase A Caregiver's Effectiveness

The Ideal Counselor (counseling tool)	244
The Ideal Nurse (counseling tool)	244
The Ideal Chaplain (counseling tool)	245
Caregiver Exercise: Perceiving The Holy Incarnate (counseling tool)	246
Dropping Our Armor (patient story)	249
Kristen And Dr. Albers (patient story)	250
Dropping The Clinical Distance (patient story)	251

More Dropping Of Clinical Distance (patient story)	252
Sometimes We're Just Not Needed (patient story)	253
Charlie (patient story)	254
Giver/Receiver Dialogue (counseling tool)	254
Becoming The Client/Patient (counseling tool)	255
Nourishing Touch (counseling tool)	256
Sensual Back Rub (counseling tool)	256
Foot Washing (counseling tool)	257
Sharing The Silence (counseling tool)	257
Tonglen (counseling tool)	258
Looking Forward To Tomorrow (counseling tool)	259
Appreciation Award (counseling tool)	260
Changing The Caregiver's "I Need" To "I Want" (counseling tool)	261
Caregiver's Report Card (counseling tool)	262
A Day's Reward (counseling tool)	262
Who Am I? (counseling tool)	263
Prayers (counseling tools)	264
Bibliography	273
Doug Smith's Workshops	284
Ordering Doug Smith's Books	286

Forward

This book draws upon my 25 years of experience in working with the dying and grieving and my 10 years of doing seminars on that work.

I have found that counseling theories can be found everywhere; anyone and everyone seems to have thoughts about what constitutes good caregiving. However, counselors, nurses, social workers, ministers, family, and friends of the dying and grieving want practical tools – not theory or philosophy. This book is for such people: those who want to <u>do something</u> for those in their care.

This book offers practical tools to address people's needs and concerns in the emotional/psychological arena as well as the spiritual/religious arena. With both areas a broad perspective is taken; a wide variety of psychological and spiritual perspectives and struggles are addressed. This is why I have chosen to use the word "complete" in the book's title: this book addresses the whole person from multiple viewpoints.

One final thing must be said before you begin using this book: thank you. Thank you for choosing to work with the dying and grieving. You have chosen to do work that is both honorable and rewarding.

Chapter One

Assessments

STRENGTH ASSESSMENTS

Oftentimes strength assessments can be more valuable than problem assessments: (1) strength assessments can have more long-lasting significance – problems, and their significance, can change daily (especially for the terminally ill and grieving), whereas strengths (especially coping styles) rarely change from day to day, (2) with strength assessments resources are uncovered that can be applied to any and every problem – no matter how often those problems change, no matter what their degree of intensity, and (3) with strength assessments independence and self-help is encouraged over dependence. Any of the following questions could be asked by the caregiver to uncover a care recipient's strengths:

    A. What are your three greatest strengths?
    B. What compliments have you received from family and friends?
    C. When family and friends have turned to you for help, what kind of help have they usually been seeking?
    D. What have you done in your life of which you are proud?
    E. Tell me about some of the things in your past in which you have felt that you have been at your best. What qualities did you show at those times?
    F. When your life is over, what things are people going to miss the most about you?

A CONSIDERATION: As caregivers, we often focus on *our* strengths rather than the strengths of our care recipients. We think: "I spent all this money on my education; I better get my money's worth." Or we think: "I have all this experience; it better be worth something." Yet, our goal is to make our care recipients feel strong, not us. So we need to assess for a care recipient's strengths and feed his or her strengths, not our strengths.

A CONSIDERATION: We need to get away from always assessing our care recipients for their problems. They are already well aware of their problems: that's why they came to us in the first place. We do not need to continually remind them of those problems. However, they have oftentimes forgotten all about their strengths. We do a better service when we remind a care recipient of his or her own strengths, and feed those strengths, releasing them from dependence upon our strengths – empowering them.

"Paradoxically, by withdrawing into ourselves, not out of self-pity but out of humility, we create the space for another to be himself [or herself] and to come to us on his [or her] own terms." - Henri Nouwen.

"I began to see that thinking I knew what a person needed or even where they were or what was going on with them was disrespectful and a form of control. I began to see that my subtle forms of 'interpretation' were disrespectful and doing the [person's] work for him or her, which in itself is a form of disrespect. I was catching on to the myriad subtle little ways that I threw in 'suggestions,' 'interpretations,' 'I remember whens,' 'I wonder ifs,' and so on. More disrespect!" - Anne Wilson Schaef.

"In our best moments as helpers, we encourage clients to look inside for the wisdom to make healthy choices. . . . To do this, we must resist our impulses to provide them with all the answers, to point out what they are doing wrong, and to single-handedly meet all their needs." - Dale Larson.

A CONSIDERATION: With a strength assessment, different from a problem assessment, we are given a map for healing; we know *how* to proceed in the journey to healing. With a problem assessment we only know *where* we need to go, but we have no idea of *how* to get there.

THE PREACHER

Tyrone was a great preacher; preaching was his greatest strength. Every Sunday his church would have standing room only. He was not a great pastoral counselor; he did not even feel there was much value in counseling. He was terrible at socializing, having very little people skills. However, his preaching was superb; that was certainly his greatest strength.

When Tyrone's wife died, his grief was intense. Yet he did not want to go to a counselor because he did not place much value in counseling. He also did not want to join some grief group because of his poor people skills.

Tyrone's best friend had a suggestion on how Tyrone might process his grief: do it through sermons. Tyrone's friend suggested that Tyrone try to make reference to his wife or their relationship in some of his sermons, setting a goal of 4-6 sermons a year, thinking that number would be simultaneously therapeutic for Tyrone as it was tasteful and instructive for his congregation. Tyrone was thereby working through his loss, processing his grief, in the best way he knew how to do that – through his preaching, his greatest strength.

A CONSIDERATION: Oftentimes, as caregivers, we need to just step back and witness someone take charge of his or her own life. It is a difficult task, but sometimes a very important one: to realize that some people don't want us, some people don't need us.

"When our agenda is to fix or cure, the focus is on ourselves as 'ego-heroes.' . . . In caring, the helper never becomes the focus of the experience." - Carol Montgomery.

"Many people are caught in the Messiah Trap. . . . Messiahs try to be helpful wherever they go. . . . By saying 'No!' to the Messiah Trap, you allow others to take responsibility for their own lives and for the development of their own self-esteem." - Carmen Renee Berry.

A CONSIDERATION: The empowering caregiver communicates the following: "Let's focus on your strengths. If you need any help from me, I'd be glad to help. However, let's first focus on your strengths."

A CONSIDERATION: Many times we have nothing to give other people; but we do have the obligation to open people up to the beauty and strength within their own lives, to give them opportunities to discover the blessings and gifts they already have.

THE DANCER

Kira's life had always centered around dance. She had started dance lessons when she was only four years old. She had majored in dance in college. She had led dance workshops around the country for her income — usually accompanied by her other love, her adopted daughter, Tamara.

One Saturday, between trips with her mom, Tamara rode her bicycle into the street, was struck by a car, and died instantly. Kira was devastated. She canceled a couple months of workshops, seriously questioning how she could ever dance again.

Kira's therapist suggested that Kira not only continue dancing, but that she make her dances an ongoing expression of her love and grief for Tamara. When her dances were to express joy, she would dance the joy she felt with Tamara and the joy she saw in Tamara. When her dances were to express sadness, she would dance the grief she felt in losing her daughter. When her dances were to express love, she would actually imagine herself dancing with or before Tamara. Kira's therapist was helping Kira grieve by feeding Kira's strength: her ability to dance.

A CONSIDERATION: The goal of caregiving is not to make the caregiver feel good and strong; the goal of caregiving is to make the care recipient feel good and strong. (A) If we are working with a terminally ill man and we know that one of his strengths is his faith, we know about a resource that he has of which we can remind him. Thus he realizes that he has some strengths and does not have to rely upon us for his well-being. He consequently will gain a sense of control. He will also be able to find meaning and value in the midst of his pain and suffering even if it is not removed. (B) If we are working with a terminally ill woman and we know that one of her strengths is her humor, we know about a resource that she has of which we can remind her. Thus she realizes that she has some strengths and does not have to rely upon us for her well-being. She consequently will gain a sense of control. She will also be able to find meaning and value in the midst of her woundedness even if it is not removed.

A CONSIDERATION: Good caregiving focuses upon the *client's/patient's* strengths and resources, not *our* strengths and resources.

FOCUSING ON JANE'S STRENGTHS

Jane was a hospice patient experiencing a great amount of anxiety. I had her close her eyes and imagine herself on a beach in Hawaii. I had her imagine palm trees swaying in the tropical breeze, the fresh smell of sweet flowers and salt air. I had her match her breathing to gentle ocean waves coming in and going out, coming in and going out, coming in and going out.

Rather than seeing Jane relax, I saw her appear to increase in anxiety. Her breathing was becoming more rapid, her hands had formed fists, her neck appeared to be straining up and forward. I had Jane open her eyes and asked her what was happening. She said, "Doug, those ocean waves were frightening me. I don't know how to swim." Then I realized my mistake. I needed to concentrate on Jane's resources, not mine or anyone else's.

I asked Jane to think of a day from her past, a day that was very relaxing and peaceful. A day immediately came to her mind. She said, "Doug, I was the mother of six children. I remember quite clearly the day the last child left home. A heavenly peace just descended upon me. My husband and I decided to celebrate by going to a bed and breakfast. While there I got to open up and read a book I'd been wanting to read for months. That's the day I remember. It was simply heavenly."

The next time Jane felt anxiety, I said, "Jane, can you close your eyes now. I want to take you back to a place I'm sure you remember. Do you remember that day that your last child left home? . . . Do you remember going to that bed and breakfast with your husband? . . . Can you picture that bed and breakfast in your mind? . . . Do you remember what it looked like? . . . Do you remember how you felt being there? . . . Do you remember opening up that book and turning one page after another without interruption, . . . one page after another, . . . one page after another? . . ."

A CONSIDERATION: Just stepping back, not imposing, not interfering, can be very important – very important. Not interfering can be a great virtue among caregivers.

THE VAUDEVILLE MAGICIAN

Jack had at one time been a Vaudeville magician. At that time magic was not just his livelihood, it was his passion; it was his religion; it was his strength.

When Vaudeville had closed down, magic was so important to Jack that he wanted to continue it in whatever way he could. He and his wife Leona decided to advertise on the back of comic books that if any child were to send them a certain amount of money Jack and Leona would send that child mimeographed pages of magic tricks. Later those magic tricks got to be in a published booklet, and Jack and Leona made a living selling that booklet.

Jack was dying in the hospital, and Leona came to me quite distraught. She had just been told by a nurse that Jack had twenty-four hours or less to live. What was additionally distressing was that Jack was hallucinating and did not recognize Leona, and Leona wanted to have some quality time with Jack during those final hours. Leona asked if I might go visit Jack, but she forewarned me to expect almost anything because of Jack's hallucinations.

I went to the hospital. As I walked into Jack's room I saw that he was propped up in the bed with some pillows. As soon as I entered the room Jack addressed me by name. He said, "Doug, we have been waiting for you." As far as I could see there was not any "we" in the room. However, I decided to go along with whatever Jack was experiencing.

He next said, "Doug, today you are going to be initiated into the International Brotherhood Of Magicians."

He followed that statement with a chain of nonsensical words that sounded like some sort of magical incantation. After he ended that chain of words he said, "Doug, come closer." I walked up to the side of his bed. "Closer," he said. "You must be closer." I leaned over.

He then said, "Doug, I'm going to teach you a trick. It's the greatest trick of all. But first you must be closer." Before he said that final "closer" my face was about a foot and a half away from Jack's face and I felt uncomfortable at that distance. But I leaned in a little further. Jack had that look that people can sometimes have when they're looking *through* our eyes. He held that expression until he knew he had my undivided attention. Then he whispered, "Doug, watch me disappear."

Then Jack died.

As you can imagine, I still get shivers recalling that event. But the importance of that event becomes clear when I think about me challenging Jack upon entering that room: "Jack, there's no 'we' in the room. You need to talk sense." Or, if midway through that magic trick I was to say: "Jack this is not a time for magic. You're dying, and we need to talk about that." If I would have said either of those things I would have ruined something that was obviously very meaningful for Jack; I cannot imagine a better death for a magician than the death that Jack died. But I also would have ruined something that ended up being meaningful for me; I was allowed to experience a reality that was not my own and was thus allowed to experience something very special, something I had never experienced before and haven't since.

I just stood there absorbing all the power of that event. Then a worry started to crop up: how is Leona going to feel that she was not here for this, and how am I going to tell her about what just happened. So, with a fair amount of fear I went back to Leona and told her the story. Leona's reaction: "Oh, Doug. I'm so glad he did that with you! I know his tricks way ahead of time. It wouldn't have worked with me! And I know he would have wanted to die in such a way. That was the best possible death he could have ever had."

A CONSIDERATION: By just focusing on problems rather than strengths we are communicating a very destructive message. We are communicating: "You're the one with all the problems, I'm the one with all the strengths." We are communicating: "You've gotten your life kind of messed up. Why don't you hand it over to me because I'm now in charge. I'm now in control, not you." We are communicating a message that encourages dependence; we are communicating a relationship of dominance.

A CONSIDERATION: Assessing only for problems could even create problems. A care recipient could think: "I need to claim problems in order to get my caregiver to give me any attention." A care recipient could think: "I guess I'm not really sick enough to receive care unless I have this problem and that problem." A care recipient could certainly even develop depression and anxiety from just hearing about all the problems typically associated with their diagnosis or their situation.

ASSESSING PERSONAL STRENGTH, PEACE, AND SECURITY

A client/patient could be asked to write down or verbalize answers to the following questions. This assessment discovers a care recipient's psychological resources.

    A. Strength:
        1. What is "strength" for you?
        2. Where can you go to get it?
        3. Who gives it to you?
        4. How can you get more?
    B. Peace:
        1. What is "peace" for you?
        2. Where can you go to get it?
        3. Who gives it to you?
        4. How can you get more?
    C. Security:
        1. What is "security" for you?
        2. Where can you go to get it?
        3. Who gives it to you?
        4. How can you get more?

THE WRITER

Jan had always enjoyed writing poems. It became her personal strength, peace, and security. It gave her an opportunity to be self-expressive, giving her the strength that can come from simply being able to be oneself. It gave her an opportunity to retreat from an over-demanding and often terrifying world, giving her a refuge of peace. It gave her an opportunity to latch onto something that was ever constant; no matter what was happening to her or her world, she always had the security of her paper, her pen, and herself.

As Jan approached death, her hospice social worker encouraged her to continue to write her poems, to express all her feelings and thoughts about her dying through poetry. Jan could thereby have strength, peace, and security even in the midst of her dying.

FOCUSING UPON MEANINGFUL SYMBOLS

A care recipient could be asked to gather two to five objects to place on a small table. These objects would symbolize what is most important in the person's life, what gives this person's life meaning and purpose, what this person most cherishes about his/her life, the sources of his/her strength. The objects could also be described as "the glue" that holds the person's life together. Possible objects could include:

A. A book or a couple of books
B. A photograph or a couple of photographs
C. Religious objects
D. Mementos
E. Art work
F. Materials gathered from nature
G. A letter, letters, or other personal documents
H. A record, CD, or tape of a musical piece.

GERTRUDE

I asked Gertrude if she would be willing, before my next visit with her, to place two to five objects on a table to represent her beliefs and values, her strengths and resources, "the glue" that holds her world together. I told her I would be honored if at that next visit she would share with me what she felt was most important for her by showing me what she had placed on that table.

When I returned I discovered that she had only put one object on the table and it was a photograph of a dog, a German shepherd dog. (I thought I had perhaps failed to properly explain the assignment.) Yet, I asked her why she had chose that picture, and only that picture, to represent her beliefs and values.

She responded by saying that five years previously she had gone through a very messy divorce where all of her former friends had sided with her ex-husband — no one had sided with her. Everyone treated her differently after the divorce, everyone except for her dog, her German shepherd dog. She said, "Doug, if you want to talk to me about my beliefs and values, my strengths and resources, or anything like that, you talk to me in those terms: that unconditional love that dog had for me that no one else had for me." (I think she understood the assignment quite well.)

"There are many situations where you as helper do solve the problem in the sense that you provide a medication, share some specific information, teach a skill, or massage a sore back. This kind of active assistance is necessary and vital in caregiving; sometimes it is all that is needed. But when we look at emotional difficulties, interpersonal dilemmas, treatment decisions, and other psychosocial problems, the appropriateness of the patient as problem-solver becomes more clear-cut. Here, even though you are active and may even teach skills or offer educational input, the responsibility for change remains with the client." - Dale Larson.

A CONSIDERATION: We might find ourselves working with people who feel they do not have any strengths. Then we might have to do some detective work: make observations, ask questions, hazard some guesses. Yet, we need to discover those strengths, and then feed them. Everyone has strengths: it is our duty as caregivers to find those strengths and feed them.

SCOTT'S STRENGTH

Scott was an Alzheimer's patient: a very difficult one. In fact, he was thought to be the most unmanageable patient on a ward of forty Alzheimer's patients. What made Scott so unmanageable was a particular habit he had. Whenever Scott would get a mess in his diaper he would immediately stick his hand into that diaper, take out what was there, and smear it on the walls.

Now that was a problem! Of course the staff would try their best to stop Scott. The staff would run to him as soon as they saw him grunting, hold him down on his back, and change those diapers before he could even reach into them. However, as anyone can imagine, more times than not, the staff was unable to anticipate Scott's bowel movements, and so they would then have the terrible task of cleaning the walls. That was certainly a problem!

One of Scott's caregivers was so imaginative that she perceived Scott's supposed problem as a strength; she saw Scott's problem as a strength in disguise. She came to the conclusion that Scott was a great artist, a truly great artist: he literally could take shit and make it into art.

Once this caregiver discovered Scott's strength, she fed the strength. She supplied Scott with finger paints and newsprint each morning. Scott never reached into his diapers again.

A CONSIDERATION: If we want to assess for problems, we would do the least amount of harm and the most amount of good by having an assessment form that mixes positively worded statements (or questions) with negatively worded statements (or questions). Such a mixture will probably give us a more accurate picture of the client/patient: not showing our biases or expectations.

PSYCHO-SOCIAL COMFORT ASSESSMENT FORM

A = Never
B = Rarely (less that one day per week)
C = Occasionally (1-2 days per week)
D = Frequently (3-5 days per week)
E = Always or almost always (6 or more days per week)

1. I am comfortable with my emotional self.   A B C D E
2. People perceive me as having a positive attitude.   A B C D E
3. I get depressed.   A B C D E
4. I get angry.   A B C D E
5. I hold in my feelings.   A B C D E
6. I feel comfortable in social situations.   A B C D E
7. I laugh.   A B C D E
8. I cry.   A B C D E
9. I like touching people and being touched.   A B C D E
10. I feel I have a sense of purpose.   A B C D E
11. I feel my family and friends need me.   A B C D E
12. I look forward to my future.   A B C D E

A CONSIDERATION: If we have to talk the language of "problems," we would do best to assess what the client/patient considers to be the problems rather than what we guess or imagine the problems to be.

A PROBLEM ASSESSMENT FORM

If we need to know someone's problems, we certainly do not have to overly emphasize them. A problem assessment form can be quite brief. Here follows an example.

From the following, choose what you feel are your four greatest problems, putting an "A" in front of the greatest, "B" in front of the second greatest, "C," and "D."

___ Depression
___ Sadness
___ Anger
___ Physical Pain
___ Hopelessness
___ Loneliness
___ Limited Physical Abilities
___ Anxiety
___ Guilt
___ Grief
___ Loss
___ Obsessions
___ Addictions
___ Fear

"The family is one of nature's masterpieces." - George Santayana.

FAMILY STRENGTH ASSESSMENT

As caregivers, we might want to not only know a person's strengths; we might also want to know the strengths of that person's family. (Often a client's/patient's strengths and his/her family's strengths are interwoven with each other.) Here are some questions that could be used to discover a family's strengths:

A. What are the three greatest strengths of your family?
B. How do members of your family complement one another so that collectively you are stronger than you would be as individuals?
C. What occasions from your family history have produced fond memories?
D. How might various members of your community be envious of your family?
E. If your family were to break apart, what would you miss the most?

"It is a reverent thing to see an ancient castle or building not in decay: or to see a fair timber tree sound and perfect. How much more to behold an ancient and noble family which hath stood against the waves and weathers of time." - Sir Francis Bacon.

"The family is the nucleus of civilization." - Will and Ariel Durant.

ASSESSING SOMEONE'S GRIEVING STYLE

Different care recipients can have different grieving styles. These styles often relate to whether the person is primarily feeling-centered, thought-centered, or action-centered. We often need to assess this style so we can provide appropriate tools for particular styles. (It would make no sense to offer a thought-centered tool to a feeling-centered person.) How a care recipient would respond to the following multiple-choice questions (responding with the answer that he/she feels is the closest to the truth) would give us some idea as to that person's adapting style.

    A. Most people who know me would describe me as:
        1. Primarily feeling-centered.
        2. Primarily thought-centered.
        3. Primarily action-centered.
    B. I would describe myself as:
        1. Primarily feeling-centered.
        2. Primarily thought-centered.
        3. Primarily action-centered.
    C. In highly emotional situations where others are expressing their emotions:
        1. My emotions come right out.
        2. I will sometimes express my emotions.
        3. I will rarely, if ever, express my emotions.
    D. When confronted with difficult situations:
        1. I will immediately try to think of a way to make the situation less difficult.
        2. I will sometimes choose a rational way out of the situation.
        3. I often find it very difficult to concentrate on anything.
    E. When I am under a great deal of stress or tension:
        1. I simply cannot stand still; I need to do something.
        2. I will sometimes do something to end the stress, and sometimes just wait it out.
        3. I am often immobilized.

WALLY'S AND DJUNA'S GRIEVING STYLES

Wally and Djuna lost their daughter, Karin, when she was only eight weeks old. She had been born quite premature and had died due to several complications with her heart and lungs.

After the death Djuna returned immediately to her work as a college professor, determined to make this the best year of her teaching career. Her evenings and weekends, if not being spent laboriously preparing for a class, were spent gardening. Gardening had always been her favorite pastime. Yet, after the death of her daughter, that gardening took on an intensity it never had before: she would dig in that ground with strong determination, she would pull out the weeds with a fervor, and she would ever-so-gently and lovingly nurture each individual plant as it grew.

Wally could not go back to his work as an accountant because his emotions were pouring out all the time. He could not focus on anything. Often he would just take himself into the basement and cry for hours. He would sometimes go out in his car to some deserted place and just yell out at the horizon. He would sometimes just get so depressed he could not communicate, unable to speak or hear anything.

Djuna thought that Wally was much too emotional, and she thought he needed to go back to work, he needed to "do something" to "get over" what she thought was his emotional quagmire. Wally felt that Djuna was not emotional enough, that she was obviously "avoiding" her grief by always "doing" things, and he felt she would eventually "crash" because of her failure to address her emotions.

They were really both fully grieving. They were just processing that grief in different ways. Djuna was a cognitively-centered and action-centered griever; she processed all of her grief intellectually and through physical activities. Wally was more of a feeling-centered griever; he processed all of his grief emotionally.

ASSESSING FOR THE PHYSICAL DIMENSIONS

Sadness, anger, anxiety, and depression (and other problems) can often present themselves through physical symptoms. When caregivers make assessments of those in their care, we might want to gather information that identifies the physical dimensions of a care recipient's emotions, thoughts, and experiences. The goal is to help care recipients relieve pain/suffering and establish comfort. The following four-part assessment form can be useful in achieving that goal.

1. Where do you feel most of your pain/suffering? Mark the areas where your pain/suffering is most felt. If there is more than one site, label each site with the letters A, B, C, D, from the most intense to the least intense, using these same letters in steps 2, 3, and 4 of this form.

    ____ head
    ____ neck
    ____ back
    ____ shoulders
    ____ chest
    ____ arms
    ____ hands
    ____ stomach
    ____ groin
    ____ buttocks
    ____ legs
    ____ feet
    ____ joints
    ____ other _____

2. Describe how the pain/suffering feels. Place the corresponding site letters in the blanks that most appropriately describe the feeling.

    ____ sharp
    ____ dull, aching, or diffuse
    ____ radiating or shooting

____ pressing or tight
____ burning
____ pulling
____ other _____

3. Describe the intensity of the pain/suffering on a scale of 0 to 5, with 5 representing the most intense, in the various sites.

	Site A	Site B	Site C	Site D
At present	____	____	____	____
Highest it gets	____	____	____	____
Lowest it gets	____	____	____	____

4. Measure the frequency of pain/suffering by checking one for each site:

	Site A	Site B	Site C	Site D
Occasional	____	____	____	____
Frequent	____	____	____	____
Constant	____	____	____	____

Here are some additional questions that could be asked to learn more about those physical variables:
   A. What makes your pain/suffering worse?
   B. Are there times of day or night when your pain/suffering is worse?
   C. What has helped in the past to control the physical symptoms of your pain/suffering?
   D. What does the pain/suffering prevent you from doing?

It is important to identify several sites of pain/suffering because they are often interrelated. The more we can learn about each site and its possible connection to others, the better we will be able to help reduce or alleviate the pain/suffering. Remember: it is always important to never assess problems (physical, psychological, or spiritual problems) without simultaneously recommending some steps that patients and loved ones can take to diminish those problems themselves, showing people how they have an ability to address and relieve their own problems.

A CONSIDERATION: We all have problems; we all have strengths. How beautiful it can be when we grow together, honoring and feeding each other's strengths, working together to solve each other's problems.

Chapter Two

Care Plans

"The more you think of yourself as a 'therapist,' the more pressure there is on someone to be a 'patient.' The more you identify as a 'philanthropist,' the more compelled someone feels to be a 'supplicant.' The more you see yourself as a 'helper,' the more need for people to play the passive 'helped.' You're buying into, even juicing up, precisely what people who are suffering want to be rid of: limitation, dependency, helplessness, separateness." - Ram Dass.

"Remember that you are facilitating another person's process. It is not your process. Do not intrude. Do not control. Do not force your needs and insights into the foreground. If you do not trust a person's process, that person will not trust you. Imagine that you are a midwife; you are assisting at someone else's birth. Do good without show or fuss." - John Heider.

ALLOWING OUR ROLES TO BE DEFINED

Instead of us imposing our roles upon care recipients (assuming *our* care plan), we might want to first discover what the expectations are of the care recipients (discovering *their* care plan). The following forms could be given out to care recipients by an institution's intake staff to discover those expectations, thus allowing care recipients some often-needed choice and control.

Social Worker or Counselor Role Definition

From the following list of items that you, the care recipient, might receive from your caregiver, put an "x" beside those that best complete this statement: "I would like my social worker or counselor to help me . . ." Cross out any item that you feel you will never want from a caregiver. Put a question mark next to any of which you are unsure. Use the blank space for anything else you wish to say.

    I would like my social worker or counselor to help me . . .
- ____ explore non-medical ways of relieving pain, depression, or anxiety;
- ____ address some emotional problems I'm having;
- ____ explore some issues related to my purpose and self-worth;
- ____ address some problems I'm having with my social life;
- ____ explore religious or spiritual issues;
- ____ address financial issues;
- ____ make some decisions about my future;
- ____ put some more fun and humor into my life;
- ____ communicate feelings towards one particular person (_____);
- ____ finish a project (_____);
- ____ do the following (_____).

Chaplain Role Definition

From the following list of items that you, the care recipient, might receive from your chaplain, put an "x" beside those that best complete this statement: "I would like my chaplain to help me . . ." Cross out any item that you feel you will never want from a chaplain. Put a question mark next to any of which you are unsure. Use the blank space for anything else you wish to say.

    I would like my chaplain to help me . . .
- ____ maintain contact with my congregation, minister, rabbi, or priest;
- ____ strengthen my life with prayer and/or meditation;
- ____ explore some of my spiritual concerns;
- ____ feel a sense of worth and dignity;

    ____ settle some religious differences within my family;
    ____ address some emotional problems I'm having;
    ____ help a particular member of my family;
    ____ find some good study materials for my struggles;
    ____ address some of my doubts, fears, and/or anger;
    ____ do the following (_____).

Volunteer Role Definition

From the following list of items that you, the care recipient, might receive from your volunteer, put an "x" beside those that best complete this statement: "I would like my volunteer to help me . . ." Cross out any item that you feel you will never want from a volunteer. Put a question mark next to any of which you are unsure. Use the blank space for anything else you wish to say.

I would like my volunteer to . . .
    ____ give me some occasional companionship;
    ____ help me with housekeeping matters;
    ____ run some errands outside the home;
    ____ help me do some "handyman" projects;
    ____ help me with my social life;
    ____ relieve some of my other caregivers of their duties;
    ____ put some more fun and humor into my life;
    ____ address some emotional problems I'm having;
    ____ explore religious/spiritual issues;
    ____ finish a project (_____);
    ____ do the following (_____).

Nursing Role Definition

From the following list of items that you, the care recipient, would like to receive from your nurse, put an "x" beside those that best complete this statement: "I would like my nurse to help me . . ." Cross out any item that you feel you will never want from a nurse. Put a question mark next to any of which you are unsure. Use the blank space for anything else you wish to say.

    I would like my nurse to help me . . .
- ____ find medication for pain relief;
- ____ find medication for other physical problems;
- ____ find medication for some emotional issues;
- ____ learn more about alternatives to medication;
- ____ learn about ways to put more quality into my life;
- ____ communicate with my physician(s);
- ____ make more decisions regarding my own well-being;
- ____ communicate my concerns and wishes to my family and friends;
- ____ communicate feelings towards a particular person (_____);
- ____ finish a project (_____);
- ____ do the following (_____).

Home Health Aide Role Definition

From the following list of items that you, the care recipient, might receive from your home health aide, put an "x" beside those that best complete this statement: "I would like my home health aid to help me . . ." Cross out any item that you feel you will never want from a home health aide. Put a question mark next to any of which you are unsure. Use the blank space for anything else you wish to say.

    I would like my home health aide to help me . . .
- ____ bathe and clean myself;
- ____ dress myself;
- ____ maintain a clean and safe environment;
- ____ achieve some mobility;
- ____ use and exercise my muscle groups;
- ____ massage away soreness and tension;
- ____ purchase, prepare, and/or serve meals;
- ____ do light housekeeping;
- ____ finish a project (_____);
- ____ so the following (_____).

A CONSIDERATION: The typical evolution of care plans involves making them longer, more complicated, and simultaneously less customer friendly. More and more paperwork, less and less time with the care recipient; more and more time spent on the *plan*, less and less on the *care*.

ONE QUESTION CARE PLANS FOR THE DYING

The typical care plan is designed to address any-and-every possible problem that any-and-every possible person could have. Yet most governing/reviewing agencies (JCAHO, for example) ask for a care plan that addresses a particular *individual's needs*, *concerns*, *expectations*, and *priorities* (not *every person* and not *problems*). - If we are willing to be creative, we can do what is being demanded of us in just *one sentence* rather than several pages. The following one question care plans better address the requests of those governing/reviewing agencies than the typical multi-page care plan.

1. Given your current capabilities (whatever they might be), what is the best way you can imagine spending the rest of your life?

2. For you, what is the best thing that can come from our relationship (nurse to patient, social worker to patient, chaplain to patient)?

3. If I could grant you three wishes concerning your future, what would those wishes be?

4. In the next couple weeks, what are your most important needs, concerns, expectations, and priorities?

However a person answers any of the above questions that is his/her care plan. How nice it would be if that was also the caregiver's care plan.

"Throughout the entire dying experience the individual is forced to confront a loss of control. [He or] she is powerless to stop imminent death and the preceding deterioration, nor can [he or] she stay the losses that befall from the moment of diagnosis until the time of death. In the effort to provide support and assist [that individual] in dealing with [his or] her feelings and experiences there is no more superior intervention than providing [that individual] with control." - Therese Rando.

TIM'S TRUCK

Tim was very sick. He had been told that he had only two or three more months left in his life.

Tim had always wanted to own a truck, ever since he had been a teenager. So one day he called up his local Dodge dealership, bought a truck over the telephone, and asked them to deliver it to his house. They brought it to his driveway and parked it there.

Whenever Tim was able, he would go out to the driveway, get into his truck, put the key in the ignition, start the truck, hold the steering wheel, rev up the engine, and just sit: sitting in that truck, staying in that driveway. Whenever anyone would walk by on the sidewalk, Tim would wave to them and honk his horn.

One day he said, "I think I'll go to Texas today. Never been to Texas." He then went out to the driveway, got in his Dodge truck, started the engine, and sat there, waving his hand and honking the horn at anyone he saw. He later went back in the house and told everyone about his trip to Texas.

On another day he said, "This looks like a good day to go to Vermont. I understand the leaves are quite colorful this time of year." He then went through his routine of revving up the engine, waving his hand, honking the horn. Then he returned to tell everyone about Vermont and the colorful leaves he saw.

THE FISHING TRIP

Herb and Floyd were residents in a life-care community in Florida, both of them getting towards the end of their lives. They had both been avid fishermen and loved to tell each other fish stories. They had informed the Activities Director at the life-care community that they wanted to go on one last fishing trip up to Minnesota. This was obviously impossible given their poor health.

However, the Activities Director did the next best thing: he got two fishing poles and took Herb and Floyd out fishing to the man-made lake on the facility's property. The Activities Director apparently made quite the sight pushing two wheelchairs with two feeble old men, each carrying his own fishing pole. They spent two hours fishing. Afterwards Floyd declared, "I had never thought I would ever go fishing again. And this was probably the best fishing trip I ever had."

Were they able to go to Minnesota? No. Did they catch any fish that day? No. But they still had a wonderful time, because someone took their wishes seriously, someone wanted Herb and Floyd to go on one last fishing trip.

"A dying person is a living person." - Herbert Reisz.

"Those who are facing death have a profound wish to feel that they are still part of the world of the living." - Egilde Seravalli.

A CONSIDERATION: Sometimes the work of being a caregiver can come down to a simple choice: do we have unconditional positive regard for our governing/reviewing agencies or do we have unconditional positive regard for our patients? Do we bend people to try to fit into our paperwork or do we bend the paperwork to try to fit our patients?

"A dying person most needs to be shown as unconditional a love as possible, released from all expectations." - Sogyal Rinpoche.

A CONSIDERATION: Governing/reviewing agencies often ask for "measurable outcomes." All we need to do is take a patient's care plan (whatever it might be: realistic or unrealistic, simple or complex, primarily concerned with the physical or primarily concerned with the spiritual) and then somehow measure that patient's particular needs, concerns, expectations, and priorities. All we need to do is take a patient's care plan, in his/her own words, divide it into 3-6 measurable outcomes, and then periodically review those outcomes as we provide the care. Recording our progress, recording something measurable, need not be terribly complex or terribly time consuming.

A CONSIDERATION: Sometimes patients can have unrealistic care plans: unrealistic needs, concerns, expectations, and priorities. Yet, even if someone's care plan is unrealistic, it is still that person's care plan. If we cannot complete the care plan literally, we need to get as close as possible. (If a dying woman wants to be in Australia and she cannot get there - for whatever reason, I must try to bring a little Australia to her. If a grieving man wants to go back in time and say something to his now deceased wife, I must try to help him do that through a role play, a guided imagery, or some other technique.) No matter how unrealistic the care plan we must supply it with as much reality as possible.

RICK'S CAMPFIRE

Rick was a young man spending his final days in a hospice house. There was only one wish he wanted fulfilled before he died. That wish was related to an annual tradition his family practiced. Each summer his family (aunts, uncles, cousins, brothers, sisters) would set a date to gather at a campsite in northern Wisconsin for a weekend reunion. The first night they gathered they would build a campfire, encircle the fire, and go around one at a time and tell the stories of what had happened to each of them since the last campfire, each person telling his or her year's story. Part of the family tradition involved those over twenty-one years old sipping a beer while they told their story. Rick's one wish was to stay alive until the summer, go to Wisconsin, sit around a campfire, tell his last story, and sip a beer while he was doing it.

We knew Rick would most likely not be alive by the summer. Even if he did by chance make it to the summer, he would not be able to stand a trip to northern Wisconsin. However, that was Rick's last wish, that was his personal care plan, his one goal, and we wanted to see how close we could get to making that wish become reality.

We set a date for the following week. We called as many relatives as we could. They came to the hospice house. We built a fire in the fireplace. We wheeled Rick out in his bed in front of the fire. His brother brought a beer and a straw. Rick sipped that beer and told his last story to his family.

ONE LAST CHRISTMAS

Becky wanted to have one more Christmas, her favorite holiday. But it was August, and all of her caregivers were fairly sure she would not even make it through September. So the caregivers decided to have Christmas in August. One Sunday they cut down an evergreen tree, brought it to her room, and decorated it with ornaments and lights, spending the entire afternoon in her room — decorating, laughing, telling stories of past Christmases. That evening a small children's choir came to Becky's room to sing several Christmas carols. The last song they sung was Silent Night: tears could be seen in many people's eyes. The very next morning Becky was found peacefully lying in her bed, having spent her last day on this earth celebrating her favorite holiday.

ONE QUESTION CARE PLANS FOR THE GRIEVING

Here are three questions that could be used to discover what a grieving person's care plan is. Any one of these questions (or a combination of all of them) could be used.

1. For you, what is the best thing that can come from our relationship (counselor to client, volunteer to client, minister to client)?

2. When we lose a loved one, we can say we have lost our "other half." Describe the half of you that is now missing: what did you previously have that you do not have now, missing parts that are crying out in need of replacement?

3. What dreams do you have that you now feel cannot come true? In other words, are there any desires you have that you now feel will not be fulfilled because of this death?

THE CANOE TRIP

Zach was a realtor and a workaholic. His only times of relaxation were spent daydreaming with his oldest son Michael, a teenager. The daydream they most often talked about involved a long canoe trip they would one day take together. That daydream never became a reality because Michael died in a car accident with some of his teenage friends. Zach's grief of losing his son was complicated with his guilt of never having made that canoe trip.

Zach could now not work no matter how hard he tried. His thoughts were preoccupied with that never-taken canoe trip with Michael. A counselor working with Zach suggested that Zach somehow needed to transform that unfulfilled daydream into some kind of reality.

Zach took a three month sabbatical from work. The first six weeks he spent building a canoe from a kit. On both sides of the canoe he painted the canoe's name, MICHAEL. The next six weeks he spent canoeing in Minnesota with MICHAEL.

The trip was filled with many thoughts and emotions, tears, anger, love. Each evening Zach wrote those thoughts and emotions in a journal he took with him. Each entry was in the form of a letter to Michael. Zach wrote about his past, reviewed his relationship with Michael, reviewed his relationship with the rest of his family, and reviewed his relationship to his work. He also, through that trip and journal, set his priorities for his life's future, placing his relationship with the remaining members of his family as his top priority. His work ended up being ninth on his list of priorities.

A CONSIDERATION: Care plans do not have to always be designed as ways of a caregiver meeting the needs of a care recipient. Care plans can be designed as ways of care recipients helping themselves.

SELF-CARE PLAN
FOR A PERSON WHO IS GRIEVING

Step One. Choose four words from the right column that you would most like to be descriptive of you in six months. Circle those four words and mark an "X" on each of the four lines to represent where you are now.

1	3	5
hopeless		hopeful

1	3	5
fragmented		whole

1	3	5
sad		happy

1	3	5
constrained		free

1	3	5
tense		relaxed

1	3	5
spent		energized

1	3	5
resentful		grateful

1	3	5
troubled		peaceful

1	3	5
socially alienated		socially integrated

Step Two. Take each of those four words from Step One, placing them in the first blanks of the following sentences. Fill in the second and third blanks with how you plan on achieving each of those states.

    A. I plan on making my life more _____ by _____
    and by _____.
    B. I plan on making my life more _____ by _____
    and by _____.
    C. I plan on making my life more _____ by _____
    and by _____.
    D. I plan on making my life more _____ by _____
    and by _____.

FROM "I NEED" TO "I CAN GET"

The following activity can enhance a client's/patient's sense of control by adapting a technique from the "rational emotive therapy" school of psychology, a form of therapy that emphasizes self-empowerment. In this exercise designed to determine and achieve a client's/patient's care plan, care recipients (the terminally ill or grieving) are led to the realization that they have choices they may not know they have, choices they can exercise if they wish.

1. The caregiver would give a "homework" assignment to complete twelve sentences that each begin with the phrase "I need . . ." (The care recipient might write, "I need people to touch and hold me." Or, "I need some private time.")

2. From the list of twelve needs, the care recipient might select three to five that could become care plan goals. In each of those three to five statements, the "I need . . ." sentences would be replaced with "I can get . . ." statements. ("I can get people to touch and hold me." "I can get some private time.")

3. Each "I can get . . ." statement would then be placed at the top of a separate sheet of paper. Below the statement several different strategies would be developed for making that statement a reality. (The person wanting more time alone might set aside forty-five minutes each afternoon for "private time." A "PLEASE DO NOT DISTURB UNTIL 4:30" sign might be placed on the door to prevent interruptions.)

MY IDEAL DEATH

A terminally ill person could write a story about what he or she perceives as the ideal death, the best possible death that could happen. The story would have only elements that are actually possible: his or her best possible death. The following questions would be addressed:

   A. Where do you die?
   B. Who and what is around you?
   C. What are you doing?
   D. What are the people doing who are around you?
   E. What has been happening in the last couple days?
   F. What has been happening in the last couple hours?
   G. What is the very last thing you do?
   H. What is the very last thing you say?

This story can be used to determine a person's needs, concerns, expectations, and priorities from his or her caregivers.

"Every one of death's diverse appearances is as distinctive as that singular face we each show the world during the days of life. Every man will yield up the ghost in a manner that the heavens have never known before: every woman will go her final way in her own way." - Sherwin Nuland.

HAWAII

When Maude was told that she had only a couple months to live, she was determined to spend those last months in Hawaii. She had never been to Hawaii, someplace she had always wanted to go.

However, there were other things she needed to do first: selling her house, saying some goodbyes, adjusting her will, settling various items of unfinished business. Her disease was also developing more rapidly than originally anticipated, so rapidly that by the time she had finished all her affairs she was not in good enough health to get on an airplane. She was even unable to leave her bedroom.

Her caregivers decided that if Maude couldn't get to Hawaii, they would bring Hawaii to her. They put a CD player in her room to play Hawaiian music. They put posters of beach scenes on her walls. Everyday at five o'clock they would give her either a pina colada cocktail or a pineapple milkshake — her choice. Every morning they would bring in some fresh flowers and fruit, greeting her with an "Aloha."

Although Maude's home was in Parsippany, New Jersey, her bedroom was just a short distance from Waikiki Beach. When she died Maude was facing a poster of Diamond Head: the waters were a little choppy, but the sunset was really quite beautiful.

GUIDED IMAGERY: THE MEDICINE MAN

The use of guided imageries can be helpful in addressing several issues. Here is a guided imagery that can be used to help discover a dying person's care plan.

"Close your eyes and imagine that you have heard about a very unusual medicine man, a great medicine man who knows the secret of finding purpose in our final years. You have decided to go and talk to him to find out what main purpose you have set before you between now and the end of your life. . . .

"To meet this medicine man, you have flown by helicopter to the top of a mountain in a deserted part of New Mexico. You find yourself seated at a campfire and he is sitting across from you. You can barely make out his features. Imagine what he is wearing. . . . How does his body appear? . . . Examine his face closely. . . . Look into his all-knowing eyes. . . .

"Now ask him what important task you are to accomplish between now and the end of your life. What do your priorities need to be for the rest of your life? . . . At first, the medicine man just stares at you in silence. . . . His eyes penetrate into the depths of your being. You watch him watching you. . . . Finally he speaks, telling you what to do. What does he say about your purpose during the remainder of your life? What does the medicine man say is your goal during your final days on this earth? What are you supposed to do? . . .

"Now respond to this medicine man. How do you react to what has just been said to you? . . . What feelings do you have toward the medicine man? . . .

"Now get ready to leave the medicine man. There is nothing more you need here. You know what your purpose is for the rest of your life. You know the task that is set for you. You know what your priorities now need to be. . . . How do you wish to say goodbye? . . . Say goodbye to the medicine man in whatever manner seems most fitting to you. . . . Slowly open your eyes. . . ."

Discussion would follow. "What did the medicine man say you're supposed to do?" "How do you feel about what was said?" "If you were to do what the medicine man suggested, how would you best go about doing it?"

A CONSIDERATION: Sometimes people cannot clarify their care plan. They might be too distraught and confused to clarify it. They might be intellectually impaired. They might be unable to communicate in any fashion. No matter what the reason is that a patient cannot clarify his/her care plan, we must still never impose *our* needs, concerns, expectations, and priorities; we must discover that patient's care plan. Some detective work might be necessary.

USING SOME DETECTIVE WORK

Hank was an Alzheimer's patient in a nursing home. Almost every night he would get up in the middle of the night, take off his pajamas, and start to walk around his unit. He would often walk into women's rooms. Of course, screaming would follow.

What desires was Hank trying to fulfill? What were his wishes? What were his needs, concerns, expectations, and priorities? Was Hank wanting to be a nudist? Was he wanting to turn the whole nursing home into a nudist colony? Or could he be a real danger perhaps: a potential rapist? What was going on? Why was he walking around without any clothes on? What was he trying to do? What was his care plan?

In a conference with Hank's family, a counselor from the nursing home was told that Hank used to sleep in the nude. In fact, there were several family jokes about it.

So the counselor advised Hank's caregivers to quit putting pajamas on him at night. Sure enough: Hank slept through the night.

Hank's care plan was quite simple: he just didn't want to wear pajamas.

Apparently Hank used to get up in the middle of the night because he felt uncomfortable in those pajamas. He would take them off. He then probably thought that as long as he was up, he might as well go for a walk.

A CONSIDERATION: With many grievers their care plan can only be practiced in some contained space: a time and a place where they can extract themselves from the rest of the world and fully center upon their necessary agenda. Can our clients/patients find such a space? Do we allow them to have such a space?

FINDING SOME CONTAINED SPACE

Pat was grieving the death of his wife, Marjorie. He had created a contained space, a private environment, for that grief. Whenever he needed to revisit his grief, or whenever that grief would unexpectedly come to revisit him, he would enter his home library.

In that library was a table on which had been placed a scrapbook labeled "Marjorie." Also in the library was a tape recorder that was queued up to repeatedly play Pat's and Marjorie's favorite song from their courtship, Neil Sedaka's "Calendar Girl."

Pat would go into that library, take the scrapbook, and sit down in a reclining chair. He would flip through that scrapbook, often pausing at certain pictures, certain mementos, closing his eyes and recalling that time with Marjorie. When he was done with the scrapbook, he would once again close his eyes as he listened to a couple playings of "Calendar Girl." After grieving in that contained space, he would leave the library and once again return to his other world, the world where he was not allowed to focus too much on Marjorie.

A CONSIDERATION: The key to the effectiveness of any care plan is its degree of patient-centeredness. As caregivers we must at all times be able to answer the following questions. What does the client/patient need? What does the client/patient want? What does the client/patient wish? – If we cannot answer those questions by looking at our care plans, our care plans are totally inappropriate and have obviously made someone or something to be more important than the client/patient. If we cannot answer those questions by looking at our care plans, we are not showing our clients/patients love, we are showing them violence.

"Love and violence, properly speaking, are polar opposites. Love lets the other be, but with affection and concern. Violence attempts to constrain the other's freedom, to force him [or her] to act in the way we desire, but with ultimate lack of concern, with indifference to the other's own existence or destiny. – We are effectively destroying ourselves by violence masquerading as love." - R. D. Laing.

"To tell another person what that person ought to do, think, or be is an affront at any time; but to do this when that person nears the end of life [or is grieving the end of someone else's life] is sanctimonious cruelty." - Avery Weisman.

Chapter Three

Addressing The Emotional/Psychological Concerns Of The Terminally Ill

LAST REQUEST

In the initial stage of the caregiving relationship, the following question could be used to discover a dying person's care plan. It could also be used to address an emotional/psychological concern in the later stages of the relationship.

"We are all sentenced to death from the day we are born. Often when people are given a death sentence, they are granted one last request. What would you want your last request to be?"

THE SMELL OF A HORSE

A dying cowboy's last request of his nurse was not some food or drink. There was no person he felt he needed to see. There was no task he wanted to finish. His last request was simple: all he wanted was to smell a horse. He said that he missed that special smell, saying that that smell was quite unique and he associated it with many fond memories from his life as a cowboy.

Two days later the nurse wheeled the cowboy's bed outside. A horse was brought up to the bed. The cowboy held his face up against the horse's head, smiled, and breathed in that special smell he associated with all his fond memories.

WERTHER'S CANDY AND A BEER

Anthony had been in a coma for several weeks. His family had been at his bedside throughout that time, faithfully awaiting his death. Anthony was attached to several machines.

One day a nurse was in the room checking the machines when Anthony suddenly bolted upright into a sitting position and blurted out "I want Werther's candy and a beer."

The nurse expressed a frightful gasp and immediately ran out of the room in search of the assigned doctor.

One of the family members casually walked out of the room, went out of the hospital and down the street to a convenience store, got the Werther's candy and the beer, and returned to the room.

Before the nurse could get back to Anthony's room with the doctor, Anthony had had one candy, two sips of the beer, and had also died.

JUST ONE LITTLE PILL

Leland made an unusual request of his nurse. He said there was only one thing he wanted before he died. "What do you want, Leland?" she asked. He said, "All I want is one pill, just one little pill." She was concerned, "Are you in pain, Leland?" "Well, not really," he said. "But I suppose you could call it a type of pain," he continued. "But it can be solved with only one pill. All I want is one. Just one. It's my dying wish: one Viagra. That's all I need and I will die happy."

A CONSIDERATION: In saying that we honor people's wishes, in saying that we allow people choices and control, in feeding people's strengths, we often create limits. ("I don't mind giving people control as long as they do what I want.") Yet, as caregivers, we might need to challenge those limitations. Are we willing to honor people's wishes when they are contrary to our wishes? Are we willing to allow people choices and control when they make decisions that we would prefer they not make? Are we willing to feed people's strengths when we do not like those strengths?

"I accept the patient as being in an okay space except for the ways the patient defines as unsatisfactory." - Sheldon Kopp.

A CONSIDERATION: Acceptance of another, showing love towards another, means that we strive to have no reservations, conditions, evaluations, and/or judgements of that person's feelings, attitudes, or actions; we regard that person as having inherent value. It is not acceptance up to this or that point and no further. It is not acceptance only of those feelings, attitudes, and actions that are in agreement with our own or complementary to our own.

GET OUT OF MY ROOM

Phyllis was angry and she would let everyone know about it. When the nurse entered her room, she said, "You know, if you were doing your job, I wouldn't be in this bed. You haven't been doing your job. I don't like you. Get out of my room!" When the social worker entered her room, she said, "You've been wasting my time. Go waste someone else's time. I don't like you. Get out of my room!" When the chaplain entered her room, she said, "You're living in a world of illusion. You need to grow up. I don't like you. Get out of my room!"

Phyllis felt she could not stop anything that was happening to her, but she could sure be angry about it. Her anger might have been her last way of asserting herself. Her anger might have been her last way of feeling any kind of strength. If any of her caregivers were to try to calm Phyllis down, to try to take that anger away from her, they could very well be doing her a disservice rather than a service.

The social worker working with Phyllis put this in her care notes: "My role is to be yelled at." That was supporting her patient's coping style; that was feeding her patient's strength. That was allowing Phyllis whatever choice and control she could have. That could have been the best of all care plans for Phyllis.

A CONSIDERATION: Supporting a person's coping style, feeding a person's strengths, might involve caregivers providing appropriate tools to that person. Those tools might especially be necessary for coping styles and strengths that are unacceptable to the general public.

THE IMAGINARY SLEDGEHAMMER

A caregiver might suggest to a person experiencing anger that the person imagine all the restraints that have ever been placed on him or her since childhood until the present. These restraints could be anything that has kept the client from becoming whatever the client has wanted to become or prevented him or her from doing whatever he or she has wanted to do. (Some examples of restraints: an interrupted education, some family responsibility, certain financial limitations, or an illness.)

Suggest that the client imagine these restraints one at a time, take an imaginary sledgehammer, and destroy each and every restraint until each one is totally smashed in his or her imagination. (The client might enhance the activity by physically going through the motions as if that sledgehammer was within his or her grasp, shouting with each swing.)

HERE: TRY ME

As caregivers, we might offer to be the target of the patient's or loved one's anger. We would then be helping someone get out the anger that is being held in.

We could offer ourselves as the recipient of verbal anger. We could allow the person in our care to create a role-playing situation in which we would play the person or thing that is felt to be the cause of the anger. Then the client could verbally dump all that anger, dumping it all on us.

We could also offer to be the recipient of physical anger by suggesting that the patient or our loved one release some of that pent-up anger by squeezing one or our arms or legs, squeezing very hard. Again, we would play the role of the person or thing that is felt to be the cause of the anger. We could even encourage him or her verbally by saying, "Squeeze harder. Get it all out."

"If you are never angry, then you are unborn." - African Proverb.

SUSAN AND HER RELEASE ROOM

I could not understand what made Susan so easygoing. If I were in her position, I would probably be weeping all the time, and I would have certainly been angry. Her life was being taken away while she was in her late forties. The physical ravages of her disease kept her from going anywhere in public: cancer was eating away at her face. Also, she would probably never be completely free of pain until she died. Susan certainly had many reasons to be sad and angry, yet she was so serene – almost cheery – with everyone. I asked her once, while visiting her at her home, "What's your secret, Susan? How do you stay so calm in the midst of all that is happening to you?"

"Follow me," she replied. "I'll show you my secret." She led me to a spare bedroom, opened the door, and said that this was her "release room," a room where she would go whenever she felt hurt, angry, or very sad. Whenever she needed to release some of these emotions, she entered this room. The room was simply furnished with a bed, one chair, and two stuffed animals, a bear and a giraffe.

When she needed to cry, Susan explained, she would lie on the bed, hold the stuffed bear tightly to her, and sob until she felt completely cried out. When she was angry, she would either sit on the chair and yell at the giraffe (toward which she projected some identity such as her disease or a person who had been unkind), or she would wring the giraffe's long neck with all her strength.

A CONSIDERATION: A coping style we frequently try to suppress is denial. (Even though denial might help a patient's agenda, we often feel it contrary to our agenda.) Denial has certainly gotten much more bad press than good. Yet could not denial assist a patient? Could not denial provide a patient with strength? Could not denial be a legitimate coping style?

NAUGHTY WORDS

Cancer had metastasized throughout Martha's eighty year old body. Her condition was apparent to her family, friends, and medical advisors, but Martha refused to allow the word "cancer" to be spoken in her presence. She also refused to let anyone around her mention the words "dying" or "death." For Martha those were all "naughty words." Whenever any of those words were inadvertently mentioned, she turned away from the speaker, faced the nearest wall, and thrashed her arms in agitation.

This was Martha's way. This was Martha's style. This was the way she coped. She, for whatever reason, felt this was the only way she could cope.

A CONSIDERATION: In my own work with the dying, I've had many people who have chosen to practice denial. However, I've yet to have a single person that I have not been suspicious that they know absolutely everything that's going on – they just don't want to talk about it. I don't need to know *why* they don't want to talk about it. I just need to honor their choice.

"In our attempt to deal with the immense sadness and anxiety connected with death, both our own and others', have we tried to make it prettier than it is? And in doing so, have we added another burden to the already overwhelming loss represented by death? The burden of dying . . . with a positive attitude." - Mona Wasow.

A CONSIDERATION: We are all in the process of living; we are all in the process of dying; we can all choose to focus on the living or focus on the dying. There can be benefits in focusing on living; there can be benefits in focusing on dying. There can be problems in just focusing on dying; there can be problems in just focusing on living. We can never say that one approach is always good and one is always bad.

A CONSIDERATION: We want to honor our patients and loved ones. We want to honor patient families too. Denial is a choice. It is not the only choice, and we do want people to realize there's another choice (we want people to have choices) – but we do not want to force any choice upon a patient or a family.

SAM

Sam's family did not think Sam could handle the fact that he was dying. In their initial meeting with the hospice nurse in the hospital's family conference room they had requested that she not inform Sam of his terminal status. They explained that they felt their request was coming from their love of Sam and their desire to protect him from something they believed he could not handle.

The nurse informed the family that she would honor their request as long as Sam did not bring the topic up himself. She explained that she would not want to hide something from Sam if he really wanted to know it. The family responded by saying that they were convinced Sam was completely unaware of the seriousness of his illness, and they reiterated their request for the nurse to not initiate any conversation with Sam about his dying.

The nurse left the family in the conference room and then entered Sam's hospital room down the hall. Before she could even introduce herself, the nurse was greeted by Sam: "Are you the one who's going to work with me while I'm dying?"

The nurse responded affirmatively.

Then Sam just started talking away. "You know I'm ninety-five," he said. "You don't live that long and not accumulate some wisdom. My family thinks I'm stupid; they treat me like I don't know anything. You don't reach ninety-five without knowing a thing or two. They're the ones that are in the dark. They're such idiots: you'd think they'd never heard of death before."

A CONSIDERATION: Caregivers can often underestimate the abilities and knowledge of care recipients. People are capable of doing much: more than we might imagine. People are capable of knowing much: more than we might imagine. Their desire to do and to know can also be great.

GLENDA

Glenda knew her death was not far away. She had chronic obstructive pulmonary disease. Any movement was difficult for her. Glenda wanted to know absolutely everything about what was going to happen. She peppered her doctors and nurses with questions about every possible detail of her future. She talked convincingly about adjusting to any adversity that might arise. Glenda asked her nurse, for example, about the possibility that she would eventually be unable to use her walker. The nurse confirmed that it was probable that she would soon become unable to use it.

When the nurse arrived the next day, she found Glenda crawling around the floor on hands and knees.

"What are you doing, Glenda?"

"I'm preparing myself for the future," Glenda replied with a big smile. "You know, I think I'll be ready when the time comes to get rid of that walker."

Glenda did not realize that she would also not be able to crawl in the future. However, she wanted to know as much about her future as she could so she could make some preparations.

VICKY

Vicky was living her final days in a hospice residence. In the room across the hall a woman was dying. Vicky took her walker over to that room and asked the gathered family if she might stay with them for the death. The family, moved by Vicky's concern, permitted her to do that.

After the death occurred, Vicky asked the family if she might be able to stay in the room when the people from the funeral home came. The family did not want to stay in the room, but they arranged for Vicky to do that. She watched as the body was wrapped up, strapped to a cart, and wheeled out of the room.

Vicky followed the body with her walker to the front of the residence. She peered out the window as the body was being placed in the funeral home car. She took her walker to another window to watch the car pull away from the property.

I met with Vicky afterwards in her room. I met with the family afterwards in the residence dining room. The family expressed how impressed they were with Vicky's obvious love and concern for their relative. I had to inform the family that Vicky had never met their relative. Vicky had done all she did simply because she needed to find out what happens to people when they die. Vicky felt no one was being honest with her, and she needed to find out what was going to happen. So she went on her little experiment.

A CONSIDERATION: Oftentimes dying patients are well aware of their situation; it can be very difficult to hide it from them. Yet their emotional/psychological response to that situation is part of their freedom. We do not need to know the reason for that response (cultural, familial, or simply personal). We just need to *accept* that response; we need to *honor* that response (no matter what form it takes).

WILLY AND CLARA

Willy and Clara had dementia. Willy would often be found in the recreation room waltzing with an imaginary partner, waltzing to some imaginary music. Clara would often sit in the same room, head down, occasionally glancing up at Willy, shaking her head in disgust.

One day Karen, a social worker, decided to dance with Willy, the two of them waltzing around the recreation room together.

Clara got out of her chair, walked up to Karen, and tapped her on the shoulder.

Karen said, "Just wait a minute, Clara. I'll be done pretty soon. And then I can spend some time with you."

Clara shook her head in disgust, sat down for only a few seconds, got up, and again tapped Karen on the shoulder.

"Just a minute, Clara. I'll be with you soon. I'll be done pretty soon."

Clara shook her head in disgust again, sat down for a few seconds, got up, and tapped Karen on the shoulder.

"Okay, Clara. What do you want?"

"There's no music," said Clara.

"Yes, Clara. For you there is no music. But for Willy there is."

A CONSIDERATION: For those who hear music, we hear music. For those who do not hear music, we do not hear music.

A CONSIDERATION: The goal of the work of caregiving is not to make me feel strong; the goal of the work is not to make me feel comfortable. The goal is to make the other person feel strong, to make the other person feel comfortable, whatever the form of that strength or comfort.

A CONSIDERATION: The goal of the work of caregiving is to find out the client's goals and to try to achieve those goals. The goal of caregiving is to care enough for someone that we honor his or her choices, whatever form those choices take.

ANDY

Andy was a thirty-six year old man with AIDS, total blindness, an esophageal ulcer, and HIV cardiomyopathy. He was receiving a great deal of pain medication: duragesic patches, nitroglycerine tablets, propoxyphere napsylate tablets, morphine sulfate liquid, and lidocaine viscous liquid.

In the early stages of his illness Andy adjusted fairly well. He had strong support from family and friends and an active sense of humor. As his ailments progressed and his physical pain became worse, his medications increased. But after a few weeks of such heavy medication, Andy decided to decrease their intake. He sought an acupuncturist to treat the pain of his peripheral neuropathy, a pain that caused an intense burning sensation. He found acupuncture helpful and was able to discontinue use of the duragesic patches.

Even though acupuncture was less convenient and gave about the same measure of pain relief as the patches, Andy chose to stay with the acupuncture because, he explained, it was something he was doing for himself, independent of the usual medical directives he received from his caregivers. Because he chose this pain treatment, rather than having it chosen for him, Andy felt empowered. He also felt a certain sense of comfort in simply being able to have the right to determine an aspect of his pain control regimen.

ELMER

Elmer was on morphine concentrate liquid and hydromorphene hydrochloride suppositories for pain because he was dying from lung cancer with celiac disease. The morphine upset Elmer and his wife because they equated it with "giving in" to the disease. To both of them it meant the disease was out of control, and therefore Elmer's fate was out of their control.

Elmer had never been someone to "give in" to anything. He had been active and self-sufficient for all his life. He needed to have some sense of control over his destiny, some sense that the disease was not victimizing him.

Elmer felt continual dull aches in his chest. He and his wife decided to treat the aches with reflexology, a therapeutic foot massage. He found the results very helpful in relieving his suffering. His wife administered the foot massage, and his morphine dosage was somewhat reduced.

It would be difficult to pinpoint exactly what helped relieve Elmer's pain. Perhaps it was the morphine (though reduced), the loving touch of his wife's hands, the reflexology itself, or a combination of all factors. The important point is not the actual mechanism but the fact that his pain relief was supplemented in a positive way by Elmer's sense of having some choices and control in his fate.

HIGH ENERGY AND REGULAR BOWELS

Russell, who suffered from lung cancer, had his own special diet: a bowl of oatmeal covered with an entire stick of melted butter and two tablespoons of brown sugar, administered three times a day. This was literally his comfort food: a bowl of oatmeal, a stick of melted butter, and two tablespoons of brown sugar. As far as Russell was concerned, the diet worked quite well because he felt it kept his energy level high and his bowels regular. That was all he needed, he believed, to be comfortable and content: high energy and regular bowels.

A CONSIDERATION: Providing choices, allowing a client/patient to take control of his or her own life, applies to people no matter what their response, or lack of response. We must give the same rights to the supposedly "unresponsive."

A CONSIDERATION: As caregivers we often label some people "unresponsive." We label them that way because they do not communicate to us in our accepted standard forms of communication: the verbal and the visual. Yet there are other ways of communicating. We can tell things about the dying by their breathing rate. We can tell things about the dying by the temperature of their skin. We can even tell how close people are to death by the smell of their bodies. These people we have labeled "unresponsive" are still responsive! Just because some people do not follow our accepted standard forms of communication does not mean we should treat them with any less respect; we must give *all* our patients choice, control, and respect.

GIVING CONTROL TO AN "UNRESPONSIVE" PERSON

As caregivers, we have the possibility of giving "unresponsive" persons a sense of control. We merely need to remember the following.

1. Upon entering the room of someone who is seemingly unresponsive, always acknowledge that person before acknowledging anyone else in the room. (The last sense to go can often be the sense of hearing. This seemingly unresponsive person could be hearing every single thing we say.)

2. In the presence of a seemingly unresponsive person, never speak about that person to someone else. (We have control of what we say, but we do not have control of what other people say. Other people might say something that is not in the best interest of the patient.)

3. Always react to any signals, any form of communication from a person (facial expressions, body posturing, breathing patterns, body temperature, sounds, odors).

4. Always offer a person choices or imply choices, no matter how seemingly insignificant the choices might appear or how seemingly unresponsive the person might be. [Example: If this person needs to be turned onto his or her side, say, "I am about to move you to your right side. I hope that is okay." Then pause to acknowledge the possibility of a response. Then, and only then, do the moving of the person.]

5. Always thank a care recipient upon leaving the room – especially someone we have labeled "unresponsive." (We have just entered a room uninvited. We have just done some things and we probably are uncertain as to whether we have been helpful or harmful. Some people have only one choice left in their life: to cooperate or not.)

Also, as caregivers, we need to acknowledge that sometimes care recipients might choose to be "unresponsive." – The above steps will help whether someone has chosen or not chosen to be "unresponsive."

KIND WORDS

Deeply anesthetized and undergoing his second open-heart surgery, Richie was fading fast. As he was fading he was receiving frantic care from a doctor and a nurse. The nurse was saying kind and encouraging words to Richie during the surgery. However, the doctor twice blurted out, "The son of a bitch is not going to die on me!"

Three weeks later, as he was being transported out of the hospital in a wheelchair, Richie heard a nurse's voice in the hall. He had the wheelchair attendant stop. Richie addressed the nurse: "You're the one who operated on me. I appreciated your kindness. I appreciated it very much. But would you please tell that doctor that I did not at all appreciate what he was saying about me. Tell him I found him quite offensive. . . . A person like that does not deserve to be a doctor."

A CONSIDERATION: In accepting another, in loving another, in giving care to another, we not only honor what and who they are now, but we also honor what and who they have been in the past. As caregivers we need to show respect for who a person is *and* for who he/she has been.

THE RADIO ANNOUNCER

Mark had been a radio announcer in Chicago much of his life. The best years in his career were in the forties and fifties when he had a popular radio show that played music of that era. As part of his radio show he would often interview musical artists who were giving performances in Chicago. In addition to giving the radio show, he would often attend many concerts, speaking to the performers and hobnobbing with various "movers and shakers" within the music industry. He was accustomed to living an active social life centered around radio and music.

Mark was fortunate to have two loving daughters to take care of him when he acquired Alzheimer's disease. During the early stages of his disease they would encourage some of his old associates and contacts to call him on the telephone or come visit him. They would periodically take him on a "field trip" to a radio station or to concerts given by some of the old performers. They would periodically review his scrapbook with him, looking at some of the old concert programs, some photographs taken of Mark with famous singers, some photographs of radio station staff and old friends. They would also always have music in the house, playing some of his old favorites: Doris Day, Frank Sinatra, Julie London, Perry Como.

As Mark's disease got more serious, his daughters had to eliminate the visits from friends, the field trips, and the concerts. But they would still go through the scrapbook with Mark even if he would often have a blank stare as they were doing so. They would also always have the music playing.

Four days before Mark died his daughters saw him tapping his feet and waving his left hand to the music. In his right hand he was holding an empty glass and mumbling into that glass as if it were an old-time radio microphone.

SPEEDBALL

Albert was in his mid-nineties. He was terminally ill and seemed unresponsive. He lived in his own home with his wife. She was in her mid-nineties also. Although she was not terminally ill, she was about as responsive as Albert was.

My first two visits with the couple consisted of me sitting in one chair, she in another, and Albert lying in the bed. We just shared silence together.

My third visit I noticed something in Albert's room that could have been there the first two visits, but I might not have been very attentive those first two visits. It was a book, a book on Albert's bedside table. That alone should have clued me into something: what was a book doing on the bedside table of someone who is supposedly unresponsive? Also, it was an unusual book to have on the bedside table of someone who was dying. The book had a title something like "The History Of Black Baseball."

I went over to the bedside table and picked up the book. Albert, whose eyes had not opened, must have somehow realized that I had that book in my hands because I heard the first sound from him. It was an "Ummph."

I turned to Albert and saw his hand move. I had never seen his hand move. He extended three fingers, then two. He did it again: three fingers then two. Again. Finally I realized that I needed to turn to page thirty-two in that book. On page thirty-two was an old photograph of a man named "Albert," nicknamed "Speedball."

I turned to Albert. "Speedball?"

I got an "Ummph" with a smile.

"Did you know Satchell Paige?"

Albert's eyes opened.

It's amazing how showing interest in someone's life work – even if it's an accidental showing of interest – can literally bring people out, even out of "unresponsiveness."

A CONSIDERATION: Looking to the past to find meaning and value is important for the family as well as the patient. A family might want to review a loved one's life.

CHRISTOPHER'S FATHER

Christopher was in his mid-thirties and his death was very near. He was living his final days in a hospice house. He was a mere shadow of his former self: he had lost over fifty pounds. His parents were now spending much of their days at the hospice house with Christopher.

A regular part of Christopher's care included his morning bath. Each morning the nursing assistant would come into the room, lift Christopher out of his bed, put him into a wheelchair, wheel him down the hall, lift him into the whirlpool bath, and then bathe him.

One morning the nursing assistant came into Christopher's room to go through the daily ritual. Christopher stopped her and told her that he didn't want to receive his bath from her. He said he wanted his father to give him his bath. Then Christopher asked if she might send his father into the room.

Christopher had the courage to ask his father to give him a bath. His father had the courage to accept the invitation.

I met with Christopher's father afterwards. He said, "I am so glad I was able to do that for Christopher. As I held him in that bathtub, his entire life was reviewed in my mind. I remembered washing him when he was only a week old. I remembered washing his scraped elbow when he fell off his tricycle. I remembered how clean he looked his first day of school. I remembered playing with him in a swimming pool during a summer vacation. I remembered seeing him come out of a shower when he was a teenager, and how later that day I bawled because I knew that he would be grown up and leaving me soon. I remembered the day he called me all excited because he had gotten his first job. I remembered when he introduced me to his first love. And then I remembered the day he told me he was dying. I remembered all of that as I was giving him his bath. . . I am so glad I was able to do that for him. I think it meant a lot for him and it certainly meant a great deal to me."

A CONSIDERATION: Sometimes the typical life review form can be quite long. Sometimes those forms can ask some rather silly questions. (How many times have you moved? What was the name of your first grade teacher? What has been your favorite color?) Why?

A SIMPLE LIFE REVIEW

Two ingredients are essential to a successful life review when a patient/client is nearing the end of life: brevity and emphasis on the positive. A life review involving 2-4 of the following inquiries might be sufficient to get an understanding of someone and to show a genuine interest. (We must always remember to not only show interest through the questions, but also through how we listen to the answers.)

>   A. Of all the events in your past, which one has caused you to have the most amount of pride? Describe what happened.
>   B. At what moment in your life were you most aware of the meaning of the word "love?" Elaborate.
>   C. When you look back on your life and think about the really fun moments, what comes to mind?
>   D. What event from your past are you least likely to forget?
>   E. How would you describe your "good old days?" Elaborate.

Although this activity emphasizes the positive, an opportunity to uncover negative events could also be provided if such events are hindering someone from moving toward the future with full attention. If you feel that might be the case, you could add another question to those above: "Is there anything from your past that has 'a hold on you' that you feel you want to let go, some event that still causes you a lot of pain or anger? Describe what happened." Emphasizing the positive may be most appreciated, but we would be doing a disservice to people in our care if we do not give them an opportunity to discuss and free themselves from past negative events as well.

AMANDA

During one of my early interviews with Amanda, she said, "I feel angry and I feel cheated." When she said that, I immediately assumed that she was angry because she was dying and she felt cheated because her future had been robbed from her. But I asked her to tell me more, and she revealed to me something very different from what I expected.

She informed me that she had been married to this man and one day discovered that he had been having an affair for seven years with a good friend of hers. Amanda was not assertive and did not confront her husband. She lived with him for another three years knowing that the affair was still going on, and then he left her. She was angry and she felt cheated: not because her future had been robbed from her, but her past. She even said to me: "Doug, how can I talk about my future? I didn't have a past." She was angry.

I told her she sounded like she was "stuck" around those ten years, and I asked her how she was going to ever get "unstuck," how was she ever going to get beyond that. She answered by saying that she needed to somehow confront that man, but modified that statement by saying that she was not assertive. She asked me if she might do it over the telephone, and would it be okay if I was there with her when she did it. I told her that if that was the only way it could be done, we would do it that way.

Once Amanda got on the phone, she didn't need any help from me. She said all she needed to say and she said it with authority. I nicknamed her "Amanda the Hun" after that visit.

LINDA

As Linda entered the last few months of her life, the physical characteristics of her illness were dramatic reminders of a psychological and physical trauma from her past. At age forty-four, Linda had cancer of the uterus with metastasis to her spinal cord and subsequent paraplegia from her mid-breast downward. When I met her for an initial interview and assessment, she volunteered that she had been sexually abused when she was only four years old by a teenage babysitter. The incident was still of major significance to her after forty years. She revealed this history before she even mentioned other important concerns of the present: the emotional state of her three young children, her own feelings about her debilitation, her worries about her husband's welfare. Linda's childhood nightmare was crying out to be confronted and explored immediately. She needed to discuss it before she could address all the other issues associated with her imminent death.

Unveiling that forty year old trauma was frightening for Linda because she had previously told only her husband. But after revealing all the details to me, Linda experienced a sense of great relief. Telling her story was so therapeutic that she decided to tell others, first her children and then her friends. As she told them one at a time, even more relief was being experienced. She even invited members of her church prayer group to visit her and hear her story. With each of these meetings, Linda gave her listeners an emphatic charge: Do your best to end the horrors of sexual abuse in whatever way you can. That charge was particularly powerful because it came from Linda, only a few weeks away from death, and it was her last attempt to somehow release herself from that trauma.

PHOTOGRAPHIC LIFE REVIEW

Whenever we enter someone's room and we see a group of photographs, we need to imagine a sign under each one saying, "Ask me." We can learn much from photographs: not only by what is seen but also by what is not seen. (If all the photographs are from the '70s and '80s, there's a natural question: "What was so important about the '70s and the '80s?" However, there's another question there as well: "What was not so important about the '60s and the '90s?")

PASS IT ON

Rather than focusing upon events that have happened, this "life review" focuses on lessons that have been learned, lessons that can be passed on to others. In this life review, meaning is borrowed from the past to lend meaning to the present and future. The care recipient would complete the following sentences:

1. I feel people need to cherish _____.

2. The best thing people can do with their lives is _____.

3. My formula for getting fun out of life is _____.

4. I have found that friendships work if people _____.

5. I have found that the secret to feeling content is _____.

6. The one thing for which I most want to be remembered is _____.

This activity could be followed by a discussion on how these lessons might be passed on to relatives, friends, and others.

"Life is not a problem to be solved but an experiment to be lived. It is enough to have suffered through into deeper meaning. Such meaning enriches and is its own reward. We cannot avoid the swamplands of the soul, but we may come to value them for what they bring us." - James Hollis.

"Death puts Life into perspective." - Ralph Waldo Emerson.

"Do not seek death. Death will find you, but seek the road which makes death a fulfilment. . . . In the last analysis, it is our conception of death which decides our answers to all the questions that life puts to us." - Dag Hammarskjold.

RECORDING A MESSAGE

If it seems appropriate, we may want to encourage a person to leave some messages for posterity. A message could be written, tape-recorded, or videotaped for relatives and friends. The message might include feelings, thoughts, or desires that have not been expressed previously. It could be given to relatives and friends before or after their loved one's death, as he or she prefers.

PEOPLE'S IMPRESSIONS

Many of us see ourselves through the eyes of other people. The following life review is done *for* the people receiving care rather than *by* them. It gathers other people's impressions and holds them up as a mirror for a care recipient to consider. One or more of the following approaches could be taken:

> A. Various people from the care recipient's past could offer remembrances of special moments they have shared. This can be done in person or through letters, phone calls, audiotapes, or videotapes.
> B. Several people could present a short history of key events and accomplishments in the person's life.
> C. Remembrances and recollections in the form of poetry, music, or artworks are a very special, imaginative way to give the person something completely unique as a tribute.
> D. A play could be performed to portray the person's life.

A CONSIDERATION: An almost universal desire amongst the dying is the desire for touch. Not everyone wants it, but most people do. Since it is not a universal desire, we would want to *assess before we express*. However, if we have discovered the desire, we need to somehow try to fulfil that desire in whatever way we can.

"It is not uncommon to find a heightened sense of life in the terminally ill, and an almost overwhelming need for human contact." - Egilde Saravalli.

A CONSIDERATION: In assessing for someone's desirability for touch we do not need another form – we already have enough forms. Assessing can be quite simple. Sometimes people's eyes will tell us whether we are to be closer or further away. Sometimes people's body language will tell us whether we are to be closer or further away. (If I take a step forward and she takes a step back: that's an assessment.) However, when in doubt, we can always ask: we need to ask.

A CONSIDERATION: Every caregiver might improve his/her caregiving by having the following written in his or her job description: "administer appropriate touch." So that every time we are evaluated for our jobs, we are also evaluated for how and when we use touch. Are we touching people? Are we doing it appropriately? Have we assessed before we have expressed?

CANDY

Candy weighed over 400 pounds and her weight had become life-threatening. Although she was only thirty-six years old, she was living in a nursing home. Each of her days in that nursing home began with four staff members coming into her room to lift her into a sitting position. One morning one of the staff members, Jan, after helping Candy get up, stayed in the room and talked. Jan asked if she might hold Candy's hand as they were talking. After giving Jan her hand, Candy looked down at the hands and started crying. Jan asked, "What's wrong, Candy?" Candy responded, "No one has ever sat down with me and held my hand. The last time I think someone held my hand was when I weighed only sixty-five pounds. I was in second grade. Thank you. Thank you. Thank you."

MABEL

Mabel was a young grandmother. On the day that she died she was lying in a bed surrounded by her children and grandchildren. Everyone was holding her. One person held one hand, one another. Her feet, shoulders, legs, arms, head were all held. Then, one at a time, each relative said some words of love they associated with their touch.

The first person to speak was a young granddaughter: "Grandma. I remember all the times you would come and visit us, and you would have a surprise behind your back. You wouldn't show us the surprise until we gave you a hug. Grandma, I would have hugged you without the surprise."

The next person to speak was a daughter: "Mom. I remember when I was a little girl and I would often come home from school crying. You would hold me until I stopped. . . . Sometimes you had to hold me a long, long time. . . . I remember your love, Mom. I remember your touch, Mom. I'm trying to send that back to you now with my love and my touch."

One word frees us from all the weight and pain of life . . . that word is love. - Sophocles.

Love bears all things, believes all things, hopes all things, endures all things. . . . Love never fails. - St. Paul.

A CONSIDERATION: We men often have more difficulty with touch than women. Sometimes we need help, sometimes we need some kind of modeling and permission.

NELSON

Nelson was in a hospital bed in his living room. Besides Nelson, there was his wife, his sister, his brother, and me: two women and two men. The pain was coming on in waves. As the pain got intense, the two women were up at the bedside comforting Nelson. They would hold his hand. Sometimes kisses. Sometimes gentle petting. As the pain got intense, Nelson's brother started pacing, back and forth, beside the bed, back and forth. I don't know what I was thinking: I was seated in a chair, perhaps thinking I was the conductor of this orchestration. I had no idea what I was thinking.

I needed to do several things. (1) I needed to assess. Nelson's brother was pacing. What was going on? Was he nervous about something? Did he want to touch his brother, but had never before touched him out of love? (2) If the brother wanted to touch Nelson, I might have to model touch for him, and it would have to be an easy touch, some kind of touch that would not be too threatening for the brother. (3) I would also need to give permission to the brother to let him know that his touching of Nelson was okay. – However, the first thing I obviously needed to do was to get up off that chair.

I got up off the chair and decided to first model some touch so the brother would know the subject of the assessment and the subject of the permission – some easy touch. I took a wet washcloth and gently tapped Nelson's forehead during those waves of pain. Wet washcloth on a forehead: easy touch. I then decided to assess and give permission with the same movement: I held the washcloth out to the brother to see if he wanted the washcloth. He grabbed the washcloth, touched Nelson's forehead just briefly, then fell upon Nelson, and held his brother as tight as he could.

ROSIE'S FIRST VISIT

It was Rosie's first home visit as a hospice nurse. She was calling on an elderly woman in rural South Carolina. In the home, in addition to Rosie and the elderly woman, there was the woman's daughter and a deaconess from the woman's church.

The dying woman would periodically voice a loud gasp. Whenever she gasped, the daughter would burst into tears and the deaconess would start speaking in tongues. This went on for over an hour.

Rosie decided to go over to the daughter and suggest that the daughter go to the bed and hold her mother's hand. The daughter went over, took hold of her mother's hand, and simply said, "Mom." Her mother took a final gasp and died. The daughter turned to Rosie and said, "I almost missed that, didn't I?"

A CONSIDERATION: We say that some people are "in touch" and some people are "out of touch." We usually associate those who are "out of touch" with those who are so busy, so caught up with this-and-that that they have forgotten what is really important. If you find yourself so busy that you are "out of touch," you might want to consider getting back "in touch." Touch can be very important for people.

A CONSIDERATION: Many of our care recipients might also desire humor. It is not a universal desire, but it is certainly often desired. Here, as with touch, we must *assess before we express*. Many people want humor, but not everyone.

"Humor is not just a defense mechanism; it's an offense mechanism." - Norman Cousins.

"Life does not cease to be funny when people die, any more than it ceases to be serious when people laugh." - George Bernard Shaw.

I FOOLED YOU

I had a non-responsive patient I would often visit. I would go to her room, walk in, and say, "Janet, it's Doug. I'm back again." Then I would spend about ten minutes in her room, most often just sitting beside her. I would hold her hand and I would just pass the time in silence. But I was always sure to greet her verbally when I arrived, and would verbally say goodbye to her when I was leaving.

One day I was getting ready to leave. Janet's hand felt very cold, and I had this suspicion that she was no longer breathing. I got up close to her, leaning forward in my chair, to see if that was in fact the case. I could not tell. So I leaned in even closer: my face less than a foot away from Janet's face. I was staring at her mouth and nose to see if there was any movement. Suddenly her eyes opened – wide open. I jumped back, falling out of my chair.

Janet started laughing. She said, "I fooled you, didn't I?"

I almost stopped breathing.

She might not have died that day, but I nearly did.

A CONSIDERATION: As caregivers we often know our patients want humor because whenever there is joke-telling, the patient is often the one to initiate it. We'll also often have patients say something like the following: "I'm sick and tired of people coming into my room and putting on a mask of seriousness. I can hear people laughing down the hall. Do you know how that makes me feel? It's dehumanizing."

LA CUCARACHA

I was visiting a hospice patient in a hospital when a nurse approached me and asked if I might want to go down the hall and meet a patient named Harry. "Is Harry a hospice patient?" I asked. "No," she replied. "Might he be one soon?" I asked. "No: I don't think so," she said. "Well, why would I want to go down and meet Harry?" "You need to ask him about the train joke." I was hooked; my curiosity got the best of me.

So I went down the hall, introduced myself to Harry, and asked him about the train joke. His response: "Which version?" "Well, you better tell me all the versions," was all I could say.

Then Harry began his explanation. "There are two versions of the train joke. And I'd be glad to tell you both.

"But first you need to know that I have multiple sclerosis and I'm in the hospital because I've developed a mild case of pneumonia. They're basically just observing me to make sure that things don't get worse. And humor helps me: it helps me cope. And I think it helps others cope as well. So, when I think that I need a good laugh or someone else does, I do the train joke – the first version of the train joke.

"I press my call light button. And when my light goes on at the nurses station, they realize that it must be time for the train joke. So, two nurses come in the room. I work myself over to the side of the bed, get out of the bed, and brace myself up against the bed's side. And because of my multiple sclerosis I cannot make it across the room on my own. But I can with a little help. So a nurse gets in front of me, and I wrap my arms around him or her. A nurse gets behind, wrapping arms around me. And then the three of us can get across the room by shuffling. And as we are doing that I make these train noises."

He demonstrated his train noises.

He said, "That causes at least one of the nurses to laugh, and I think that really helps them. . . . And that's the first version of the train joke."

He then continued. "Now a couple days ago I decided to try a variation on the first train joke. I pressed my call light button. My light went on at the nurse's station. Two nurses came into my room: they were both women. We got into the train position. We started shuffling across the room. . . . And I was not making a sound, and they were puzzled. . . . When I got midway across the room, I jerked forward and I jerked back. I said, 'La Cucaracha.' . . . When I said that, the nurse in back started laughing, and it soon spread to the nurse in front and me in between. And we were laughing so loudly that our grips were loosening. And my surgical pants, which I like to wear, soon slipped to the ground. . . . As you can imagine, that didn't help to dissipate the laughter. . . . And the harder we laughed, the more our grips loosened. And soon all three of us followed the same route as the pants. And that didn't help either. . . . So, here I am on the floor with my pants off, rolling around with these two women. Now we're laughing so loudly that we're attracting people in the hall. They're looking in at us, we're looking up at them, and of course we can't stop laughing then at all."

SMILING AND LAUGHING PERMITTED HERE

If patients want to signal visitors that humor is okay in their rooms, they could pick one or more of the following signs to place in their room. Or: they can make up one on their own.

      A. "THIS IS A FROWN-FREE ZONE."
      B. "DANGER: EXCESSIVE SERIOUSNESS CAN PROVE HAZARDOUS TO YOUR HEALTH."
      C. "NO BUSINESS TRANSACTED HERE EXCEPT FOR FUNNY BUSINESS."
      D. "I COULD DIE LAUGHING IF YOU WOULD BE WILLING TO TELL ME A JOKE."
      E. "I AM NOT AFRAID OF DEATH. I JUST DON'T WANT TO BE THERE WHEN IT HAPPENS."
      F. "EVERYONE ALLOWS JOY TO COME TO THIS ROOM: SOME WHEN THEY ARRIVE, SOME WHEN THEY DEPART."

"Having humor while you're terminally ill is like making Death sit upon a Whoopy Cushion." - James Thorsen.

"Laughter can be more satisfying than honor; more precious than money; more heart cleansing than prayer." - Harriet Rochlin.

"I've taken my fun where I've found it." - Rudyard Kipling.

"Humor brings insight and tolerance." - Agnes Repplier.

LUCY

Lucy was struggling with dementia. She would often urinate in her bed. One day, Lucy's younger sister, Lydia, was changing Lucy's nightgown as Lucy silently endured the changing. Then suddenly Lucy bolted upright in her bed, winked at Lydia, and said, with a mischievous grin, "By Elmo, Lydia, I can still pee-pee and poo-poo with the best of them." Lucy started giggling, and Lydia started laughing so loud she started snorting.

"Sometimes a laugh is the only weapon we have." - Roger Rabbit.

WOLFGANG AND RUDOLF

Wolfgang lived alone in his home, except for his dog, a very protective dog, a schnauzer named Rudolf. Whenever our staff went to visit Wolfgang, who was almost always in bed, Rudolf would also be in that bed, growling at whoever came close to Wolfgang. This made our staff quite nervous.

One morning, the home health aide who was working with Wolfgang, a woman named Barb, had cornered several of us in our staff kitchen to tell us how nervous she was to make the visit that day. She was nervous because she not only needed to touch Wolfgang, but she needed to touch him in a rather intimate way. Wolfgang needed to have a condom catheter placed upon him. Needless to say, Barb was very worried over how Rudolf would respond, and, of course, all the rest of us were quite curious over how Rudolf would respond. We were so curious that we asked Barb to announce on the intercom when she was back at the office so that we could all gather again in the kitchen to hear her story.

At the end of the day Barb came back to the office, announced over the intercom that she was back, and then we gathered in the kitchen to hear her story. She told us that Rudolf was indeed present for her visit, in the bed, growling at her, inches away from her hands as she was applying that condom catheter. Barb said she was sweating, she was shaking, and it took her about three times the normal length of time to finish that procedure. . . . As soon as she finished, she stood back and gave a great sigh of relief. As soon as she stood back, Rudolf lunged. . . . Not for her, but for the condom catheter. Rudolf grabbed that condom catheter in his teeth and started pulling back on it. . . . This startled Barb. She yelled out loudly at Rudolf. . . . Apparently she yelled loud enough to startle Rudolf, who immediately let go of the condom catheter, which snapped back. . . . You know who was next startled in that equation: Wolfgang. After the pain subsided (and it took a little while), Wolfgang just started laughing. He said, "Okay, Barb, you can go tell everyone. Because I know you will."

"A sense of humor can help you overlook the unattractive, tolerate the unpleasant, cope with the unexpected, and smile through the unbearable." - Moshe Waldoks.

"Humor, like hope, allows one to acknowledge and endure what is otherwise unendurable." - Gail Sheehy.

A FUNNY LIFE REVIEW

The following activity uses the principle of recalling a past event and reliving it in the present to bring more humor into the present situation. Caregivers would ask those in their care to choose three questions from the following list. Suggest that they not answer them right away, but save their answers for the next visit. Giving them some time to respond will not only assure a good time for the next visit, but it will also provide them with some light moments in between the visits.

A. What do you remember as a funny thing that happened to you in grade school?
B. What is the funniest thing that ever happened to you during a meal?
C. What is the funniest thing that ever happened to you when you were not fully clothed?
D. What is the funniest thing that ever happened to you in an automobile?
E. When did you injure yourself and cause you or someone else to laugh?
F. What is the funniest joke that you have ever heard?
G. What is the funniest thing that you have ever seen a child do?
H. What is the funniest thing that you have ever seen an older person do?
I. What is the funniest thing that you have ever seen on television?

FUNNY VIDEOS

Video stores are stocked with humorous videotapes. Think of some of your favorites, or take recommendations from your patients, or ask your movie-going friends for some particularly funny ones. When people are ill or limited in their mobility, they and their caregivers can watch these tapes together. The experience is even more fun if you can share popcorn, ice cream, or candy. (However, we must always remember to assess before we express: "I heard about this funny video the other day. It was about this and that. . . . I wondered if it might be okay if I brought it next time?")

AFFIRMATIONS

Affirmations are not just for those who are healthy and involved in some sort of diet or exercise program; they can also be used with patients and loved ones who are dying. One to three of the following affirmations could be chosen by a terminally ill person to be his or her personal affirmation(s). Or, even better, a person could create his/her own affirmation(s). Each affirmation used would be posted on a place visited everyday (on a mirror or a refrigerator). Each time the person sees the affirmation, the affirmation is internally (or verbally) repeated three times.

   A. Every day, in every way, I am getting more at peace with myself, my family, my environment.
   B. I am a powerful person because I am filled with love.
   C. I accept and love myself just as I am.
   D. I have already done what I have needed to do with my life.
   E. My life has truly been full of joy.
   F. I am letting go of my life in peace and joy.
   G. My body might be leaving this world, but my influence will surely remain.
   H. I am going into my future with thankfulness and courage.

Other affirmations could be gathered from books and calendars that are available at bookstores and libraries.

A CONSIDERATION: As caregivers we receive so much from giving; in giving we really do receive – we can become richly blessed. That can also be a truth for our care recipients; care recipients can receive a sense of joy and purpose when they are allowed to show care to others.

"The hand that gives, gathers." - German Proverb.

RANDOM ACTS OF KINDNESS

Often the loss of job and the loss in family role definition cause people living in their final years to have a lack of self-worth, meaning, purpose. These following activities involve little in the way of time or physical energy, yet they can create great amounts positive satisfaction for all involved - simultaneously giving and receiving value.

> A. A person could bake some cookies, make some lemonade, and set up a table outside his or her home. A sign would be on the table saying: "FREE LEMONADE AND COOKIES."
> B. A person could go to a nursing home or a home for the mentally retarded and ask to visit someone who never receives any visitors, visiting for at least half an hour.
> C. A person could go to a neighborhood playground or shopping mall and pass out free balloons to children.
> D. A person could go to a shopping mall and pass out flowers. Each flower could have a little tag on it saying: "Have a good day. Please give this flower to someone else." After passing out the flowers, the person could just sit back and watch different people walking by with the flowers.
> E. A person could send one or five dollar bills to people randomly picked out of a telephone book, and then imagine how the money was used.
> F. A person could sit outside a beauty parlor and compliment everyone that comes out.

END-LIFE CRISIS

When people have what is often referred to as a "mid-life crisis," they can change occupational goals, adopt new political causes, go back to school, seek out new personal friends, alter their philosophies of life, even begin to wear new clothes and new hair styles. Many of these changes can result in a person acquiring a new sense of energy and a new sense of purpose. So it is with a "mid-life crisis."

What about an "end-life crisis?" Is there any reason why people cannot have an "end-life crisis" as well as a mid-life crisis.

What is wrong with people in their final years studying for a high school equivalency exam or enrolling in a college course? What is wrong with people in their final years deciding to join a political group like the National Organization for Women, the Sierra Club, or a Right To Life chapter? What is wrong with people in their final years going on a spiritual retreat or changing religions? What is wrong with people in their final years wearing fluorescent orange shirts and bright green pairs of pants?

A CONSIDERATION: A dying person's thoughts, his or her attitudes, can certainly affect his or her health and quality of life. Do we encourage constructive thinking and discourage destructive thinking? Do we encourage independence, whenever possible, and discourage dependence? Have we helped to create an environment whereby our clients/patients are empowered to discover their own self-worth, freed from the past, **equipped for the future?**

ELIMINATING SELF-BLAMING OVER ILLNESS

In looking back on life people can often have thoughts of self-blaming. Much of this self-blaming is the result of irrational thoughts. Such irrational self-blaming can hinder asserting control, hindering the activation of constructive choice-making. These irrational beliefs can be changed through cognitive shifts that involve a person changing thought patterns from irrational personalization to reasonable depersonalization. The following activity helps people make those kinds of cognitive shifts.

1. Make a list of the various self-blaming beliefs that often accompany your thinking, listing all the thoughts that you have in which there is a blaming of the self for some problem that you have. Make the list quite long, trying to generate between five and ten self-blaming thoughts. [Examples: "If I would have had a more healthy diet when I was younger, I would not be so sick now." "If I only had more positive thoughts, I could get over this illness." "God is punishing me because of my lack of religiosity."]

2. Do some brainstorming on some other possible causes of your problems, reminding yourself that some causes are simply unknown and that some things happen out of pure randomness.

3. Going through the self-blaming list one item at a time, make a cause-related statement that is not self-blaming, using similar vocabulary as the self-blaming sentence. [Examples: Across from the statement "If I would have had a more healthy diet when I was younger, I would not be so sick now" write "People can get sick whether they eat or not eat healthy food." Across from the statement "If I only had more positive thoughts, I could get over this illness" write "If positive thinking could eliminate all illness and body decay, optimists would never die. Yet, optimists die of the same diseases as everyone else."]

4. Keep a diary of negative events. After each negative event list a supposed self-centered cause and then a cause that is not self-centered.

5. Post statements around your living space reminding you that external causes are of great influence on health and welfare, and these causes are often completely out of anyone's control.

A CONSIDERATION: Everyone has dirt in their lives. Some people grow roses in the dirt, and some people just grow weeds.

THE GRASS CAN SOMETIMES BE BROWNER

People approaching death often feel cheated out of life. They ask, "Why me? . . . Why now? . . . Why couldn't I have gotten a warning? . . . Couldn't I just be given ten more years, or even ten more months?" Frequently accompanying this feeling of being cheated, is a fantasy about having a better existence than the current one, a feeling that they would be so much better "if only . . ." This activity helps people to examine their true state, which they may discover is not all that bad. They may in fact come to see negatives in their fantasy world and positives in their real world.

1. Close your eyes and imagine that all your fantasies came true. Imagine that this fantasy world will last forever, that nothing will ever diminish or destroy it.

2. Write down all the elements in that fantasy world. [Example: "I would have no aches and pains. . . . I would not age. . . . I would be able to eat anything I wanted, go anywhere I wanted to go. . . ."]

3. Create an honest, detailed picture of what life would be like in the fantasy world. Consider every angle, even the negative ramifications. [Examples: "Doesn't pain protect us from some things? What are the positive purposes that pain might have? . . . There are advantages to youth, but what are the disadvantages? What are the advantages of age? Are there some gains that come from age which younger people do not experience? . . . Wouldn't eating anything, whenever we wanted, destroy some wonderful eating pleasures that come from anticipating a special food and finally eating it? Wouldn't the foods we really enjoy become less likable if they were all we ever ate? . . . Would it really be an enjoyable state never to experience any changes?"]

4. Now focus on your current life. Consider every angle, even the possible advantages. [Examples: "What pleasures in life would you have missed if your life stopped at age thirty? . . . What people would you have not met? . . . Have you even experienced some joys in the last twenty-four hours, even with all the negative things going on?"]

"Looking for alternatives – better sights than we see, better sounds than we hear, a better mind than we have – keeps us from realizing that we could stand with pride in the middle of our life and realize it's a sacred mandala." - Pema Chodron.

GUIDED IMAGERY: DIALOGUE WITH DEATH

The following guided imagery could be read to the care recipient with pauses between sentences to allow him or her to verbalize the images, thoughts, and responses that come to mind. Or care recipients could listen silently and later write or dictate a report of the images and responses that they imagined as the dialogue is read aloud. - This dialogue could be adapted for different occasions; it could be restructured as a "Dialogue with Pain" or a "Dialogue with Stress."

"Close your eyes and imagine yourself sitting across from an empty chair. Now imagine that the personification of death is sitting in that chair. What would Death look like if it were a person sitting there? . . . What does the face of Death look like? . . . Describe the clothes Death is wearing. . . . What do the hands of Death look like? . . .

"What would you want to say to Death? . . . Verbalize what you want to say in the present tense, just as though Death is actually sitting in that chair across from you. . . . Say everything you want to say to Death. . . .

"Now put yourself in that chair and visualize yourself as Death looking at you. Verbalize Death's response to you. If you were Death, what would you say to the person in front of you? Say everything that Death would say. . . . How would Death respond to the message that you had previously directed toward Death? . . .

"Although you cannot eliminate the existence of Death, you have the power to exercise some control over Death. In replying to what Death has just said, go back in your imagination to your original place and tell Death what you want Death to do. Verbalize some orders to Death. Tell Death how you expect Death to behave from this moment forward. . . . Tell Death also how you want Death to change in physical appearance, and say what you expect Death to wear for the next visit. . . .

"Now tell Death to get up from the chair and leave the room. . . . As you visualize Death starting to exit, tell Death that you realize that you will see Death again, but you expect Death to wait for an invitation before returning. . . .

"For the moment, say goodbye to Death . . . and slowly open your eyes. . . ."

The above activity might seem rather silly to people. Yet there is a profound truth being explored and expressed here. For many people the personification of Death can in fact change. For many people Death can change from an intruder to a welcome guess, from something very ugly to something that might even be beautiful, from an enemy to a friend. This activity helps people realize that our relationship to Death can change; Death can change.

GUIDED IMAGERY: MY FUNERAL

The following guided imagery could be read to the participant or recorded for the participant's use.

Lying down on a floor, close your eyes and try to make your body as quiet as you possibly can. . . . Relax deeply. . . . Relax until you feel as though your body and the floor are one. . . . Your life has left you. Only your body remains on the floor. . . .

Your body no longer moves. Your body is dead. Your physical being is gone. . . . Only your consciousness survives and your consciousness realizes that it is the day of your funeral. . . . Your funeral is about to begin. . . .

You see your body lying in a casket at the end of a funeral parlor. Picture the lid open on your casket and see your dead body lying inside. . . . Notice how you appear. . . . Notice how you have been preserved. Notice what you are wearing. . . .

See the people who have come to your funeral. Look around at who has come. Recognize the individuals. Look into their faces. . . . Notice their expressions. . . . Notice their emotions. . . . Notice those who are mingling with others. . . . Notice those who are silent and reserved. . . .

Imagine people coming up to the casket one at a time. Who is the first person who comes up to your casket? . . . How does this person react to seeing your body? . . . What would you like to say to this person? Remember you are dead and cannot say anything. . . . Notice the second person who comes up to your casket. What reactions does this person have? . . . What do you want to say to this person? How do you feel being unable to say those words? . . . Who is the next person to look at your body? How does this person react? . . . What thoughts do you have about this person? . . .

    Looking around, is there someone missing that you hoped would be there? . . . Who is the missing person? . . . What has caused this person to be absent? . . . What would you like to say to that person? . . .

    Notice your emotions as you picture your funeral? . . . Focus on those feelings. . . . Experience your feelings. What do you feel? . . .

    Notice the music that is playing at your funeral. . . . Listen to the music as it is being played. . . . Is the music what you wanted to hear? . . .

    Notice the flowers. . . . Are there many? Are there few? . . . Visualize and smell the flowers at your funeral. . . . How do you feel about these flowers? . . .

    Notice who is getting up to give your eulogy. . . . Listen to what this person says. . . . How do you feel as you listen? . . .

    The funeral is now ending and the people are leaving. . . . Notice how people look as they are leaving the service. . . . Prepare yourself to leave the service and to return to your body. . . .

    Now take your attention back to your present physical body, the live body, the body that is laying on the floor this very moment. . . . Feel the weight of your head. . . . Feel the weight of your pelvis. . . . Feel your heels. . . . Feel your upper body. . . . Feel your upper body move as you take in each breath. . . . Feel the life-giving air enter your body, allowing its life-giving energy to swirl throughout your entire body. . . . You are alive! . . . Your life is not over yet! . . . You have more time. What do you want to do with this time? . . . What did you learn from imagining your funeral? . . . What do you need to do? Who do you need to talk to? . . .

    Slowly open your eyes. . . .

This guided imagery would be followed by a discussion examining the following questions. What negative experiences or images did you have in that guided imagery: what did you not like? How might we increase the possibility that those negative things which you experienced and imagined will not become reality? What positive experiences or images did you have in that guided imagery: what did you like? How might we increase the possibility that those positive things which you experienced and imagined will become reality?

A CONSIDERATION: Not only do our clients/patients want to control much of what precedes death, having options, having choices. Our clients/patients can also want to control the timing of death itself, having options there, having choices there.

BILL'S CHOICE

Bill was dying in a hospital. His family had gathered: his wife and his four children. The family was told by a doctor that Bill would most likely die within the next twenty-four hours. The family did not want him to die alone, so they set up a schedule so that someone would be at his bedside every minute. Just in case he lasted longer than twenty-four hours, they decided to commit themselves to a three day schedule.

When that schedule expired they set up another three day schedule.

On the fifth day of the watch, one of Bill's sons was on his shift. The son wanted to make a telephone call he did not want his dad to hear. He went out into the hallway to make that call. He was gone no more than five minutes. When the son returned, Bill was dead.

I believe Bill might have chosen to die at that moment. Sometimes people just want to die alone. They might not want to be a "burden" to anyone. They might not want to "favor" anyone by dying on that person's watch. They just might not want to be around people in this most personal and vulnerable of moments. They could have any number of reasons.

ESTHER'S CHOICE

Esther was living with her daughter and her grandson. Her grandson was four years old, closing in on five. Everyday the boy would ask his grandmother, "Are you going to die today, Grandma?" Everyday Esther would reply, "I don't think so."

One day the boy said, "Grandma, please don't die on my birthday: I'm going to be five. . . . It's okay to die *after* my birthday, but not *on* my birthday. Okay, Grandma?"

"I'll try my best," said Esther.

Esther died the day after her grandson's fifth birthday.

KAMMY'S CHOICE

Kammy was twenty-nine, the mother of two girls, ages three and six. She was dying of cancer of the liver.

Kammy would always hurry back from her therapy to be with her children: she did not want to lose any time that she knew was becoming more and more precious. She also did not want to die in a hospital away from her children; nor did she want to die at home with her children seeing her die. She just did not want to die; she did not want to leave her children. But she also knew everything was not going to be left up to her to decide. She had some choices, but certainly not many.

Her disease progressed rapidly.

Kammy had a good friend named Linda. Linda talked to her every day. They were the best of friends. Their relationship had even gotten stronger during the illness.

After receiving a suggestion from someone at her church, Kammy decided to go to a faith healer living in a city that was a six hour drive from her home. Two of her church friends drove her there, where Kammy had arranged to stay at a bed-and-breakfast the night before she was scheduled to meet the faith healer. She had not told Linda she was going, probably because she knew Linda would want to come along. She had also insisted that Donald, her husband, not come along, but stay at home with the girls.

Kammy died that night at the bed-and-breakfast.

Donald, Linda, and Kammy's nurse, in looking back, felt that Kammy knew that she would die on that trip. She did not want to die in a hospital; she did not want to die at home; she did not want to have her husband, children, or best friend watch her die.

A CONSIDERATION: As caregivers we can make mistakes in trying to postpone someone's death against his or her wishes. As caregivers we can make mistakes in trying to hasten someone's death against his or her wishes.

TRICIA'S PATIENT

Tricia told me about an experience she had her first year out of nursing school. She was caring for a woman in her seventies, a woman who had signed the appropriate paperwork asking that she not be kept alive through any artificial means. The woman was dying and she was having difficulty in eating, losing a lot of weight, but insisted on no artificial feeding. She would frequently talk to Tricia whenever Tricia visited, trying to assure the young nurse that it was okay to die: that there was no reason to fear death.

The dying woman's oldest son, who hadn't seen his mother for over a year, insisted on force-feeding his mother through a Dobhoff tube (a tube that was inserted in her nose in order to force nutrition into her). The son made sure that his wishes were carried out even though he knew they were contrary to his mother's own wishes. As soon as that Dobhoff tube was inserted, the woman refused to communicate in any fashion to anyone: not communicating for the entire five weeks that tube was in her nose. Finally the son relented and decided to remove the tube.

The day after the tube was removed Tricia was giving the woman a sponge bath. After the bath the dying woman broke her silence, saying, "Thank you, deary. Thank you. You've been very kind to me. You've been very kind. Not everyone has been kind to me."

The woman died two weeks later. Apparently she refused to say anything else to anyone else. She didn't say anything to her doctor. She didn't say anything to her son.

DORREEN'S BROTHER

Dorreen's brother wanted no technological interventions used on him to postpone the natural dying process, and he had communicated that to relatives and appropriate health care authorities. But his wishes were not honored. When Dorreen, a nurse of fourteen years, was informed of her brother being in a hospital, she was also informed that he had been resuscitated after not breathing for eight minutes (consequently having brain damage), was hooked up to an IV drip, and was no longer breathing on his own, but only through a breathing machine. Dorreen was furious that her brother's wishes had not been honored.

Dorreen drove ten hours to get to the hospital that was holding her brother. When she was taken to see him, she felt she was not being shown the brother she remembered; there was only the physical shell that used to house the person she had known as her brother. She was told that there was a less than one percent chance that her brother would ever leave the hospital alive.

Dorreen asked the doctor in charge to take her brother off the ventilator. The doctor refused, saying that he believed such an act to be inhumane. Dorreen's fury was building. She gave her doctor until noon of the next day to follow her brother's wishes, her wishes, and the family's wishes.

Later that day her brother's doctor left town. The physician designated to take his calls also refused to cease life support. The new physician said, because he was not the primary doctor, that he couldn't make that decision.

Dorreen demanded an ethics committee consult. She was told the hospital did not have an ethics committee.

Dorreen could not get anyone at the hospital to follow her brother's clearly stated wishes. She felt that she was being forced into taking matters into her own hands. She stopped the half-dozen IV pumps, turned off the monitor, pulled out the catheter that had been inserted in her brother's heart, removed an arterial line, and had one of her sisters, a respiratory therapist, remove the breathing tube. Then Dorreen gave her brother a bath.

Then the wait began. For several hours, her brother's breathing was rapid, shallow, and wet. Dorreen clearly remembers hearing that awful, gargling, drowning sound, that sound which she was forced to hear.

CATHY

Cathy was young to face death. She desperately wanted to live for her young children. But everyone around her, including her parents, saw futility in her desire to fight her devastating illness. During the last week of her life, Cathy's parents were at her bedside, witnessing her pain and praying for its relief, believing her pain could only be relieved through death. They encouraged her to let go, hoping that their permission could assist Cathy in that dying process.

Cathy's parents, with good intentions, continued this approach for several days. As they gently rubbed her back or held her hand or stroked her hair, they told Cathy that she had fought a brave fight, but that it was now time to let go.

Cathy always responded with a resounding "No!" no matter how weak she was. No matter how much pain she was in, she could gather together enough energy to say "No!"

Her parents used guided imagery by portraying the image of a reunion with her favorite relative, her grandfather. They talked about all the good arrangements that were being made for the future care of her children. They expressed all their love towards Cathy. Yet, even in a semiconscious state, Cathy always protested, "No! No! No!"

On the last day of her life, Cathy's struggle was obvious to everyone who entered her room. Some people saw her struggle as a conflict between the known and the unknown. Others likened it to the labor of giving birth. Some saw it as a battle with God's will. Some saw it as just plain stubbornness. However interpreted, Cathy continued to voice her insistent "No!" It was her final word.

Cathy did not want to die. She did not want to surrender to the dying process. Why should she have to surrender? Others might want to surrender, but not Cathy. "No! No! No!"

A CONSIDERATION: What few choices we have in determining how we enter this world. What few choices we have in living our own lives – being manipulated politically, economically, socially, environmentally. What very few choices we have as we become seriously ill. Can we not at least have a few choices in how we exit this world?

A CONSIDERATION: Some tools and techniques are only appropriate for use by professional caregivers. Some tools and techniques can be used by professional caregivers as well as family members. Some tools and techniques are only appropriate for use by family members. Professional caregivers and family members can sometimes fill the role of the other, but can never be completely equal to the other.

INVASION OF PRIVACY

Mary, a social worker, approached me during a seminar. She had tears in her eyes. "Do you know that hospice can be an invasion of privacy?" I'm sure I had a puzzled look on my face, wanting to hear her, wanting to understand what she was saying.

"My husband died five months ago," she said. . . . "The hospice people just came into our house with their forms. They acted like we wanted them or needed them. We did not want them. We did not need them. A doctor had forced us to get hospice." Tears were coming down her cheeks.

"They acted like they knew everything. They didn't know anything. They didn't know me. They didn't know my husband. They were acting like they were members of our family, but they were not. They didn't know anything about our family.

"And they thought they were helping me. . . . They were interfering. They were getting between my husband and me. . . . And they had no right to be in my home."

A CONSIDERATION: Family members can sometimes be quite important. They often become indispensable as death is near.

DOTTIE'S SON

Dottie had been unresponsive for five days. Death appeared to be imminent. Her son had been notified, and he was driving down to see her. From his home in Toronto, he would need to drive for twenty hours to reach his mother's bedside.

Even though Dottie was unresponsive, her nurses would periodically inform her about her son's progress. "He'll be here in fifteen hours." "It's only twelve more hours now." "Eight more hours, Dottie. Eight more hours." Even though there was no assurances from Dottie that she heard a single word, the nurses continued to inform her of the son's progress. "Four more hours. It's now only four hours."

The son arrived. As soon as he entered the room, he said, "Mom, I'm here."

Dottie opened her eyes for the first time in five days. She then spoke: "My boy. I knew you'd make it. I knew my boy would make it. All along I knew."

Dottie died an hour later. She and her son were holding hands.

"But be glad for me if I can die in the presence of friends and family. If this happens, believe me I came out ahead. I didn't lose this one." - Raymond Carver.

A CONSIDERATION: We are told that there are more non-traditional families than traditional families; there are more exceptions to the rule than there are examples of the rule. If that is in fact the case, we probably need to look at the rule. What do we mean by family? At a minimum we would probably have to include the following three qualities: connectedness, interdependence, and intimacy. Yet whatever definition we produce, we would have to acknowledge that those qualities can come in a variety of forms, a variety which is often quite beautiful.

MANNY AND NATHAN

Manny was dying of AIDS. He was in the hospital having all of his physical needs being addressed by physicians, nurses, and various other hospital personnel. But his spirit was slipping; his attitude was failing.

Then one afternoon his partner, Nathan, abducted Manny from the hospital and took him to a bed and breakfast owned by some friends of theirs. That afternoon and evening Nathan and Manny watched a videotape of "I Love Lucy" reruns, they danced to Bette Midler, they drank champaign and ate caviar, and they talked about the good times they had had together in their partnership.

Nathan brought Manny back to the hospital late that night. Manny was totally exhausted, completely spent from his time with Nathan.

Manny lived for about six more weeks. He told everyone that he couldn't have been happier than the day he was abducted from the hospital. He said that it was the very best day of his entire life.

THE BIRTHDAY PARTY

Priscilla would be alive for her eightieth birthday, but it would almost certainly be her last birthday. A couple weeks before the event, her daughter called about thirty of Priscilla's relatives to see if they might be available to call Priscilla on her birthday. A schedule was formed, staggering the telephone calls throughout the day. As each telephone call came in, the daughter held the phone up to Priscilla's ear. Priscilla received telephone calls from relatives in twelve different states that day, each telephone call filled with greetings and fond memories.

THE WEDDING ANNIVERSARY

Carlos was dying of emphysema. He had been informed that he had only a couple months to live, but he wanted to be alive for his fiftieth wedding anniversary which was nine months away.

His three daughters decided that they would design a different fiftieth wedding anniversary every month for as long as he lived. Each anniversary celebration, each month, would have a different theme. One month they had a tacky gift party. Another month they had a re-marriage service. Another month they had an accordion player serenade the couple. Another month: a thirty-one flavor ice cream party. Their parents had a ball at each celebration.

Carlos ended up dying a couple weeks after the real fiftieth wedding anniversary. But in the meantime he had eight other wonderful celebrations.

FAMILY DISCUSSION

The terminally ill are often comforted by knowing that their family members are prepared for the death. Family members could be led through the following activity to assist in that preparation.

1. Each family member would go off alone one afternoon, each taking a pen and a piece of paper labeled "My Opinions Concerning Death."

2. Each family member would write for 20 to 30 minutes. People could follow a stream-of-consciousness style – they should not worry about sentence structure, spelling, or punctuation, just scribble the thoughts down on paper as they come to mind. If anyone has difficulty getting started, the following questions may help.

    A. What causes people to die?
    B. What is the worst death that you can imagine?
    C. What is the best death that you can imagine?
    D. What is your opinion about an afterlife?
    E. How do you feel about the eventuality of your own death?

3. When everyone has finished writing, each person shares with the rest of the family what he or she has written. No value judgments or critical comments are allowed. Everyone's opinion is accepted as having equal value and validity with everyone else's.

COUPONS

The family of the care recipient might want to offer him or her some coupons, redeemable whenever the recipient chooses. Here are some samples:

    A. "This coupon is good for a 10-minute back massage."
    B. "This coupon is good for one ice-cream cone. You choose the flavor."
    C. "This coupon entitles you to have me as your slave for a whole afternoon."

D. "This coupon means that I will read to you for an hour from a book of your choice."

E. "This coupon is good for a manicure."

F. "This coupon means that I will be the guardian of your peace and quiet for a whole day."

G. "This coupon entitles you to a three-hour outing to a location of your choice."

SHARING DREAMS

Several books about dreams and dying suggest that not only do people facing death often dream about death, but their family members also are likely to dream about it. A useful exercise to increase the sense of family connectedness and intimacy involves setting a time once a week for families to gather and share their dreams. Each family member could describe one dream from the past week. Then all the other relatives could discuss their feelings and thoughts about that dream.

GIVEAWAY CEREMONY

The giving away of a person's possessions can take on great meaning when done in a group setting. This giveaway ceremony can be done by the dying person before he or she dies or by the executor (or other designated person) after the death.

1. Invitations for the event would be sent out to all the people who would be receiving a gift.

2. As each item is given away, special memories of the item would be shared and reasons would be given for why the particular item was going to a particular recipient.

3. Each recipient would be asked to give some verbal response after receiving the gift.

FAMILY LITANY AS DEATH IS NEAR

Sometimes the dying are simply ready to let go; they're tired; they realize their time has come to leave this life. When this occurs, a family might want to gather to say together the following litany, placing the dying person's name in the space that is blank.

Family spokesperson: "_____, in knowing that you have led a good and complete life,"
Family: "We release you."

Family spokesperson: "_____, in knowing that we are not at all angry with you,"
Family: "We release you."

Family spokesperson: "_____, in knowing that you have all our love,"
Family: "We release you."

Family spokesperson: "_____, in knowing that we have heard and received your love,"
Family: "We release you."

Family spokesperson: "_____, in knowing that there is no more that we can do for you,"
Family: "We release you."

Family spokesperson: "_____, in knowing that your suffering will soon be relieved,"
Family: "We release you."

In giving this litany to a family, the caregiver would communicate to them that only they will know whether there is a time or place to do this. The caregiver can mention that other families have found this to be helpful. But only this particular family will know if it is right for them. The family would also decide whether they do the litany in the presence of the dying person or in another room.

CLYDE'S WIFE

A nurse named Trevor described Clyde as very stoic; Clyde's emotions, if he had any, were apparently very difficult to read. Trevor described Clyde's wife as alternating between periods of intense struggling to stay alive with periods of wanting to have her life finished. As no one was certain of how Clyde felt, no one was certain of what Clyde's wife was feeling either: she could no longer speak or write, and she appeared to be battling conflicting desires.

Clyde and his wife's marriage had been rocky for the last several years. They had had some beautiful times early in their marriage, but much time had passed since then. They were now quite distant from one another, physically and emotionally.

Trevor advised Clyde to go into his wife's room and tell her it was okay to die if she wanted to, that she didn't have to fight any more to stay alive. Clyde did that, but his wife did not give up her fight.

Trevor asked Clyde what might his wife be waiting for? Why was she holding on? Was there something that had not been done? Something that needed to be said? Trevor asked, "Is there something in your relationship which is incomplete?"

Clyde said he thought he knew what needed to be done. He told Trevor he would be right back as he went into his wife's room. He held both of her hands. He looked into her eyes and said, "I love you." She took three breaths and died. Clyde then left the room, convinced that each of those three breaths stood for a word. Her response: "I love you."

NAOMI'S HUSBAND

A nurse named Naomi wanted to share with me the story about her husband's prostate cancer. He had received bad news after bad news, disappointment after disappointment, one blow after another. Never any good news, always bad news, and it kept coming.

Naomi said, "I was a nurse. And I knew that we were being told he was dying and that we did not have much more time together. And yet, instead of showing care or using my nursing experience, I just distanced myself, knowing that he was going to die. . . . And then he didn't die. . . . He didn't die."

She continued, "And then I suddenly discovered that I loved my husband – I discovered that I loved him so much – and I had not expressed any of my love in the last twenty years of our thirty-seven year marriage. And when I realized that I just started crying. And I cried and I cried and I cried.

"I knew that my distancing was an attempt at protecting me. I didn't want to get into all the emotional stuff: I felt I somehow didn't want to have to bother with the emotions. . . . But I love him so much now. And I tell him that I love him: I now tell him that every day. I love him. I love him so much. And it took his dying for me to realize that."

Chapter Four

Addressing The Emotional/Psychological Concerns Of The Grieving

NO TIME TABLE

I was introduced to Frank and Betty shortly after they had celebrated their seventieth wedding anniversary. Frank was dying, and Betty was determined that after living with Frank for seventy years there was no way that she was going to hand him over to someone else for his last couple weeks. She was going to be his principle caregiver to the very end, no matter how difficult his care might become. But his care became very difficult, especially for a woman in her nineties.

Fortunately, at the time, I was working at a hospice that had a hospice house. We invited Frank and Betty to move into one of the rooms together. That way Betty could be Frank's principle caregiver, and if she needed any help all she had to do was stick her head out into the hall and call for help. They accepted the invitation.

Part of the reason why it was necessary for Frank and Betty to move into the house was because they had not had any children other than a daughter who was stillborn the first year of their marriage. Frank and Betty had named their daughter Sarah.

Although I had met Frank and Betty shortly before they entered the hospice house, I never got an opportunity to talk to them afterwards. Each time I went to visit I would find Frank asleep in the bed and Betty asleep in the lounge chair.

One morning a nurse was making her rounds when she looked into Frank and Betty's room and saw that the two of them were lying together in the bed holding hands. The nurse walked into the room. As the nurse got closer to them she realized that Frank was not breathing. Betty was looking out the window. With tears in her eyes Betty turned to the nurse and said, "Frank asked me to come into bed with him and then he asked me if it would be okay if he went to be with Sarah. I told him it would be okay, but I miss him now already."

A CONSIDERATION: We can grieve someone we have lost minutes ago; we can grieve someone we have lost seventy years ago. We can grieve someone we've known for seventy years; we can grieve someone we've known for only a few moments. We can grieve someone whose death is way premature; we can grieve someone whose death might even be long overdue.

"No two people experience grief in exactly the same manner. Whether male or female, old or young, Swedish or Native American, Protestant or Roman Catholic, grief is an individual process." - Elizabeth Levang.

"No story of loss replicates any other." - Thomas Attig.

"If there is one thing I have learned . . . it's that we all grieve in our own ways and on our own schedule." - Candy Lightner.

STANDING, WAITING

Nick was developmentally disabled. He was in his forties, living in a house with other people who were developmentally disabled.

Nick's father would come visit him every Friday afternoon around 2 p.m.. They would then go out on a walk. Every Friday Nick would always be waiting for his father at the house's front door at 1 p.m.. Nick would have his coat draped over his arm, standing, waiting, until his father arrived. Then, at 2 p.m., the two of them would go out for their Friday walk.

Nick's father had an extended illness and had to miss an occasional Friday. Yet Nick would still go to that door at 1 p.m., coat draped over his arm, standing, waiting. On the days his father did not come Nick would wait for about two hours, then return to his room, realizing that his father was not going to come that Friday.

Then Nick's father died.

Every Friday, for the next six and a half years, until he himself died, Nick would go to that door, coat draped over his arm, standing, waiting.

"There are no absolutes in grief. There are no reactions so universal that all, or even most, people will experience them. There is only one unalterable truth: All relationships are unique." - John James & Russell Friedman.

A CONSIDERATION: Every death is different from every other death. None are necessarily more easy for the survivor; none are necessarily more difficult. Sudden death or protracted death: one does not necessarily cause more grief than the other – each can be terribly difficult. Death by suicide or death by natural causes: one does not necessarily cause more grief than the other – each can be terribly difficult. Death of an 8 year old or death of an 80 year old: one does not necessarily cause more grief than the other – each can be terribly difficult.

A CONSIDERATION: As no deaths are necessarily more difficult for the survivor, no recovery tools are necessarily more fitting, whether the grief is the result of a sudden death or a protracted death, death by suicide or death by natural causes, death of an 8 year old or death of an 80 year old. The care recipient and the caregiver must explore many options for recovery, finding something that works and then working with what they find.

KEEPING A GRIEF DIARY

Buy a blank book to serve as your grief diary – something that looks nice. Whenever you have remembrances of your lost loved one or whenever you have some emotions related to grief, record your thoughts and feelings in your diary. Don't shy away from any thoughts – share the good and bad. Don't shy away from any emotions – share whatever you feel. Portray a complete picture of your loved one. Portray a complete picture of you.

This diary can be shared or kept private. It's your diary intended for your thoughts and feelings, your ups and downs: do with it what you like – just do it. It will help.

Eleanor M. McNear
49 Saint Paul Ave.
Trenton, NJ 08638

MEMORY BOOK

A person could make a "memory book" to remember and honor the deceased. This memory book is designed to be an ongoing, ever-expanding memorial.

1. The cover of the book could be made from some special material (a former article of clothing, a favorite pattern of the person who has died).

2. The book could hold several items:

    A. Birth certificate.
    B. Various photographs.
    C. Diplomas.
    D. Wedding announcement.
    E. Menus from favorite restaurants.
    F. Reminders of vacations taken.
    G. Person's favorite passages from literature or scripture.
    H. Newspaper announcements (birth, school events, marriage, retirement, etc.).
    I. Letters sent and received.
    J. Funeral service program.
    K. Sympathy cards.

3. If an entire family is doing the project, each family member could be responsible for gathering materials from a particular time in the deceased person's life or from a particular role that person had (father, husband, businessman, golfer, community activist, etc.).

4. At first every other page could be blank. The blank pages would be used in the future to make comments (thoughts, feelings, additional remembrances) when reviewing the book.

5. The book could be placed in a special place.

MEMORY COLLAGE

A client/patient could gather a bunch of old magazines, a large poster board, scissors, and glue. A collage could then be made out of pictures and words from the magazines, images and thoughts that remind him or her of the person who has died. The collage could then be shared with family and/or friends.

MEMORIAL QUILT

The project is to make a quilt with each square representing either a special time in the departed person's past or a different role (or activity) in that person's life. Some suggestions:

    A. Fabric paint or embroidery could be used as well as special items or mementos stitched onto the cloth squares.
    B. The project could be done by a single participant, a couple bereaved persons, an entire bereaved family, or several friends and family members.
    C. When the quilt is finished, a party could occur, inviting family members and friends to come admire the quilt and share stories about the person who is being memorialized.

MEMORY JAR

A grieving person might want to set aside a memory jar to help in the grieving process.

1. A large jar is placed in a convenient place.

2. Whenever the survivor has a memory of the person who died, he/she writes that memory on a piece of paper and places it in the jar.

3. The survivor then periodically takes some time (perhaps the first day of each month) to sit down with the jar and review the memories that have been placed in the jar since the last review.

THE MEMORIAL SCULPTURE

Many people were coming to visit Brad. During visiting hours there would usually be at least four or five people in his room, always talking: reminiscing, joke-telling, clowning around. Brad had always been very popular.

One day, a couple weeks before he died, Brad's mother entered his room just before visiting hours were to officially begin. She found him crying. "What's wrong, dear?" she asked. He responded, "Mom, I know I have a lot of friends, and everyone comes and visits me, and everyone seems to have a good time when they're here. But have you noticed that no one ever touches me anymore; they don't touch me. People used to give me hugs all the time. They'd put their arms around my shoulders, kissed me hello and kissed me goodbye. Sometimes a handshake. But now, no one touches me, no one hugs me, no one kisses me. No handshakes. It's tearing me up inside. It's tearing me up. No one, no one anywhere, should have to die without being touched and held."

Brad's mother later shared Brad's remarks with some of his friends. His friends realized their wrong and were moved to show more physical expressions of their love; there was plenty of touching in Brad's room after that.

Brad's friends also decided to make a memorial to Brad after he died. Twenty-seven of his friends gathered one day to put their hand prints in a mold. A wall sculpture was then made for the hospital. The sculpture had twenty-seven pairs of hands appearing to reach out from the wall. At the bottom of that sculpture was the last sentence of Brad's conversation with his mother: "No one, no one anywhere, should have to die without being touched and held."

A "FITTING" MEMORIAL

One day during the last couple months of her life, Lisa asked her three best friends to come over to her house for a special ceremony. The four of them had spent much time together, and they had many things in common. They had all enjoyed some of the same sports. They had some of the same tastes in men. They all liked going out to eat and having a good bottle of wine with their dinner. They had read some of the same books. They even had the same tastes in clothes, even wearing many of the same sizes of clothing.

On that day Lisa gave away all her favorite clothes to her three friends. With each gift she shared a story regarding that particular item of clothing, telling of the times she had worn each item, where she was, what she was doing. Lisa in giving away those clothes was doing her own life review as she expressed her deep love for her friends. She was also giving her friends a way of remembering her, a memorial they could even wear.

A "DEAD DENNY PARTY"

When Denny was alive his favorite form of relaxation/entertainment was to put on an old sweatshirt and jeans, take a stereo out to his backyard, and listen to Grateful Dead music while he drank Chianti and smoked a big cigar. After Denny's death his friends held an annual "Dead Denny Party" on his birthday. His friends would gather in sweatshirts and jeans in someone's backyard, listen to Grateful Dead music, drink Chianti, and smoke big cigars.

RELATIONSHIP LIFE REVIEW

Grievers can sometimes benefit from simply telling their story. A client/patient could write down the answers to the following questions, then share his/her story with someone special, a counselor, or several people.

1. When did the two of you first see each other? Where were you? What transpired between the two of you?

2. What was the fondest moment you recall from the early part of your relationship? Where were you? What transpired?

3. What was the roughest time in your relationship? What transpired? How did the two of you get through that time?

4. What was the fondest moment you recall from the later part of your relationship? Where were you? What transpired?

5. What will you most miss about this person? What will you miss the least?

6. Describe your last couple days together. How were the last couple days like all your days together? How were they different?

7. If you could put two sentences on this person's tombstone, what would you put?

THE FUN(NY) TIMES

Write down your answers to the following questions, then share your answers with one or more people.

1. What was the funniest thing the two of you ever did?

2. What do you feel was the funniest thing this person ever said or did?

3. What was the funniest thing the two of you ever saw (movie, TV show, event)?

4. What did this person most like to do for fun?

5. What could you do or say to cause this person to smile?

"All relationships include both positive and negative interactions. We know that you can complete grief only by being totally honest with yourself and others." - John James & Russell Friedman.

GUIDED IMAGERY: DIALOGUE WITH THE LOST ONE

Close your eyes. . . . Remember your loved one at a time when the two of you were at your best together. . . . Remember your loved one's appearance at that time. . . . Now imagine your loved one sitting in a chair across from you. . . . Imagine the two of you breathing together. You and your loved one breathe in together, . . . and out together, . . . and in together, . . . and out together, . . . and in together, . . . and out together. . . . Look at your loved one's total appearance. . . . Look at your loved one's face. . . . Look into your loved one's eyes. . . .

You are now going to have a dialogue with your loved one. You are going to be imagining yourself asking some questions and making some statements. You are going to imagine your loved one responding to your questions and statements. . . . Looking into the eyes of your loved one, imagine yourself giving thanks for all your times together. Imagine yourself thanking this person. . . . What does your loved one say in response to what you have just said? . . . Looking into the eyes of your loved one, imagine yourself asking forgiveness for all the times you caused your loved one to hurt. . . . What does your loved one say in response? . . . Looking into the eyes of your loved one, imagine yourself giving forgiveness for all the times your loved one hurt you. . . . What does your loved one say in response? . . . Looking into the eyes of your loved one, imagine yourself verbalizing some of your greatest fond memories in your relationship. . . . What does your loved one say in response? . . . Once again thank this person for your times together. . . . Once again imagine yourself breathing in unison with this person. Breathing in together, . . . and out together, . . . and in together, . . . and out together. . . .

You are now about to say goodbye to this person. You will say goodbye, but you can always revisit this person whenever you close your eyes. You will say goodbye, but you will always know that this person is as close to you as your very lungs, breathing in, . . . and breathing out, . . . and breathing in, . . . and breathing out. . . . Slowly say goodbye to this person, watching their image slowly disappear, . . . knowing that your loved one is as close to you as your very lungs, . . . breathing in, . . . and breathing out, . . . and breathing in, . . . and breathing out. . . .

SERVICE OF REMEMBRANCE

The usual funeral service occurs within a week of the death, a time when most grievers are still somewhat in a state of numbness and confusion. It might help to have an additional service three to twelve months after the funeral service, a service that can receive adequate planning, free of that numbness and confusion.

1. Choose a place.

    A. A church.
    B. A place frequented by the deceased (a restaurant, a park, a country club, a church, or even a bar).
    C. One's home.

2. Choose an officiant.

    A. A minister.
    B. A good friend of the deceased.
    C. A family member.

3. Choose attendees.

    A. Selected family members.
    B. Selected friends.
    C. Selected business and community associates.

4. Choose a format.

    A. Selected readings.
    B. Selected speakers.
    C. Selected music.
    D. Food and/or drinks could be served.

5. Send out invitations clearly indicating the purpose and design of the service.

LITANY OF REMEMBRANCE

The following can be periodically said by the person who is grieving. A good time to say the litany is when the griever is feeling any sadness or guilt. The departed person's name would be placed in the blank

"For the good times we spent together, for all those fond memories, for all those special moments we shared: _____, I give you thanks. Thank you for all of those special moments."

"For all the times I said or did something that hurt you, for all the times I caused you any pain or suffering: _____, I ask your forgiveness. Please know that I loved you and did not want to cause you any hurt."

"For all the times you said or did something that hurt me, for all the times you caused me any pain or suffering: _____, I forgive you. I believe you loved me and did not want to cause me any hurt."

"For the early days in our relationship: _____, I will always remember. How could I ever forget?"

"For the easy times in our relationship, when the two of us experienced oneness with each other in thought and action: _____, I will always remember."

"For the rough times in our relationship, when the two of us had separate ideas and agendas: _____, I remember them too. But I will always remember the bigger picture, the greater context."

"For our last good moments together: _____, I will always remember. How could I ever forget?"

"For our future together: knowing that you are no longer with me physically, but you are still a very great part of me nonetheless — a very great part. Thank you."

"_____, I give thanks to you for sharing your life with me. I am so thankful we were able to share our lives together. You have meant so much to me; you mean so much to me now. Thank you. Thank you. Thank you."

A CONSIDERATION: Grief is not just confined to losing a person through death. Intense feelings of loss can come from the ending of a marriage by separation or divorce. A move can produce feelings of grief. A rape. A job loss. Loss of a body part or body function. Financial loss. Loss of dignity and respect. Loss of a pet.

SEEING-EYE DOG

One of the most difficult counseling situations I ever had involved Jonathan whose seeing-eye dog of ten years, Angel, died. Angel was Jonathan's live-in partner, his dearest family member, his closest work associate, his trusted servant, his most faithful friend, an actual extension of himself, a literal part of his being – his eyes. When Angel died, all of that was lost.

LOSING EVERYTHING

While doing a summer internship at a facility for the developmentally disabled, I became quite fond of two men. They went by the names of Bob and Fred. Everyday Bob and Fred would be together, seated on a bench, playfully pushing and shoving one another, and giggling. Monday, Tuesday, Wednesday, Thursday, Friday, morning, afternoon, evening: pushing and shoving one another, and giggling.
One day in the middle of the summer, on a Wednesday, I showed up for work and saw that Fred was not on the bench. I asked the staff, "Where's Fred?" I was told that he had died the night before. On the bench was Bob pushing and shoving empty space, and crying. That is what he did on Wednesday, Thursday, and Friday: pushing and shoving empty space, and crying.
The following Monday I showed up for work, and Bob was not on the bench. I asked the staff, "Where's Bob?" I was told that during the weekend he had gone up to a cement wall and had beat his head against the wall until he lost consciousness.
In losing Fred, Bob had lost more than just a companion. He had lost his job. He had lost his purpose, his meaning in life. As far as Bob was concerned, his job, his purpose, his meaning in life was to push and shove Fred and giggle.

"Sometimes, when one person is missing, the whole world seems depopulated." - Lamartine.

NO "ME"

Madeleine was destroyed. "He wasn't my other half; he was all of me. I feel like I am absolutely nothing without him. Nothing. There's no 'me' left. All there is is grief, pain, guilt, longing, despair, numbness. No 'me.' When he died, whatever was 'me' went with him."

"Guard your grief. There will be those who will try to minimize your grief, to cheer you up when you don't want this to happen. . . . Your grief is yours, and you have a right to have it." - Joan Furman.

"Grief is itself a medicine." - William Cowper.

AWAY ON A BUSINESS TRIP

Melanie's husband died from a heart attack while away on a business trip. She never saw his body and had great difficulty in acknowledging his death. Melanie's counselor was unable to do anything with her until she was first willing to acknowledge the death.

A CONSIDERATION: Because grieving is a process, a counselor might want to use a series of tools designed to follow one another, emphasizing the process, helping the process along – a systematic approach to grief counseling.

A SYSTEMATIC APPROACH

STEP ONE: LOSS INTENSITY GRAPH

In counseling people who are trying to recover from a particular loss it often helps to view their historical relationship to loss – what losses they have experienced and how they have responded to those losses.

1. List 4-8 of the greatest loss experiences you've had in your life (death of friends and/or family members, divorce, job loss, loss of health, etc.).

2. Of those losses, which one caused you the most pain, the loss that was the most debilitating for you?

3. Take a piece of paper and begin a bar graph by drawing a bar at the extreme left of the page. This bar would go from the bottom of the page to the top. Within the bar, make a notation identifying the loss, and dating the loss.

4. Take the other losses you have listed, sorting them in order of intensity, placing your second greatest loss next to the greatest, then the third, etc. A bar would represent each loss, each bar's height determined by its proportional relationship to your greatest loss. (If your second greatest loss was half intense, the second bar would be half the height of the first.) Within each bar there would be a notation identifying the loss. Below the bar would be the date of the loss.

5. After completing the graph, identify the loss (a loss that involves a relationship with a person) that seems to have the most amount of unfinished business related to it? Of all the losses in your graph, which one (related to a personal relationship) do you believe needs the most amount of work? Put some shading inside that bar.

6. Share this graph with a counselor, friend, or family member (whichever is the most comfortable for you).

STEP TWO: RELATIONSHIP COMPLEXITY GRAPHS

These graphs can be used after a relationship has ended, whether by death, divorce, or some other loss. It helps those grieving to realize the gamut of feelings they have towards the missing person, helping people to avoid enshrinement (just praising) or bedevilment (just blaming). Do these graphs for the bar you shaded in Step One.

1. List 3-5 of the most positive memories you have about this person, and 3-5 of the most negative memories you have about this person.

2. Take a piece of paper and begin a bar graph on your positive memories. Draw a bar at the extreme left of the page. This bar would go from the bottom of the page to the top. Within the bar, make a notation identifying your most positive memory. Record the date below the bar.

3. Take the other positive memories you have listed, sorting them in order of intensity, placing the second greatest positive memory next to the most positive, then the third, etc. A bar would represent each positive memory, each bar's height determined by its proportional relationship to your most positive memory. (If your second greatest positive memory is half intense, the second bar would be half the height of the first.) Within each bar there would be a notation identifying the memory. And below each bar would be the date of its occurrence.

4. Take a second piece of paper and begin a bar graph on your negative memories. Draw a bar at the extreme left of the page. This bar would go from the bottom of the page to the top. Within the bar, make a notation identifying your most negative memory. Below the bar put the date of the memory.

5. Take the other negative memories you have listed, sorting them in order of intensity, placing the second greatest negative memory next to the most negative, then the third, etc. A bar would represent each negative memory, each bar's height determined by its proportional relationship to your most negative memory. (If your second greatest negative memory is half intense, the second bar would be half the height of the first.) Within each bar there would be a notation identifying the memory. Below each bar would be the date of occurrence.

6. Share these graphs with a counselor, friend, or family member (whichever is the most comfortable for you).

STEP THREE: 5, 4, 3, 2, 1 – RECOVERY HAS BEGUN

This activity can help care recipients put some closure on their grief, helping people finish some business that might feel unfinished. This activity is to focus upon the person identified in Step Two.

1. You are to first write five things you apologize for saying or doing to your lost loved one. (Step Two might have reminded you of some things.) Begin each of the statements by writing your lost loved one's name in the first blank.

    A. _____, I apologize for _____.
    B. _____, I apologize for _____.
    C. _____, I apologize for _____.
    D. _____, I apologize for _____.
    E. _____, I apologize for _____.

2. Now write four things for which you forgive your loved one. (Step Two might have reminded you of some things.)

    A. _____, I forgive you for _____.
    B. _____, I forgive you for _____.
    C. _____, I forgive you for _____.
    D. _____, I forgive you for _____.

3. Now write three declarations of love.

    A. _____, I love you because _____.
    B. _____, I love you because _____.
    C. _____, I love you because _____.

4. Now write two wishes related to your loved one.

    A. _____, I wish I could _____.
    B. _____, I wish you could _____.

5. Now complete the following sentences by writing in the name of your loved one in the blanks.

_____, I ask that you please accept my apologies and my expressions of forgiveness, my declarations of love, my unfulfilled wishes, and now this my goodbye.

_____, I know that you are no longer here with me physically. Yet you are still with me in many ways, and you will be with me in the future. But in some ways I need to say goodbye to you. In some ways I need to let go of you. Goodbye _____. Goodbye.

After this exercise has been completed, the person can imagine himself/herself sitting across a table from the loved one. The written material could then be verbalized as if being said to the loved one. (It is not necessary that this activity be shared with a counselor, friend, or family member; it might have a lot of material best left private.)

A SYSTEMATIC APPROACH

STEP ONE: THE TREASURES

1. Think of five things that you greatly treasure that the person who has died did or said to you. Write five corresponding declarations for each of these, beginning each declaration with the person's name. [Examples: "Sam, I treasure the time you first told me that you loved me. I remember that special evening." "Mom, I treasure all the times you held me when I came home from school crying. I still feel the warmth of your hugs." "Terri, I treasure your first day of school when *you* told *me* not to worry."]

2. Think of five things that you greatly treasure that you and your loved one did together. Write five corresponding declarations for each of these, beginning each declaration with the person's name. [Examples: "Sam, I treasure the time we vacationed in San Diego together: the long talks, the walks along the beach, our fish and wine dinners." "Mom, I treasure all the Sunday evening telephone conversations we had: the tears and laughter we shared in those conversations." "Terri, I treasure the times we went shopping together to buy you clothes, how you wanted to know my opinions, how you trusted my judgment."]

3. Review your declarations several times in the next couple weeks. [Examples: You could share them with a counselor or friend. You could read them to an empty chair, imagining the person who has died sitting in that chair. You could write them in a letter to the person who has died. You could post them on your refrigerator door. You could read them before a mirror.] After spending a couple weeks with this material, you can go on to the next activity.

STEP TWO: THE TRAGEDIES

Death is often a very vivid reminder of our humanity, our vulnerability, our imperfections. Since we are all human, all vulnerable, all imperfect, we have to forgive and we have to be forgiven.

1. Ask forgiveness for five things you did or said to the person who died. Write five corresponding declarations for each of these, beginning each declaration with the person's name. [Examples: "Sam, please forgive me for the time I cheated on you. I know I was completely in the wrong." "Mom, please forgive me for not spending more time with you towards the end of your life. None of the excuses I gave were acceptable." "Terri, please forgive your father and I for reneging on that promise to take you to Disneyland. I feel so bad now that we didn't have that time together."]

2. Give forgiveness for five things that were done or said to you by the person who died. Write five corresponding declarations for each of these, beginning each declaration with the person's name. [Examples: "Sam, I forgive you for refusing to come to my dad's funeral. That hurt me, but I forgive you." "Mom, I forgive you for not speaking to me after my divorce. I wanted so much to talk to you, but I do truly forgive you." "Terri, I forgive you for the story you told your teacher about me and your dad. It hurt us, but I forgive you."]

3. Review your declarations several times in the next couple weeks. Try using a form of review you did not use in the previous activity. [Examples: You could share them with a counselor or friend. You could read them to an empty chair, imagining the person who has died sitting in that chair. You could write them in a letter to the person who has died. You could post them on your refrigerator door. You could read them before a mirror.] After spending a couple weeks with this material, you can go on to the next activity.

"The garden of Love is green without limit and yields many fruits other than sorrow and joy. Love is beyond either condition: without spring, without autumn, it is always fresh". - Rumi.

"What lies behind us and what lies before us are tiny matters compared to what lies within us." - Ralph Waldo Emerson.

STEP THREE: THE TRANSITORY AND IN-TRANSITORY

1. Choose 6-10 of the declarations from the previous two activities. Transform each of those declarations into three statements: one using the past tense, one the present, and one the future. [Examples: "Mom, I loved you so much when you held me when I came home from school crying. I am thinking of those times right now. Although you are not with me now physically, I will always carry those moments in my heart." "Sam, I was so hurt when you refused to attend my dad's funeral. I forgive you for that and all the other times you hurt me. In spite of all those hurtful things, I will go into the future cherishing the many good times we had together."]

2. Review your declarations several times in the next couple weeks. Try using a form of review you have not used for the previous activities. [You could share them with a counselor or friend. You could read them to an empty chair, imagining the person who has died sitting in that chair. You could write them in a letter to the person who has died. You could post them on your refrigerator door. You could read them before a mirror.]

"You don't heal from the loss of a loved one because time passes, you heal because of what you do with the time." - Carol Crandell.

"Outside our private envelopes of pain, life lights torches, sings songs, beckons with all its senses to draw us out. We must eventually open: take part." - Esteban Alviso.

A SYSTEMATIC APPROACH

STEP ONE: ACCEPTING THE REALITY OF THE LOSS

1. List 4-8 roles this person filled for you, roles that belonged exclusively (or almost exclusively) to this person. [Examples: (1) the person who occupied the other half of my bed, (2) my dinner partner, (3) the person who walked with me in the evening.]

2. Having each of these roles in mind, write corresponding paragraphs that use the person's name, acknowledge your remembrance and appreciation of the role, and acknowledge the loss you feel that the role is now not being filled. [Example: "Sally. I'm remembering you as the person who sat across from me at the dinner table. I miss looking across at you, watching you, listening to you, having you listen to me. I'm now realizing how much that meant to me. Thank you for being there. It's a big loss for me to not see you sitting there across that dinner table."]

3. Sit across from an empty chair and read these paragraphs aloud to that empty chair. Do this on three separate occasions in the next couple weeks. Only after you've finished this activity can you continue with the next one.

STEP TWO: WORKING THROUGH THE PAIN

1. Reviewing all the paragraphs from the previous activity, identify 4-8 emotional, physical, and/or spiritual pains you are experiencing because of all those losses. [Examples: (1) anger, (2) sadness, (3) headaches, (4) upset stomach, (5) hopelessness.]

2. With each identified pain, take a separate sheet of paper and write two strategies you can follow to alleviate that pain. [Example: "Anger. (1) Whenever I feel anger arising within me, I will close my eyes, focus on my breathing, counting ten complete breaths. (2) I will try to learn a couple yoga poses that are designed to calm the emotions.]

3. Post these sheets of paper throughout your home and read each of these papers at least three times in the next week.

4. After that week, begin implementing at least one strategy for each pain. Only after you've started implementing the strategies can you continue with the next activity.

STEP THREE: FILLING SOME OF THE GAPS

1. From the first activity, choose 2-3 of the roles that you or someone else can possibly fill. [Example: The role of someone to walk with me in the evening.] Remember, however, that not all of the roles can or ought to be filled.

2. In the next couple weeks, find a way of filling each of these roles that you have identified and begin to have them filled. [Example: I will persuade Fred to walk with me on Tuesday evenings and Rebecca on Thursday evenings.]

3. Do not proceed with the next activity until you feel some degree of comfort in how these roles are now being filled. You don't have to feel completely comfortable, but you have to feel some comfort.

STEP FOUR: MOVING ON WITH LIFE

Develop 2-4 rituals for saying goodbye to your loved one. Each ritual would somehow acknowledge how you benefitted from this person. However, each ritual would have to end with some form of goodbye, acknowledging that this person is no longer physically with you. [Examples: (1) Write a long letter to the deceased person summarizing all your fond memories, ending the letter with a very clear goodbye. (2) Gather a couple objects that remind you of the person, say a prayer or meditation of thanksgiving for the person, then give away or bury the objects. (3) Go through a picture album, recalling your memories with each picture, compress the album to less than half the original size, then label the album with the beginning and ending dates of your relationship.]

"Seeing into darkness is clarity. . . . This is called practicing eternity." - Lao-Tsu.

A LETTER TO FINISH THE UNFINISHED

After a griever has extensively examined his/her grief with a counselor or friend, examining the negative and the positive aspects of the relationship with the loved one, reviewing the history of the relationship (all the key events and gamut of feelings), exploring the various implications of the loved one's death, he/she could be encouraged to write a letter to this person to give some finish to all that is unfinished. These would be the steps the griever would take:

1. Set aside at least an hour in a place where you will not be disturbed.

2. Begin the letter in the typical format addressing this person by the name or title that best represents how you remember him/her. [Examples: "Dear Mom," "Dear Tommy," "My Dearest Sweetheart," "To My Best Friend."]

3. Follow the addressing with a sentence similar to this: "I have been examining our relationship lately and I have discovered that there are several things I need to say."

4. After the opening sentence, write about all the things for which you feel you need to apologize, the things you did and said for which you are feeling some regret. Have 2-5 sentences in this section.

5. After apologizing, write 2-5 sentences covering those things for which you want to offer forgiveness, the things your loved one did or said that made you sad or angry.

6. After offering forgiveness, write 2-5 sentences covering some of the positive feelings you had towards this person, feelings that you could have expressed more often during this person's life. Cover the various things you appreciated, admired, and loved about this person.

7. End the letter in a way that somehow summarizes the letter's contents, being sure to use the word "goodbye" somewhere in that closing.

Just writing this letter can be quite therapeutic. Its benefits can sometimes be enhanced by reading it to an empty chair, imagining your loved one in the chair. It could be posted in a place where you would see it often. You could read it before a mirror. You could put it in a photograph album that has pictures of your loved one.

A CONSIDERATION: For the grieving, personal affirmations can be very important, breaking people away from numbness, depression, anger, despair. There are certainly some things that *cannot* be changed by our attitudes towards them, and there are certainly some things that *can* be changed.

"What ruins the picnic – the rain or one's attitude about the rain? This is a trick question. The answer is both. The rain really does ruin the picnic, but you cannot do anything about the rain, you can only deal with your reaction to the rain. The same is true of almost all losses. What causes my grief – the loss or my reaction to the loss? Again, the answer is both. While we cannot undo what has happened, we can do something about our reaction." - John James & Russell Friedman.

AFFIRMATIONS

One to three of the following affirmations could be chosen by a person to be his or her personal affirmation(s). Or, even better, a person could create his/her own affirmation(s). Each affirmation used would be posted on a place visited everyday (on a mirror or a refrigerator). Each time the person sees the affirmation, it is internally (or verbally) repeated three times.

    A. Although I have lost much, I am a survivor.
    B. I can choose my future: happiness or sorrow, contentment or depression. It is my choice.
    C. I accept and love myself just as I am.
    D. The more I love myself, the more I can love others.
    E. I will get through this, and I will relearn how to find happiness and give happiness.
    F. I am a temple in which the spirit of God dwells.
    G. This is a day that God has made, and I rejoice in it.
    H. Today I will make at least one person smile, and I will smile with them.
    I. I will survive.

There are many books and calendars available in bookstores and libraries that have daily affirmations also.

GUIDED IMAGERY: EXPERIENCING UNITY

The following could be read to someone or it could be placed on a tape recording for periodic use. It is designed to awaken the senses, to refresh the spirit. It can take away tension. It can eliminate preoccupation with personal problems.

"You are walking along a beach. You are breathing in the fresh ocean air.... Feel the summer air fill your lungs with gentle warmth.... You feel the air's warmth enter your lungs.... Warm, fresh, ocean air... It is about five o'clock in the afternoon. The sun is just resting above the horizon, about to go to sleep for the night.... The sun is brilliant, glowing orange. The sky is a hazy blue. The sand beneath your feet is a warm, soothing beige.... As you walk along the beach, you can feel the massaging warmth of the sand through your toes....

"Your lips are brushed with a thin coating of salt. You lick your lips and taste the salt.... You hear the refreshing splashes of the waves coming in and going out, ... coming in and going out with the same rhythm as your breathing, the breathing of the warm, fresh, ocean air. Coming in and going out.... Coming in and going out.... A distant seagull, flying toward the setting sun, cries out. Its cries become more and more distant. More and more distant....

"As you are walking along the beach, you see in front of you a sand dune, bending and bulging on the horizon. The sand dune is covered with flowers, splashes of yellow, blue, orange, pink.... You reach the sand dune and sit down, ... stretch your arms to the sky, ... and gaze in wonder out to the sea.... The ocean shimmers in silver, reflecting the last rays of the setting sun.... As the sun slowly dips into the water, you become more and more relaxed.... The lower the sun, the deeper your relaxation.... The warmth of the ocean air enters your lungs and relaxes you even more, ... and more, ... and more.... All of your being begins to be absorbed into everything that surrounds you.... You are the radiant sun.... You are the shimmering sea.... You are the massaging warmth of the sand.... You are the flowers splashed with color.... You are the ocean air swirling in your lungs.... You are the distant gull crying in joy to the horizon.... You are the world at peace, ... at rest, ... comfortable, ... relaxed...."

A CONSIDERATION: Oftentimes a patient, client, or loved one can construct barriers to healing, walls blocking potential growth. A little nudging might be necessary. A little challenge. An intervention.

TOM WAS A GRUFF MAN

Tom was a gruff man, very gruff. Tom never spoke to people; he always shouted at them. One day I was in Tom's home, in his living room, along with his wife and sister, when he suddenly shouted, "I want the women out of the room! I want them out now!"

After the women left, Tom turned to me and shouted, "Doug, I have a problem!"

"What's your problem, Tom?" I calmly responded.

"I can't cry, dammit! I can't cry!" shouted Tom.

"You sound angry," I calmly responded.

"I am angry! I can't cry, dammit!"

"People are usually sad when they want to cry. Are you sad, Tom?"

There was this pause. Then Tom shouted, "Yeah, I'm sad, dammit! I'm sad!"

I calmly said, "Tom, I want you to come over here and give me a hug."

"What?!" He shouted.

"I want you to come over here and give me a hug."

"No! I'm not going to give you a hug!"

"Tom, just come over here."

He took a step forward and gave me this look as if he were trying to determine my sexual preferences.

"Tom, just come over here," I repeated.

Tom slowly walked over, still giving me that look.

"Now wrap your arms around me." He wrapped what felt like two baseball bats around my shoulders.

"Relax, Tom," I said. . . . He tightened up even more.

"Relax, Tom. It's okay to relax." . . . He loosened up a little.

"It's okay, Tom. It's okay to relax." . . . He loosened up some more.

"Relax, Tom. . . . If you would like to cry, it's alright. . . . It's alright. . . . Tom, I want you to know that it's alright." I heard two swallows, a gulp, some quivering, some shaking, then, all at once, tears started gushing out, going down the back of my shirt.

Tom cried for at least five minutes. . . . I then felt his hands behind my back, wiping away his tears before he was going to ever stand back.

Tom then stood back, and he had this peacefulness in him I had never seen before. He softly said, "You know, Doug, that felt real good." There was this pause. Then he shouted, "That felt real good, dammit! That felt real good!"

"We fear that once acknowledged grief will bowl us over. The truth is that grief experienced does dissolve. Grief unexpressed is grief that lasts indefinitely." - Judy Tatelbaum.

A CONSIDERATION: Tears can often be cleansing. They can be therapeutic. Meaningful. Profound.

THE BEST SERMON

A clergyman told me that he had been a minister at a large congregation for a couple years when his best friend Ray died. Ray was a member of the congregation. Although this minister wanted to do the eulogy, he asked one of his assistants to do the funeral service.

It came time for the eulogy. The minister mounted the pulpit. Before he could even say a single word of his prepared eulogy he started crying, and he couldn't stop crying. He finally just left the pulpit, unable to say any of the eulogy.

At the end of the service, three of this minister's parishioners came up to him together and said, "That was the best sermon you have ever preached."

"What soap is for the body, tears are for the soul." - Jewish Proverb.

A CONSIDERATION: After the tears, after the expression of emotion, after getting out all the hurt and pain, resolve needs to be added – resolve to heal, to grow.

"You cannot prevent the birds of sorrow from flying overhead, but you can prevent them from making nests in your hair." - Chinese Proverb.

MY COMMITMENT TO MYSELF

Good intentions can carry much more weight when they are written down, especially if written down in the form of a contract. The following might help to convert the good intentions into measurable accomplishments.

I, _____, make the following commitments to myself and those I love. I make these commitments as my personal contribution to my healing process, realizing that I must help myself if I am going to ever heal. I agree to do the following, commencing on the dates stated.

1. I will revitalize my body by committing to the following physical activities:

    a. _____ Date: _____
    b. _____ Date: _____
    c. _____ Date: _____
    d. _____ Date: _____

2. I will revitalize my mind by committing to the following mental activities:

    a. _____ Date: _____
    b. _____ Date: _____
    c. _____ Date: _____
    d. _____ Date: _____

3. I will revitalize my social life by committing to the following social activities:

    a. _____ Date: _____
    b. _____ Date: _____
    c. _____ Date: _____
    d. _____ Date: _____

Signed: _____ Date: _____

Witnesses (required):

_____

_____

BECOMING PRO-ACTIVE WITH THE RE-ACTIVE

There are many normal responses to grief. However, to never emerge from those responses, to get stuck in a response, can sometimes be harmful to health. The following activity helps people to not get stuck in those responses.

1. From the following grief responses, choose the four that are the most intense for you.

   A. numbness
   B. confusion
   C. exhaustion
   D. denial
   E. anger
   F. hate
   G. cynicism
   H. guilt
   I. sadness
   J. hopelessness

2. With each of the four responses you have chosen, write a sentence that describes the form the response often takes.

   A. Example: "Anger: Since the death I often get angry at the drop of a hat, getting angry at people, at me, at God, at anything and everything around me."
   B. Example: "Guilt: I often feel guilty for not spending more time with mom."

3. After each of the previous descriptive sentences, write another sentence related to the grief response that expresses a future possibility that is positive and/or constructive, a possibility you intend to see come to pass.

   A. Example: "Anger: I will lessen my anger by going to the library and checking out a book on managing anger, reading (not skimming) every word in the book."
   B. Example: "Guilt: I will lessen my guilt of not spending time with mom by spending more time with the rest of the family, less time on non-family activities and more time on family activities."

4. Have the above sentences available in a convenient location so that whenever you experience each of those grief responses again, you can reread your sentences on future possibilities, thus reminding yourself of where you want to be and how you believe you'll get there.

INTENTIONS

Often in grief, time can seem as though it is standing still. This activity helps those who are grieving move ahead in their journey to recovery.

1. Write a paragraph on your intentions for improving your physical well-being.

2. Write a paragraph on your intentions for improving your intellectual well-being.

3. Write a paragraph on your intentions for improving your emotional well-being.

4. Write a paragraph on your intentions for improving your social well-being.

5. Write a paragraph on your intentions for improving your spiritual well-being.

6. Complete this activity by writing a paragraph of encouragement to yourself, cheering you on to accomplish all the above.

"It's not how much you do, but how much love you put into the action." - Mother Theresa.

A CONSIDERATION: As the loss of a loved one can often be felt as a shock, so healing from that loss might involve some kind of counter-shock. The journey to healing often has to involve the griever being somehow opened up, awakened, realigned to perceive everything in a new way, to adjust to a new environment, to relearn the world.

OPENING UP TO WONDER

Much of our lives are occupied by habit. Each day we go to the same job. We leave the same house, get in the same car, and travel the same route to get to our job. Much of our job can be quite repetitive, doing the same things, doing them in the same way, interacting with the same people. Often with those who grieve much of life can take on the attribute of being repetitive, trivial, empty.

1. Each time you get ready to leave your home, look around at your home, trying to see something about it you have failed to notice in a long time.

2. Each time you drive your route to work, try to see something in that route you have not previously noticed, or you have failed to notice in a long time.

3. Each time you interact with someone who is part of your habitual environment, try to perceive something about that person's appearance, personality, and communication style you have not previously noticed, or you have failed to notice in a long time.

LIFE-GIVING ENERGY

1. Take your imagination back to the time when you had the life-giving energy of a young child. Imagine the life-giving energy that is present in all children.

2. Take your imagination back to the time when you and your mother participated in the life-giving energy of birth. Imagine the life-giving energy that is present in all childbirths.

3. Take your imagination back to the time when your mother and your father participated in the life-giving energy of their love for one another, the love that gave birth to you. Imagine the life-giving energy that is present in all love shared by couples.

4. Take your imagination way back to the time when this world received its first life-giving energy that brought it into being. Imagine the life-giving energy that brought all worlds into being.

5. Bring forward into your present consciousness, into your present state of being, the life-giving energy of creation which was expressed through this world and all other worlds that came into being. All of that life-giving energy. All of that is in you.

6. Bring forward into your present consciousness, into your present state of being, the life-giving energy of love which was expressed in your parents and all other lovers of all time. All that life-giving energy. All of that is in you.

7. Bring into your present consciousness, into your present state of being, the life-giving energy which you and your mother participated in at your birth, the life-giving energy that is present in all childbirths. All of that life-giving energy. All of that is in you.

8. Bring into your present consciousness, into your present state of being, the life-giving energy of youth, the life-giving energy that is in all children. All of that life-giving energy. All of that is in you.

CREATING A BUDDY SYSTEM

We could ask a griever if he or she would like to belong to a buddy system of fellow grievers. The system would include a group of 2-5 grievers, all having had similar losses (all spouse losses, all child losses, all losses due to suicide). Whenever one member of the group is in bad straits, he/she could call another member of the group to come over to visit or just talk on the telephone.

BEING MY OWN BEST CAREGIVER

Whenever you are feeling sad or depressed, choose one or more of the following as an act of kindness towards yourself.

    A. Visualize yourself as a healthy, sane, beautiful person.
    B. Stimulate your body with some vigorous, pleasurable activity or exercise.
    C. Write in a journal about all the wonderful and exciting things you are aware of in your environment.
    D. Surround yourself with people you know will be kind and nurturing to you.
    E. Practice some form of meditation.
    F. Eat highly nutritious foods and beverages.
    G. Take a nap.
    H. Have a hot bath.
    I. Receive a massage.
    J. Play relaxing music.

"Grieving is circular and repetitive. We cycle through grief over and over; it's the old 'two steps forward, one backward.' We make progress, advance forward, then we backtrack, retracing our steps. Grieving isn't continuous, but it is recurring." - Elizabeth Levang.

"One of the basic things that education through grief counseling can do is to alert people to the fact that mourning is a long-term process, and the culmination will not be to a pre-grief state. The counselor can also let them know that even though mourning progresses, there will be bad days. Grieving does not proceed in a linear fashion; it may reappear to be reworked." - William Worden.

THE MONTHLY CHECKUP

On the first day of each month after the death (for the first 6-12 months), the client could write down the answers to the following questions. This could be the client's own way of measuring and encouraging the healing process.

1. In what ways are you feeling better in the grieving process, better than you felt a month ago? Try to come up with one to three ways.

2. In what ways might you be feeling worse, worse that you felt a month ago? Try to think of at least one.

3. In the upcoming month, how might you be able to increase the better feelings and decrease the worse feelings? Establish one to three concrete, measurable goals for the month.

"Hope is grief's best music." - Proverb.

TODD'S WISHBONE

Todd had loved his mother. She had died when he was only eight years old.

Todd's mother had gotten very ill the end of one summer and the illness had gotten worse during September and the beginning of October. His mother was very open with Todd about how sick she felt, but she never used the word "cancer" with him. Todd had confessed that back then he probably wouldn't have understood what the word meant.

Towards the middle of October he asked his mother if she would be better by Thanksgiving because he so much liked her Thanksgiving dinners. She said she could not guarantee anything, but she would try her very best to make a Thanksgiving meal if she felt well enough by then to do it. But her illness got worse throughout the entire month of October.

During the first week in November she started making the Thanksgiving dinner. She took a whole day to make an apple pie. She put it in the freezer, and then she rested for two days. She next made candied yams: it took another whole day to do it. She put the candied yams in the freezer, and then rested for another two days. Thus, throughout the month of November, she prepared the meal, one item at a time, with a couple days of rest in between each item.

Finally, on the day of Thanksgiving, Todd's mother, with Todd helping, put a turkey into the oven and warmed up all the other ingredients, and then she had Todd help her put everything on the table. Todd told me that he can still visualize the food laid out on that table. He also said that when he really puts his mind to it, he can actually remember many of the tastes and smells of that meal as well.

Todd's mother died the day after Thanksgiving.

Todd still has the wishbone from that turkey. He has told his wife and others that he wants to be buried with that wishbone in his right hand so that when he sees his mother again they can break that Thanksgiving wishbone together.

ROSE

The first words Rose uttered in our counseling session were "I might as well die." Those words accurately described her entire state of being after her husband's death. From the day of his death until five months later when our counseling sessions began she literally began to die. She had mostly kept at home, surviving on whatever was brought to her home by her children. She had not initiated any contact with any of her old friends. She had been steadily losing weight. She had lost all affect in her face and body. She had even stopped reading books and watching television. She just sat at home, waiting – waiting to die.

At the end of each of my sessions with Rose I would walk her out to the parking lot where her oldest son would be sitting by his car smoking a cigarette, waiting to drive her home. After our fourth session, the session where I came to the conclusion that I was not going to be of much, if any, help to Rose, I escorted her out to her son's car when a soccer ball rolled up and stopped at her feet. A young boy who had been kicking the ball around the parking lot came up and stopped in front of Rose and looked at the ball. Rose looked at the ball. I looked at the ball. Rose's son looked at the ball. All four of us just looked at the ball resting right in front of Rose's feet.

Rose looked up at the boy standing there, then down at the ball. She looked up at the boy again, then down at the ball again. Rose then, with her left foot, gently pushed the ball away from her towards the boy. The boy trapped the ball under his right foot. Then the boy, instead of running away with the ball, decided to gently kick it back to Rose. It rolled up against her feet. She looked down just once and gave it a swift kick back – smiling.

What I couldn't do in four forty minute counseling sessions that boy did in less than two minutes: Rose had stopped dying and started living.

Chapter Five

Emotional/Psychological Tools For Use With Either The Terminally Ill Or Grieving

CONSCIOUS BREATHING

Breath meditations have many advantages over other meditations: 1) breathing is something that just about everyone can do – a transcultural activity, an ecumenical activity, 2) breathing is not something we have to fit into our schedule – we're already doing it, 3) breathing, in many languages, is associated with the spiritual – Greek, Hebrew, Sanskrit, many Native American languages, and 4) breathing is a form of meditation that helps us transcend the physical plane without trying to leave the physical plane. - Any of the following meditations could be tried, internally verbalizing the first phrase (or word) with each in-breath, internally verbalizing the second phrase (or word) with each out-breath. Each meditation would be practiced for five or ten minutes.

- A. In-breath: "Breathing in, I am breathing in."
  Out-breath: "Breathing out, I am breathing out."
      OR   In-breath: "In."
                Out-breath: "Out."
- B. In-breath: "Breathing in, I am calm."
  Out-breath: "Breathing out, I smile."
      OR   In-breath: "Calm."
                Out-breath: "Smile."
- C. In-breath: "Breathing in, I am born anew."
  Out-breath: "Breathing out, I am fresh."
      OR   In-breath: "New."
                Out-breath: "Fresh."
- D. In-breath: "Breathing in, I am solid."
  Out-breath: "Breathing out, I am strong."
      OR   In-breath: "Solid."
                Out-breath: "Strong."

IN WITH THE GOOD, OUT WITH THE BAD

1. Take four full breaths. With each inhalation, fully breathe in, imagining yourself breathing in the feeling of peace. With each exhalation, fully breathe out, breathing out all in you that is not associated with peace. Between each inhalation and exhalation, observe a short pause to acknowledge what you have just done.

2. Take four full breaths. With each inhalation, fully breathe in, imagining yourself breathing in the feeling of power. With each exhalation, fully breathe out, breathing out all in you that is not associated with power. Between each inhalation and exhalation, observe a short pause to acknowledge what you have just done.

3. Take four full breaths. With each inhalation, fully breathe in, imagining yourself breathing in the feeling of contentment. With each exhalation, fully breathe out, breathing out all in you that is not associated with contentment. Between each inhalation and exhalation, observe a short pause to acknowledge what you have just done.

4. Take four full breaths. With each inhalation, fully breathe in, imagining yourself breathing in the feeling of joy. With each exhalation, fully breathe out, breathing out all in you that is not associated with joy. Between each inhalation and exhalation, observe a short pause to acknowledge what you have just done.

GUIDED IMAGERY:
FORGIVENESS, LOVE, AND PEACE

The following guided imagery could be read to a patient/client or recorded for that person's use.

    Close your eyes and concentrate on your breathing. Fully concentrate upon your breathing. . . . Breathe in and breathe out. . . . Breathe in and breathe out. . . . Breathe in and breathe out. . . . As you are concentrating on your breathing, bring to your awareness that which is causing you to suffer. . . . Bring to mind the source of your suffering. . . . Bring to mind the anger connected to your suffering. . . . Bring to mind the sadness connected to your suffering. . . . Imagine gently placing all of your suffering inside the very center of your being, in the center of your body. Your suffering is at the very center of your body. . . .

As you are breathing, imagine the air you inhale swirling around that suffering, that suffering that is at the very center of your being. . . . Feel the air that you inhale swirl around your suffering. . . . With each breath you take in, imagine the air swirling around that suffering. . . .

Breathe in the air of forgiveness. . . . You are breathing in forgiveness. . . . You are imagining forgiveness swirling around your suffering. . . . Every breath you take in is a breath filled with forgiveness. . . . Forgiveness moving through, in, and around your suffering. . . . Fully breathe in the air of forgiveness. Forgiveness coming to your suffering. . . .

Now, with each breath that you expel, imagine the air moving out from your suffering. It is the air of forgiveness. . . . You are now breathing out forgiveness. . . . As you continue to breathe out forgiveness, make a smile of forgiveness. . . . Breathe out forgiveness. . . . And smile. . . .

Now with each breath that you take in, imagine the air swirling around that suffering at the very center of your being. . . . Breathe in the air of love. . . . You are breathing in love. . . . You are imagining love swirling around your suffering. . . . Every breath you take in is a breath filled with love. . . . Love moving through, in, and around your suffering. . . . Breathe in the air of love. Love coming to your suffering. . . .

Now, with each breath that you expel, imagine the air moving out from your suffering. . . . You are now breathing out love. . . . As you are breathing out love, make a smile of love. . . . Breathe out love. . . . And smile. . . .

Now, with each breath that you take in, imagine that the air is once again swirling around your suffering. . . . Breathe in the air of peace. . . . You are breathing in peace. . . . You are imagining peace swirling around your suffering. . . . Every breath you take in is a breath filled with peace. . . . Peace moving through, in, and around your suffering. . . . Breathe in the air of peace. Peace coming to your suffering. . . .

Now, with each breath that you expel, imagine the air moving out from your suffering. . . . You are now breathing out peace. . . . As you are breathing out peace, make a smile of peace. . . . Breathe out peace. . . . And smile. . . .

You are breathing in forgiveness. Total forgiveness. . . . You are breathing out forgiveness. Forgiveness. . . . You are smiling the smile of forgiveness. Total forgiveness. . . . You are breathing in love. All-encompassing love. . . . You are breathing out love. Love. . . . You are smiling the smile of love. All-encompassing love. . . . You are breathing in peace. Total peace. . . . You are breathing out peace. Peace. . . . You are smiling the smile of peace. Total peace. . . . There is forgiveness with our suffering. Forgiveness. . . . There is love with our suffering. Love. . . . There is peace with our suffering. Peace. . . . Forgiveness. . . . Love. . . . Peace. . . .

PEACE IN MY BODY, PEACE IN YOUR BODY

A caregiver might suggest the following to a care recipient: it brings peace to the care recipient, and also helps the care recipient feel useful to others.

1. Sit in a straight-backed chair, feet flat on the floor. (If this is uncomfortable, you could sit in a lounge chair with feet elevated.) Rest your hands on your lap with the palms up. You have just put yourself in a position to receive some blessings of peace from the universe.

2. Close you eyes lightly. You are now going to focus your attention upon those blessings of peace.

3. As you exhale each breath, release the tension in each part of your body, starting with your feet and going up to your head, one part of your body with each exhalation or two.

4. When your body feels more relaxed than when you began this activity, focus your thoughts on the word "peace." Imagine the emotional state of being that comes with being at peace with yourself, at peace with your family, and at peace with the world.

5. Now let go of the word "peace" and just be aware of the feeling connected with the word. If other thoughts enter your mind, just observe those thoughts and let them go.

6. After a few minutes, send your feelings of peace to someone else. Imagine embracing that person with all your feelings of peace. Share all of your peace with that person.

7. Take a deep breath. Make a full exhalation of that breath. Take one more deep breath and open your eyes.

"We work on ourselves . . . in order to help others. And we help others as a vehicle for working on ourselves." - Ram Dass.

A CONSIDERATION: Those of us who help others realize that we receive benefits in helping them. In giving, we receive; in helping others, we help ourselves. This can not only be true for us; it could also be true for our care recipients.

HELPING OURSELVES BY HELPING OTHERS

This activity takes advantage of the fact that we can help ourselves by helping others. It also helps to keep people from becoming too absorbed in their own problems.

1. Feel your sadness. It is natural for you to be sad because of what you are going through at this time; you have every right to be sad. . . . Now think of someone or some people in your community who might be more sad than you. . . . Name this person (or people). . . . Think about what you might do to help this person (or people) be less sad. In what way could you help this person (or people)? . . . Go do it: go do whatever you can do to make this person (these people) less sad.

2. Feel your anger. It is natural for you to be angry because of what you are going through at this time; you have every right to be angry. . . . Now think of someone or some people in your community who might be more angry than you. . . . Name this person (or people). . . . Think about what you might do to help this person (or people) be less angry. In what way could you help this person (or people)? . . . Go do it: go do whatever you can do to make this person (these people) less angry.

3. Feel your depression. It is natural for you to be depressed because of what you are going through at his time; you have every right to be depressed. . . . Now think of someone or some people in your community who might be more depressed than you. . . . Name this person (or people). . . . Think about what you might do to help this person (or people) be less depressed. In what way could you help this person (or people)? . . . Go do it: go do whatever you can do to make this person (these people) less depressed.

4. Feel your hopelessness. It is natural for you to feel hopelessness because of what you are going through at this time; you have every right to feel hopelessness. . . . Now think of someone or some people in your community who might feel more hopelessness than you. . . . Name this person (or people). . . . Think about what you might do to help this person (or people) feel less hopelessness. In what way could you help this person (or people)? . . . Go do it: go do whatever you can do to make this person (these people) feel less hopelessness.

"I slept and dreamt that life was joy. I awoke and saw that life was service. I acted and behold, service was joy." - Rabindranath Tagore.

THE JOY OF SERVING

Helping others can often be uplifting. Helping others can often be of help to us. Try doing any of the following to uplift and help others:

A. Go to a nursing home and ask to visit someone who hasn't had a visitor in a long time.
B. Volunteer at a soup kitchen.
C. Hand out dollar bills at a street corner to anyone who looks like they might appreciate a dollar bill.
D. Make a batch of cookies and deliver them to neighbors.
E. Read to someone who cannot read or cannot see to read.
F. Find someone pulling weeds, raking leaves, or shoveling snow and volunteer to help them in their work.
G. Go to a grocery store and volunteer to help people carry groceries.
H. Find someone sitting alone and ask if you might sit with them.
I. Find someone in a computer chat room who might be lonely and converse with that person.

"So much of grieving and healing is about courage. It takes courage to find strength in the midst of helplessness and hopelessness. It takes courage to triumph over our fears and embrace living. It takes courage to integrate loss into our personal history and pursue new meaning in life." - Elizabeth Levang.

REFLECTIONS

The purpose of this activity is to allow people to be conscious of the image they convey to themselves and to others. The activity also helps people realize that we have some choices in conveying what we want to convey: to a certain extent we can show what we want to show, we can become what we want to become.

Go stand before a full length mirror. Either have few clothes on or clothes that do not hide your body's shape and expressions.

1. You are to become the personification of anger.

    A. Make a facial expression that conveys anger: the most accurate representation of anger you can make with your face.
    B. Convey a posture that is your best interpretation of anger. Fully examine in the mirror what the posture of anger looks like.
    C. Walk back and forth before the mirror, walking in the most angry way you can walk. Show nothing but anger head to toe.
    D. With the most angry voice you can create, say the following two or three times: "I am the personification of anger. I have an angry face. My body is filled with anger. I walk anger. I talk anger. I am anger."

2. You are to become the personification of sadness.

    A. Make a facial expression that conveys sadness: the most accurate representation of sadness you can make with your face.
    B. Convey a posture that is your best interpretation of sadness. Fully examine in the mirror what the posture of sadness looks like.
    C. Walk back and forth before the mirror, walking in the most sad way you can walk. Show nothing but sadness head to toe.
    D. With the most sad voice you can create, say the following two or three times: "I am the personification of sadness. I have a sad face. My body is filled with sadness. I walk sad. I talk sad. I am sad."

3. You are to become the personification of submissiveness.

    A. Make a facial expression that conveys submissiveness: the most accurate representation of submissiveness you can make with your face.
    B. Convey a posture that is your best interpretation of submissiveness. Fully examine in the mirror what the posture of submissiveness looks like.
    C. Walk back and forth before the mirror, walking in the most submissive way you can walk. Show nothing but submissiveness head to toe.
    D. With the most submissive voice you can create, say the following two or three times: "I am the personification of submissiveness. I have a submissive face. My body is filled with submissiveness. I walk submissiveness. I talk submissiveness. I am submissiveness."

4. You are to become the personification of courage.

    A. Make a facial expression that conveys courage: the most accurate representation of courage you can make with your face.

B. Convey a posture that is your best interpretation of courage. Fully examine in the mirror what the posture of courage looks like.

C. Walk back and forth before the mirror, walking in the most courageous way you can walk. Show nothing but courage head to toe.

D. With the most courageous voice you can create, say the following two or three times: "I am the personification of courage. I have a courageous face. My body is filled with courage. I walk courage. I talk courage. I am courage."

5. You are to become the personification of joy.

   A. Make a facial expression that conveys joy: the most accurate representation of joy you can make with your face.

   B. Convey a posture that is your best interpretation of joy. Fully examine in the mirror what the posture of joy looks life.

   C. Walk back and forth before the mirror, walking in the most joyous way you can walk. Show nothing but joy head to toe.

   D. With the most joyous voice you can create, say the following two or three times: "I am the personification of joy. I have a joyous face. My body is filled with joy. I walk joy. I talk joy. I am joy."

6. You are to become the personification of self-respect.

   A. Make a facial expression that conveys self-respect: the most accurate representation of self-respect you can make with your face.

   B. Convey a posture that is your best interpretation of self-respect. Fully examine in the mirror what the posture of self-respect looks like.

   C. Walk back and forth before the mirror, walking in the most self-respectful way you can walk. Show nothing but self-respect head to toe.

   D. With the most self-respectful voice you can create, say the following two or three times: "I am the personification of self-respect. I have a self-respectful face. My body is filled with self-respect. I walk self-respect. I talk self-respect. I am self-respect."

Reflect upon how we can actually *become* an emotion: we can become the total personification of an emotion. We will all, sooner or later, experience all emotions, but we do not have to *become* those emotions. If we want to become the personification of an emotion, we have some choices as to which emotions we wish to personify. We needn't waste our time and energy *becoming* emotions we do not want to *become*.

CRUSHED

Herman was literally crushed when his wife died. His regular job as an air traffic controller was emotionally demanding before her death; now he had the impending grief reactions of anger, sadness, and depression to complicate that job. Also, he was now the only parent to three young children. Physically, he was suffering from severe neck, shoulder, and back pains. He described himself by saying: "I feel like I have the whole world on my shoulders."

BODY REVITALIZATION

Does the patient need a physical and emotional lift? If so, the following might be suggested.

1. Get in a relaxing mode by doing some deep, focused breathing.

2. With your eyes closed, picture your whole body and identify places that feel dull, . . . places that feel alive, . . . places that feel pain.

3. Direct your focus toward the part of your body that is most in need of positive energy. This part of you could be in pain, aching, tense, or just tired. Imagine moving the sensations felt in the "alive" places to the places of pain, fatigue, and dullness.

4. While focusing, choose a color that you associate most with vitality. Imagine that color permeating that part of your body with invigorating energy.

5. Feel that part of your body become stronger with each inhalation of breath. Feel strength with each inhalation, and feel relaxation with each exhalation.

"I NEED A HUG" CARD

A caregiver could carry around cards for his or her patients. Each card would have printed upon it four words: "I NEED A HUG." The cards would be delivered in such a way as to respect someone's desire, or lack of desire, for touch. ("Marilyn. This is a 'I NEED A HUG' card. I give these cards to all my patients. So, if there is ever a time when you might want a hug from me, for whatever reason, all you need to do is show me the card. . . . There might be other people who enter your room, people you would like to hold you, and you might find it difficult to ask them. I'm sure if you showed them the card, they'd be glad to respond. . . . Now you can do with this card whatever you like. If you don't want to use it, that's fine. However, Marilyn, I want you to know: it will always be good with me. Always. Okay?")

PERSONAL MANTRA

Mantras can be used to encourage psychological change and growth. A care recipient might want to create a personal mantra.

1. Design a personal mantra by choosing three of the following words to place in this statement: "I am a worthy person, worthy of _____, _____, and _____."

    A. love
    B. peace
    C. contentment
    D. comfort
    E. security
    F. rest
    G. energy
    H. companionship
    I. respect
    J. joy
    K. freedom
    L. hope

2. Say this mantra upon waking, before each meal, and before going to sleep, saying the mantra for as many days as it takes to be convinced of the undeniable truth of the mantra.

THE BIRD MEDITATION

The following meditation helps clear the mind and keep it clear.

1. Close your eyes and imagine swans flying across the sky. One swan enters your field of vision on the left and flies out of vision on the right. Another swan enters and leaves. Imagine several swans flying across the sky.

2. Now picture a completely blank sky, a peaceful blue.

3. If another thought or picture enters this peaceful blue sky, imagine it being swept away on the back of a swan, carried out of sight like the previous swans.

4. Continue to imagine the serenity of that peaceful blue sky.

GUIDED IMAGERY: GARDEN OF TRANQUILITY

We, as caregivers, can be most helpful when we remind our care recipients that the effectiveness of this guided imagery, and any guided imagery, is because of a power possessed by the care recipient, the power of their own imagination, a power that lets them establish their own comfort.

"With eyes closed, pay attention to the process of breathing that is going on inside your body. Instead of thinking in terms of you breathing the air, think in terms of the air breathing you. . . . The air, of its own accord, is entering your body and then leaving your body, entering and leaving, entering and leaving, entering and leaving. . . . You are making no effort whatsoever. You are merely allowing, allowing the air to come in and go out, come in and go out, come in and go out. . . . You are making no effort. You are merely allowing. . . .

"Now allow a picture to enter into your mind. The picture is that of a very large garden with red roses everywhere. . . . You are in that garden and you are walking among all those red roses. Your walking is almost like floating. You are floating through this large garden of red roses. . . . You breathe in the deep fragrance of these red roses. . . . These are roses of life-giving energy. . . . These are roses of joy. . . . These are roses that bring a comforting smile to your face. . . .

"Find the most beautiful red rose that you can find. . . . Look at its beauty. Examine closely all of that beauty. . . Inhale the fragrance of this red rose. . . . Examine its intricacies. . . . This red rose that you see is a symbol of your life energy. It is a symbol of your passion. It is a symbol of your enthusiasm. . . . Breathe in that energy. . . . Breathe in that passion. . . . Breathe in that enthusiasm. . . .

"Up ahead of you, you see that the garden of red roses changes into a garden of violet roses. . . . You walk and float towards the violet roses, walking and floating to the center of that section of the garden so that all you see now is violet roses. . . . In the center of this part of the garden is a large chalice, a chalice that is emitting a violet flame. . . . The flickering of this violet flame conveys sanctity. . . . This is a sacred violet flame. It is the flame of harmony. It is the flame of cleansing. It is the flame of forgiveness. . . . All of these violet roses carry the same symbolism. These roses symbolize harmony. They symbolize cleansing. They symbolize forgiveness. . . .

"In the midst of all of these violet roses, you feel that all of this symbolism is directed towards you. You are in harmony with all that is around you. . . . You are being cleansed. . . . You are being forgiven. . . . Feel the forgiveness. . . . Breathe in the fragrance of forgiveness. . . . You are completely forgiven. . . . All people have forgiven you, and you have even forgiven yourself. . . . You forgive yourself for not being perfect. . . . You accept yourself for everything that you are. . . .

"Up ahead of you, you see that the garden of violet roses changes into a garden of pink roses. . . . You walk and float towards the pink roses, walking and floating to the center of that section of the garden so that all you see is pink roses. . . .

"In the center of this section of the garden is a beautiful bed of pink rose petals, soft pink rose petals beckoning to be laid upon by you. . . . You walk and float towards that beautiful bed of pink rose petals and lie down upon them. . . . You smell the comforting fragrance. . . . You feel the relaxing softness. . . . You realize that these pink roses symbolize love. . . . You are encircled by love. . . . You smell love. . . . You feel love. . . . Your inner being says, 'I know I am loved.' . . . You are loved. . . . You are loved completely. . . .

"After resting upon these roses of love, you slowly rise and start walking and floating towards the section of the garden that is filled with white roses. . . . Soon, you are completely surrounded by pure white roses. Everywhere you look there are pure white roses. . . . These are creamy white roses of purity. . . . Here you are surrounded by perfect peace. . . . Here you are surrounded by divine peace. . . . Breathe in the fragrance of peace. . . . Here all your worries and fears are gone. . . . Here is your true home, your home of peace. . . . You are at peace. . . . Everywhere is peace. . . . You are at peace. . . .

"And now, of your own free will, you are choosing to come back to this room. In coming back, you will be returning with everything that you have received in this garden. . . . You are returning with energy, passion, and enthusiasm. . . . You are returning, having experienced complete forgiveness. . . . You are returning, knowing that you are fully loved. . . . You are returning, knowing that you are at peace, totally at peace. . . . You may now slowly open your eyes. . . ."

NOT-IN-LABOR MEDITATION

We often base our happiness on what we *have*. Happiness can also be based upon what we *do not have*. We can be happy that we are not in labor! We can be happy that we are not living under a dictatorship! We can be happy that we are not starving! We can be happy that we do not have a migraine headache! Whenever we feel sad or depressed we can merely contemplate all the things we do not have, and be happy! We can be extremely happy for all the things we do not have!

RECIPE FOR COMFORT

This recipe for comfort can be used whenever someone is experiencing any kind of suffering: stress, anxiety, disturbing thoughts, anger, sadness, or some type of physical pain. The recipe can be written on a recipe card and placed in a convenient place to be pulled out whenever needed. The goal of this activity is to completely forget whatever thought or experience might have initiated that suffering.

1. Name three continents and two countries in each of those continents.

2. Snap your fingers ten times.

3. Recite the alphabet backward.

4. Blink your eyes ten times.

5. Hum the tune of your favorite song.

6. Take twenty deep breaths, counting to yourself with each exhalation.

7. With your eyes closed, try to picture all the details of the setting of your favorite vacation.

A CONSIDERATION: We, as caregivers, typically list anger, depression, and denial as problems. Is being ill and being angry about it a problem? Or, is being ill and not being angry about it a problem? Is being ill and being depressed about it a problem? Or, is being ill and not being depressed about it a problem? Is being ill and mentally resisting it a problem? Or, is being ill and not mentally resisting it a problem? A strong case can be made for labeling anger, depression, and denial as problems. However, an equally strong case can be made for *not* labeling them as problems.

"We can support others as they use coping capacities that work well for them. Respecting their individuality requires that we enable them to remain in character and cope on their own terms and in their own ways, even if their ways differ from ours." - Thomas Attig.

ANGER TIME

Caregivers can encourage friends and relatives of care recipients to give them a daily, regularly scheduled "anger time." During this 15 to 20 minute period, the client or loved one would be left alone. Everyone else would be out of hearing range. Encourage them to shout, throw or pound things – whatever they wish to do to express their anger.

RELEASING ANGER

Not everyone is willing or accustomed to expressing anger openly. This exercise can help people who have difficulty expressing strong, negative emotions.

Caregivers can suggest that the person in their care close his or her eyes and picture an imaginary chalkboard and chalk. Ask the care recipient to write about his or her anger on the chalkboard. Urge the care recipient to use the most graphic language he or she can, including words the care recipient might be embarrassed to say aloud. Suggest that the care recipient write furiously, imagining bold strokes of the chalk. In this way, the care recipient's anger is expressed in what is said and in how it is written. Now suggest that the care recipient stand back, in his or her imagination, and look at the chalkboard. The care recipient would read and reread what he or she has written. Finally, ask the care recipient to take an imaginary eraser and furiously erase everything.

OH, TRACTOR!

If the person in your care is in a setting where swearing would be considered inappropriate, suggest that he or she use creative alternatives to common swear words. When the urge to swear hits, the care recipient would have two or three words to summon from his or her new "swearing" vocabulary – whatever words he or she chooses. [Examples: "Tractor!" "Fudge!" "Sugar!" "Cork!"] These have sounds that can be pronounced with feeling. The care recipient can spit them out with all his or her might without offending anyone who might be within earshot.

HITTING, RIPPING, AND STOMPING ANGER AWAY

Caregivers can suggest any of the following activities to help patients or loved ones vent their anger:

> A. Lie facedown on a mattress and pound your fists into the mattress as you yell and scream. Do this until you are completely exhausted or until you break into tears. Let the tears flow.
> B. Roll up a newspaper or magazine and hit it against a bedpost or door frame, as you shout the name of a person or thing that is the focus of your anger. Do this until you are completely exhausted or until you break into tears. Let the tears flow.
> C. Find a newspaper or old telephone book, a crayon or marking pen. Write in bold letters a word that comes to mind about your anger. Say the word with feeling. Rip the piece of paper to shreds. Then stomp on it. Keep doing this until you run out of paper, words, or energy.
> D. Find someone who is willing to have a pillow fight. Project all the causes of your anger onto this other person. Have a pillow fight until you either start crying, or laughing, or you expend all your energy.

IT IS OKAY TO CRY

Many people have reasons to cry, but for some personal reasons, they don't. They may feel embarrassed to cry, or see crying as a sign of weakness. They may have wanted to cry for a long time but have not found a time or opportunity when they felt it was fitting or comfortable to shed their tears. This short, simple exercise is intended for them: Every once in while, caregivers might want to remind their care recipients that it is okay to cry, that it is always all right to give ourselves permission to cry. (Caution: Do not think that people "must" cry. As crying is not necessarily a sign of weakness, not crying is also not necessarily a sign of weakness. Some people are "intuitive" – feeling centered people, and some people are "instrumental" – action/cognitive centered people. Neither is more mature or superior.)

A CONSIDERATION: Tears can sometimes be one of the most therapeutic of counseling tools. Tears can sometimes be one of the most heartfelt of prayers. Tears can sometimes be one of the most healing of medicines.

"Let tears flow of their own accord; their flowing is not inconsistent with inward peace and harmony." - Seneca.

"Sorrows are out best educators. A person can see further through a tear than a telescope." - Lord Byron.

THE TRUTH SHALL SET YOU FREE

How can we help our care recipients gain the freedom that comes from knowing the truth? The six questions in this exercise are aimed at discovering the truth within oneself. Caregivers can provide these questions in written form for loved ones or patients to use at their leisure, or these questions can be discussed and explored together during a visit. If we do have a conversation, we can enrich the experience for both of us if we admit and explore our own irrational thinking.

1. What belief do I want to dispute and surrender? (That belief could be considered "irrational," such as "I must be physically attractive and healthy in order to be loved by anyone.")

2. Is it possible for me to support this belief rationally?

3. What evidence might support the truth of this belief?

4. What evidence might support the falseness of this belief?

5. What is the worst possible thing that could happen to me if this belief is, in fact, true?

6. What value do I have in my life even if this belief is true?

After exploring these questions honestly, many people discover that some of their beliefs have little or no basis. The result of that discovery is a great freedom from past fears, hurts, anger, or depression. Even when some truth does play a role in one of those fears or hurts, it is really not so terrible. There is a gain in perspective. In spite of fears, hurts, anger, and depression, people discover that there is still much of value in life. Realizing this fact can free people to think and act more rationally and responsibly.

"The truth shall set you free." - Jesus.

FINDING RELIEF FROM STRESS

The following seven-part outline can help to uncover and ease the cause of stress. This activity would be most appropriate for those who describe themselves as being more cognitive than emotional.

1. Analyze the stress: How would you define your major stress problem? Name three or four contributing factors that cause or heighten the stress. How much time each week do you spend being aware of your concerns connected to this problem? What will eventually happen if you do not address this problem?

2. Identify three or four possible methods of alleviating the stress connected with this problem.

3. List the advantages and disadvantages of each of the methods.

4. Analyze these advantages and disadvantages so that you can identify the two best approaches to alleviating the stress.

5. Carefully examine the disadvantages of each of these approaches and consider how you might compensate for them.

6. Follow through with the two best approaches you have chosen.

7. Analyze the results: How are the actual results different from the expected results? What might be done to improve these results? How might the positive results be continued over time?

"The greatest discovery of my generation is that human beings can alter their lives by altering their attitudes of mind." - William James.

COUNTERING IRRATIONALITY

"Counters" are thoughts or activities that can stop untrue ideas in their tracks. Sometimes humorous, counters act as a red light to irrational thoughts that are starting to spin out of control. A single word like "Nonsense!" or "Hogwash!" is an example of a counter. When an irrational thought begins, "My life is over . . . ," it can be interrupted with a counter: "Kibosh! Nothing but kibosh!" Or it can be stopped with a sentence: "Nobody's life is over until it's over." Whenever care recipients catch themselves thinking or saying an irrational thought, they could blurt out a counter. Here are some useful tips:

> A. Counters need to stop irrational thinking abruptly in order to be effective. Some of the best are short and punchy, like "Pish!" Say them aloud as soon as the irrational thought or expression arises.
> B. The best counters are ones you have created yourself.
> C. Develop several forms of counters: words, phrases, sentences, philosophical arguments; the greater the variety, the better. Consult a thesaurus if need be.

If a caregiver is prescribing this activity, the caregiver needs to always remember that some irrational thoughts can serve a positive purpose. That irrational thought might be an important attempt to gain some control in a situation that often feels uncontrollable. The irrational thought could serve a purpose only known to the care recipient. We cannot force our views, methods, or judgments onto care recipients.

"There is no situation, however seemingly hopeless or terrible . . . which we cannot use to evolve." - Pema Chodron.

"Affliction comes to us all, not to make us sad, but sober, not to make us sorry, but wise, not to make us despondent, but by the darkness to refresh us." - Henry W. Beecher.

"The art of living lies less in eliminating troubles than in growing with them." - Bernard Baruch.

TIME FOR REFRAMING

All of reality is open for interpretation: a glass of water can be perceived as half full or half empty. The object of this activity is to find the best possible interpretation that is consistent with reality – that is how we "reframe" our interpretations of reality.

From the following list of painful circumstances choose two, three, or four to reframe. What is the best possible interpretation you can make of this situation, an interpretation that does not alter reality, an interpretation that only alters the perception of that reality. [Example: The flu. Because I have the flu I do not need to go to work or do any strenuous activities around the house. I can use this time to read a book I've always wanted to read. I might want to also rent a few videos I've wanted to see, but haven't had the time.]

    A. Losing your car keys.
    B. A snow storm.
    C. A relationship breakup.
    D. A sprained ankle.
    E. A job loss.
    F. Having Jehovah Witnesses show up at your door.
    G. A neighborhood grocery store closing down.
    H. Someone not acknowledging a gift.
    I. A pet dying.
    J. Losing your wallet.
    K. Your television set breaking down.

Once we learn the process of reframing, we can reframe anything that happens to us – anything. Is there anything you might need to reframe concerning some of your current thoughts, negative or depressing thoughts you might have regarding your current situation?

"In some ways, suffering ceases to be suffering at the moment it finds a meaning." - *Viktor Frankl.*

"Character cannot be developed in ease and quiet. Only through experience of trial and suffering can the soul be strengthened, vision cleared, ambition inspired, and success achieved." - Helen Keller.

"It is the darkest nights that prepare the greatest dawns." - Sri Aurobindo.

DESIRES AS REALITIES

Instead of saying "I wish that my pain would go away," a person could affirm "I am free from pain." Whenever doing this stating of desires as realities, people need not pay attention to rationality or feasibility; just make the affirmation. Such affirmations are perceived by the persons affirming them not as lies, but as truths in the making, truths that are in the process of collecting enough subjective backing that they will soon become objective reality. For added effect, each affirmation could be followed by the statement "I am now in the process of creating this reality or a better reality."

1. Write down one of your present desires as a present reality. (Instead of "I wish I was not lonely," write "I am not lonely." Instead of "I wish I felt stronger," write "I feel stronger.")

2. Repeat your new statement three times each evening before going to bed and three times each morning when getting up. As you are repeating the statement, visualize the statement as if every detail of it is happening in the present moment. (For added effect you might want to say the statement while looking at yourself in a mirror.)

3. If you wish, you could also post the statement on a refrigerator, mirror, toilet lid, drinking glass, lamp shade, bedroom door, or anything that you will often see.

BEING THANKFUL

With each of the following categories, write a couple paragraphs about a particular item in that category that you remember with thanksgiving.

1. A place. [Example: I remember a lake by the house where I was growing up. I remember standing in a shallow part of the lake having a school of fish swim around and through my legs. I was filled with the wonder of life, the gift of life. . . . That was also the lake where I, at six years old, learned to swim. My dad threw me out of a boat and said, "Swim." I learned the importance of determination that day. . . .]

2. An object. [Example: My dad's model railroad setup: he allowed me to run it sometimes, showing that he trusted me . . .]

3. A special event.

4. A teacher you had.

The Greek word transliterated as "anemnesis" means that in remembering something from the past in the present we make it present, we make it *real* in the present. No matter how negative things might seem in the present we always have the power to borrow something positive from the past, bring it into the present, and make it real in the present.

SINGING

1. Start by singing the "Happy Birthday" song to yourself three times. The first time with mild affect and a gentle voice. The second time with medium affect and a normal voice. The third time with great affect and a loud, exuberant voice.

2. Get a CD or tape with one of your favorite, uplifting songs on it. Play it a couple times learning the words, taking them into your consciousness until you feel you are ready to accompany the song with your own voice. You will sing the song three times. The first time as a background voice. The second time as if part of a duet. The third time in a loud, exuberant voice as if you are the main performer and the CD or tape is your background accompaniment.

This might be an activity to repeat periodically, choosing a different song each time.

PICTURE THIS

The following exercise involves having a client/patient do some painting. Three paintings will be done, each expressing certain emotions. They would be done in a certain order with some specific instructions connected with how each painting is to be done and what is to be done after the painting is completed.

1. The first painting is to be entitled "Sadness/Depression." The painting could involve finger painting, brush strokes, or flinging the paint at a canvas (Jackson Pollock style). Colors would be chosen that express the title. The paint would be applied with movements that also express the title. Everything in the painting is to embody the feelings of sadness and depression.

2. A day or two later the second painting would be done, a painting entitled "Contentment/Joy." The painting could involve finger painting, brush strokes, or flinging the paint at a canvas. Colors would be chosen that express the title. The paint would be applied with movements that also express the title. Everything in the painting is to embody the feelings of contentment and joy.

3. A day or two later the second painting would be done, a painting entitled "Determination/Hope." The painting could involve finger painting, brush strokes, or flinging the paint at a canvas. Colors would be chosen that express the title. The paint would be applied with movements that also express the title. Everything in the painting is to embody the feelings of determination and hope.

4. A day or two later the first painting would be discarded. Burn it, bury it, or take it to a place where there is a lot of garbage (a large garbage container or a dump) and throw it in the garbage.

5. A day or two later the other paintings would be displayed either at home or office. The paintings would be displayed for as long as it takes to be reminded of the ever-present existence of contentment, joy, determination, and hope.

POSITIVE EXCHANGES

This activity requires two family members – a caregiver and a care recipient. Each person would list five or six tasks that the other could do to please the one making the list. The tasks should be stated in positive terms rather than as complaints. Not all five or six tasks need to be completed, but the person who carries out the tasks should choose three that can be done within the coming week. You may want to do this activity every month.

A CONSIDERATION: We, as caregivers, need to continually remind ourselves that the goal of caregiving is to feed the strengths of our clients/patients, not to feed our strengths. The goal is to empower clients/patients, not empower us.

I CAN BE MY OWN FAMILY

A caregiver can assign "homework" of completing eight sentences, each beginning, "I need my family to _____." (Examples: "I need my family to show me more patience." "I need my family to prepare my meals for me." "I need my family to give me more opportunities to laugh.")

From the list of eight, three needs could be selected as things that the person in your care can make into personal goals. Each statement would be reworded to reflect goals that he or she can achieve alone. (Examples: "I need to show myself more patience." "I need to prepare my own meals for myself." "I need to give myself more opportunities to laugh.")

After the new statements are composed, the care recipient would map out a strategy for accomplishing those objectives. Or, several strategies might be incorporated to move toward reaching those goals.

DO NOT STRAIGHTEN OUT

As caregivers, we sometimes succumb to the temptation of trying to "straighten out" the people in our care. We can sometimes act like parents trying to mold children before they grow up and move out of our orbit. But we forget that the people in our care have grown up, lived full lives, and have the right not to be straightened out or changed to meet our desires, expectations, or values. Before plunging ahead to tell our patient or loved one what he or she must do ("Have a more upbeat outlook; things could be worse," or "Work a little harder on your physical therapy," or "Just try a little harder to eat some more food."), we might try these steps.

1. Stop.

2. Look.

3. Listen.

4. If you feel the urge to do anything else, stop.

5. Look.

6. Listen.

7. If, once again, you feel the urge, stop.

8. Look.

9. Listen.

"When we honestly ask ourselves which persons in our lives mean the most to us, we often find that it is those who, instead of giving much advice, solutions or cures, have chosen rather to share our pain and touch our wounds with a gentle and tender hand. The friend who can be silent with us in a moment of despair or confusion, who can stay with us in an hour of grief and bereavement, who can tolerate not-knowing, not-curing, not-healing and face with us the reality of our powerlessness, that is the friend who cares." - Henri Nouwen.

"Sometimes our best service to those we love is to simply stand by, be silent, be patient, be hopeful, be understanding, and wait." - Leo Buscaglia.

"Be not angry that you cannot make others as you wish them to be since you cannot make yourself as you wish to be." - Thomas A. Kempis.

"Why don't you just sit down and shut up?" - Dainin Katagiri Roshi.

Chapter Six

Addressing The Spiritual/Religious Concerns Of The Terminally Ill

"Do we not all have a right, not only to have our bodies treated with respect, but also, and perhaps even more important, our spirits? Spiritual care is not a luxury for a few; it is 'the' essential right of every human being, as essential as political liberty, medical assistance, and equality of opportunity." - Sogyal Rinpoche.

"The willingness to allow [care recipients] to be themselves by supporting them with our presence is essential. In the spiritual realm, presence implies an 'unconditional acceptance' of people." - Patrice O'Connor.

"Our work . . . would change remarkable if we thought about it as ongoing care rather than as the quest for a cure." - Thomas Moore.

"No one wishes to be 'rescued' with someone else's beliefs. Remember your task is not to convert anyone to anything, but to help the person in front of you get in touch with his or her own strength, confidence, faith, and spirituality, whatever that might be." - Sogyal Rinpoche.

"Don't be so arrogant as to suppose that the truth is no bigger than your understanding of it." - Michael Green.

MY SPIRITUAL TRAVELOGUE

Journals have often been encouraged as a form of spiritual practice or emotional/psychological growth.

1. The dying person would start with a bound book of blank pages. The book would be divided into three sections, one entitled "Thoughts on God" or "Thoughts On The Existence Of A Reality Greater Than Myself," one entitled "Thoughts On My Value And Lack Of Value As A Person," and one entitled "Thoughts On Afterlife."

2. The dying person would make a dated entry in at least one of the sections each day.

3. This participant would then periodically share the contents of his or her journal with a trusted friend, family member, counselor, or caregiver.

A DYING PERSON'S DREAM JOURNAL

Dream journals can often allow people to talk about and explore subjects they might not normally want to talk about or explore: sex, God, fears, etc.

1. The dying person could create a journal of all of his or her memorable dreams, especially those in which the subject of death is somehow present.

2. After recording the dream, the participant would address in the journal the following three questions:

>A. What message is there in the dream that might have relevance to my past, especially in regards to any "unfinished business" I might have: something I needed to do but have yet to do, someone with whom I have needed to speak but have yet to, etc.?
>B. What message is there in the dream that might have relevance for my current situation? Is there something I need to be doing now that I am not? Is there something I am not doing now that I need to do?
>C. What message is there in the dream that might have relevance for my future, especially related to what my priorities might need to be?

A CONSIDERATION: We, as caregivers, might often assume that what is nourishing for us must be nourishing for everyone, therefore we feel compelled to share our nourishment. Yet, what is *nourishing* for us could be *toxic* for others. Rather than trying to impose our nourishment on others, we might want to rather help care recipients find what is nourishing and comforting within their own beliefs or tradition.

"O man, do not be afraid of death at all. Thou art immortal. Death is not the opposite of life. It is only a phase of life. Life flows on ceaselessly. The fruit perishes but the seed is full of life. The seed dies but a huge tree grows out of the seed. The tree perishes but it becomes coal which has rich life. Water disappears but it becomes the invisible steam which contains the seed of new life. The stone disappears but it becomes lime which is full of new life. The physical sheath only is thrown but life persists." - Sivananda.

"Do not allow death to disturb you, do not let the demise of flesh be the cause of pain or anguish. It is merely riddance of your vehicle, the sloughing off of your clothes." - Shantidasa.

"To be afraid of death is like being afraid of discarding an old worn-out garment. - Mohandas Gandhi.

"Death is no more traumatic than taking off an old coat." - Eknath Easwaran.

"What, I pray you, is dying? Just what it is to put off a garment." - St. John Chrysostom.

GUIDED IMAGERY:
A CHRISTIAN CONVERSATION

The following guided imagery could be read to the participant or recorded for the participant's use.

Close your eyes and imagine that you are being transported to Gethsemane. . . . You see Jesus all alone, kneeling and praying. . . . You see his power. You also see his vulnerability. You see all of his internal struggles. No one understands him. He feels alone. He feels unloved. . . . You quietly walk over to his side and kneel next to him. You kneel there in silence. . . . After a short while, Jesus turns to you with love in his eyes and asks, "What can I do for you?" . . . You look Jesus in the eyes and say, "Please tell me how you feel as you are facing death." Listen to Jesus talk about death while he is in Gethsemane. . . . Imagine his words, his tone of voice, his facial expressions. . . . What does Jesus say about death while he is in the garden of Gethsemane? . . .

Now imagine that you are being transported to the foot of the cross. . . . You see Jesus hanging alone on that cross. He is in great pain. He feels completely deserted. . . . After a while, Jesus sees you standing below him. With love in his eyes, he asks, "What can I do for you?" . . . You look Jesus in the eyes and say, "Please tell me how you feel as you are dying." Imagine how Jesus talks about death as he is hanging on the cross. . . . What does he say about death while he is hanging on that cross? . . .

Now imagine that you are being transported to the throne of the resurrected Jesus. You see Jesus relieved of all his pain, basking in the glory of God. . . . You quietly approach the throne. You kneel in silence. . . . After a while, Jesus turns to you with love in his eyes and asks, "What can I do for you?" . . . You look Jesus in the eyes and say, "Please tell me how you feel after you have died." Imagine how Jesus talks about death after he has experienced the resurrection. . . . What does Jesus say about death after the resurrection? . . .

GUIDED IMAGERY:
A JEWISH CONVERSATION

    Close your eyes and imagine that you are going back to the time of Moses. You are going to be with Moses beside him in his life's journey. . . . You are with Moses as he stands before the burning bush. He is receiving God's call and promises. . . . Moses claims to be a nobody. Yet God says he will empower Moses; he will comfort him and strengthen him. God says he will pour out blessings upon Moses. . . . After receiving all of God's blessings and promises, Moses turns and sees you, and asks, "What can I do for you?" . . . You look at Moses and say, "Please tell me how you feel at this time in your life." Imagine how Moses would describe his life now after receiving all of God's blessings and promises. . . .

    Now imagine yourself with Moses later in his life. Imagine yourself with Moses in the desert after he has witnessed the idolatry of Israel. Although Moses still has faith in God, he now feels despair and little hope for he and his people. . . . This despairing Moses now turns to you and asks, "What can I do for you?" . . . You look at him and say, "Please tell me how you feel about life now." Imagine how Moses describes life at this point in his journey. . . .

    Now imagine yourself meeting Moses at the very end of his life. He realizes that God will deliver all his promises even though his people have been unfaithful. He realizes that God can even feed people in the desert. . . . Look upon Moses at this point in his journey. . . . Moses turns to you and asks, "What can I do for you?" . . . You say, "Please tell me how you view life now at the end of your life." . . . What does Moses say? . . .

GUIDED IMAGERY:
A BUDDHIST CONVERSATION

      Close your eyes and imagine yourself meeting Gautama in his youth, before he had ever witnessed suffering, before he had ever witnessed death. Imagine him in his protected environment, removed from all hardships and pain, isolated within his wealthy family's compound. . . . Look upon this protected, innocent youth named Gautama. . . . This young man turns to you and asks, "What can I do for you?" . . . You look at him in all his innocence and say, "Please tell me how you feel at this time in your life." Imagine how Gautama would describe this time of his life. . . .

      Now imagine yourself meeting Gautama when he first discovers suffering and death. Imagine his shock at discovering pain for the very first time. . . . Look upon this shocked and disturbed young man, this man whose protected world has just been dramatically challenged by the existence of pain and death. . . . This now disturbed young man turns to you and asks, "What can I do for you?" . . . You look at him and say, "Please tell me how you feel at this time in your life." Imagine how Gautama would describe his discovery of pain and death. . . .

      Now imagine yourself meeting the Buddha just as he has gotten up from sitting under the bodhi tree. Imagine his whole being aglow with the realization of enlightenment. . . . Look upon the Buddha, this man who has now become aware of the way to overcome suffering, the way to transcending pain and death. . . . The Buddha turns to you and asks, "What can I do for you?" . . . You look at the Buddha in the glow of his enlightenment and say, "Please tell me how you see death." Imagine how the Buddha would describe his enlightened perspective of death. . . .

GUIDED IMAGERY:
A NATURALIST CONVERSATION

Close your eyes and imagine yourself standing before a great oak tree in the middle of the season of Summer. This great oak tree towers before you with its deep, strong roots, and its branches reaching out in all directions, each branch lavishly decorated with thousands of green leaves. . . . Look with wonder upon this mighty, richly decorated oak tree, this oak tree with many leaves. . . . You see that this tree has survived for many generations and has witnessed much throughout its years. . . . After you have examined this oak tree for a little while, a gentle voice comes from the center of its huge trunk, asking, "What can I do for you?" . . . You look at this great oak tree and say, "Please tell me how you feel in the midst of this Summer." Imagine how this oak tree would describe its Summer condition. . . .

Now imagine that you are standing before this mighty oak tree in the middle of the season of Autumn. Its leaves are glorious and multicolored. Most of its leaves are still on the tree, but many have fallen to the ground. . . . Look at this tree at the height of its beauty and the waning of its liveliness. . . . After you have examined this oak tree in this stage of transition, a beautiful voice comes from the center of its trunk, asking, "What can I do for you?" . . . You look at this great oak tree and say, "Please tell me how you feel in the midst of this Fall." Imagine how this oak tree would describe its Fall condition. . . .

Now imagine that you are standing before this mighty oak tree in the middle of the season of Winter. Its branches are bare; there are no more leaves. Several branches have been broken by an ice storm and lie scattered on the ground beneath the tree. . . . Look at this tree that has been stripped of all its beauty, standing in all of its vulnerability, shivering in the harsh winter wind. . . . After you have examined this oak tree in this stage of devastation, a quivering voice comes from the center of its trunk, asking, "What can I do for you?" . . . You look at this great oak tree and say, "Please tell me how you feel in the midst of this Winter." Imagine how this oak tree would describe its Winter condition. . . .

Now imagine that you are standing before this mighty oak tree in the early part of the season of Spring. Little buds are sprouting all over its branches. Singing birds have returned to its branches and greet the tree with encouraging song every morning. . . . Look at this tree as it witnesses new life around it, upon it, and within it. . . . After you have examined this oak tree in this stage of rebirth, an excited voice comes from the center of its trunk, asking, "What can I do for you?" . . . You look at this great oak tree and say, "Please tell me how you feel in the midst of the Spring." Imagine how this oak tree would describe its Spring condition. . . .

A CONSIDERATION: Oftentimes a client's/patient's spiritual quest has been, and is, the quest for *meaning* rather than the quest for *happiness*. Or, all happiness might be based on meaning, purpose. As caregivers, we might often need to help a client/patient find meaning, purpose.

"The purpose of life is not to be happy – but to matter, to be productive, to be useful, to have it make some difference that you lived at all." - Leo Rosten.

"When people are serving, life is no longer meaningless." - John Gardner.

"Fear not that your life shall come to an end; rather fear that it will never have a beginning." - St. John Cardinal Newman.

"The goal of life is not happiness but meaning." - James Hollis.

PURPOSE

Gary was an active man in his early fifties. He simply liked doing things. He was a vice president of a bank, always working well beyond the hours expected of him. He was active in his community, belonging to several civic groups. He was active physically: he enjoyed running marathons.

It was during the running of a marathon that Gary felt some funny sensations in his feet. He pulled out of the race.

The next week Gary was diagnosed with amyotrophic lateral sclerosis (ALS), Lou Gehrig's disease, a gradual paralysis that typically begins with the feet and ever so slowly moves up the body. The person with ALS maintains full mental awareness, but the rest of the body loses its functioning inches at a time. For Gary, it was a seven year process of watching his body lose its functioning more and more each day.

Gary was determined that no matter what that disease did to him he would remain an active person. He would have some meaning in his life, some purpose, no matter what he lost.

Gary decided to continue to be vice president of that bank for as long as he could, even if he had to go to work in a wheelchair, even if that wheelchair would provide him with embarrassing situations: and it did provide him with many embarrassing situations.

One day Gary was in his office bathroom and could not get up off of the toilet on his own. He called out for help. The only person to hear his call was his secretary, who had to go into the bathroom and lift Gary up off of the toilet. Gary decided that day that he could no longer be vice president of that bank. But he was determined to not be defeated by that loss; he knew he could find something else to do, something else to give him a sense of meaning, a sense of purpose.

By this time he had a van made for him which he could operate with his hands. He decided that he would use that van to go around his city and teach people about his new area of expertise – ALS. So Gary went to various civic groups and schools teaching people about ALS: this was his new purpose. He taught people about ALS for quite a long time and he felt good in doing that. But the disease did not stop: it was beginning to effect the muscles in the upper part of his body. Then one day he got in an accident while driving the van. That day Gary had to once again acknowledge that he could no longer do something: he could no longer drive that van. But he was determined to not be defeated by that loss; he knew he could find something else to do, something else to give him a sense of meaning, a sense of purpose.

Now Gary was confined to his home. He called up the local junior college and asked if he might tutor students in his home. If students could come to his home, Gary would tutor them in basic computer skills, knowledge Gary had. He did that tutoring for some time, and that was his new purpose. But the disease did not stop: it began to effect the muscles around his diaphragm and his lungs. He had trouble projecting his voice; his students had trouble hearing him. Once again Gary said to himself that he would not be defeated. Once again he said to himself that he could find something else to give him meaning.

By this time Gary could use only one of his arms to any degree of control. He had his son make a special swivel device to rest his elbow on. Gary, then, with his right hand and his computer designed the software system for his local hospice, a software system that would help them track the health status of all their patients. Gary did that with one hand. It was his new purpose.

GIVING ASSIGNMENTS

A one hundred and four year old woman was dying in her home, surrounded by several generations of her family. She had been an active matriarch, always involved in several family projects, always trying to address the needs of her many relatives, always wanting to know that she was needed.

As her death was near, the family had gathered. Family members were going into her room, one at a time, sharing memories, saying their goodbyes.

One of her granddaughters, who was sixty, had lost a child many years ago. Her final message to the dying matriarch was the following: "Grandma, I know you're going to heaven. I've always known that. Would you do a favor for me when you're there? I need you to look after somebody: my son, Jeremy. He never was very good at taking care of himself. But you've always been good at taking care of lots of people. Grandma, would you please watch out for Jeremy?" The one hundred and four year old showed a big smile, thankful that she had something more she could do for the family.

LETTER FROM MY HIGHER SELF

The following activity is intended to prevent people from going into despair over what they might perceive as their life's lack of purpose.

1. Soon after a person has been informed of a terminal diagnosis, that person would write a list of all the compliments he or she has received from family members, friends, and associates. Next, this person would write a list of some of his or her most cherished life accomplishments.

2. The material in these two lists would then be put in the form of a letter addressed to the person. At the bottom of the letter would be the words "yours truly." The dying person would then sign his or her name under the salutation. This is a letter written to the care recipient from the care recipient.

3. The letter would then be placed in an envelope with the recipient's name on the outside of the envelope.

4. The letter would then be given to a trusted family member or friend with the instructions that the letter would be delivered if the care recipient would ever be in a state of mind where he or she was questioning the value of his or her life.

A CONSIDERATION: A person's purpose, meaning, can be an important issue up until the very last moment of life.

LEAVING NOTHING TO CHANCE

Kate was a very successful business woman; she had worked her way up the corporate ladder with great determination. In her late forties Kate had had a successful battle with colon cancer. After that battle she enjoyed the next three years without any problems. Then she had another battle with that cancer, this battle being more arduous than the first. But she won that battle too. Then six months after the second battle, Kate went on a long-anticipated two month tour of Europe. A couple weeks after returning from the European trip she called Judy, her minister, asking if they might spend the afternoon together. Judy found much of the conversation that afternoon quite different from Kate's usual conversations. Kate spent most of the time reminiscing: she had reviewed much of her life, the good times and the bad, talking about what she had felt to be some of her best accomplishments and some of her worst failures. Judy reported that Kate appeared to be in good health and good spirits throughout the entire afternoon, although she had expressed, a couple times during the afternoon, some fears of a possible third battle with that colon cancer.

Two days after Judy's visit with Kate, Judy was informed by a mutual friend named Troy that Kate had died. Judy responded, "I can't believe it. I just saw her a couple days ago and she appeared to be perfectly fine." Troy said, "Think about it, Judy. Think about it. Did Kate ever leave anything to chance?" "What do you mean, Troy?" "Just think about it, Judy. Think about it. Did Kate ever leave anything to chance?"

Judy reflected back on that afternoon with Kate and then saw her visit in a completely different light. She said to Troy, "That was Kate's goodbye to me. We were doing a final life review. She even made a couple confessions to me. She also told me how much she was dreading another battle with cancer. Then we hugged each other goodbye — Kate was not a hugging person. Kate was actually telling me she was going to take her life; she was giving me several signals. She took her life: that is what she did. Kate was in charge of her life and she was determined to be in charge of her death."

CAROL'S GRANDMOTHER

Carol's grandmother was dying in spasms of pain, having great difficulty breathing. The spasms of pain and difficulty in breathing had lasted for several days and nights. Carol was spending most of those nights with her grandmother, trying to sleep in the same room on an inflatable mattress on the floor. One night Carol, seeing her grandmother's body racked with pain and hearing her continually cry out, picked up a pillow and held it in her hands for a long time, struggling with the possibility of ending her grandmother's life, wanting to end her struggling. She finally resisted the temptation, put the pillow back on the mattress, and laid down for a fitful night of sleep.

During the night Carol opened her eyes to see two of her aunts standing beside her grandmother's bed. The two aunts were crying and pouring out expressions of love towards Carol's grandmother. These aunts had never before expressed those feelings of love.

Carol thought, "Had I ended my grandmother's life earlier that evening I would have cheated my aunts of that opportunity to say those things. I would have cheated my grandmother of the opportunity to hear those things." She thought, "Who can ever know why people go through so much pain? Could it have been that immense pain, and only that immense pain, that opened up the hearts of those two women?"

GOD'S BREATH

The words for the following breath meditation come from a hymn found in many Christian hymnals. The meditation could be used with people of the Jewish and Hindu faith, as well as other faiths, because of the natural association between "breath" and "spirit" in many languages. The out-breath phrases could be said aloud or silently.

> In-breath: (silence)
> Out-breath: "Breathe on me, Breath of God."
> In-breath: (silence)
> Out-breath: "Fill me with life anew."
> In-breath: (silence)
> Out-breath: "That I may love what Thou dost love."
> In-breath: (silence)
> Out-breath: "And do what Thou wouldst do."
> (repeat for as long as it feels good)

OBJECT MEDITATION

Meditating upon an object can create a peaceful mind. Object meditations might also be considered for those who cannot do breathing meditations because of a particular illness they might have: COPD, ALS, lung cancer.

1. Any object that elicits comfort can be the focus of a daily meditation.

    A. A crucifix
    B. A statue of the Buddha
    C. A mandala
    D. A menorah
    E. A copy of the Koran
    F. A flower
    G. A family photograph
    H. A stone
    I. A candle

2. Ten to fifteen minutes would be spent centering all of your attention upon this object of comfort. Whenever other thoughts intrude, close your eyes, and then open them up again upon the object of concentration.

A CONSIDERATION: Part of being open to a client's/patient's spirituality is a general openness to the existence of the mysterious, the unexplainable. The truly good caregiver wants to be receptive to the predictable and the unpredictable, the material and the immaterial, the explainable and the unexplainable.

HAZEL

When I first met Hazel I was informed that her doctors expected her to live no longer than two months. Hazel didn't concur. She intended to extend her prognosis, and she did: another nine months.

During that time Hazel had a profound influence on many people. Although her brain tumor prevented her from speaking more than one-word or two-word sentences, Hazel was often the center of interaction wherever she went. She had a special way of spontaneously evoking conversation in others.

Over the last five months of her life she insisted on attending her church almost every Sunday. Even though she had to attend services on a gurney, and even though she could not hide the disturbingly obvious physical effects of her disease and therapy treatments, Hazel was always surrounded by people busily conversing. Hazel's contribution to any conversation was most often not with any words but with a watchful, knowing expression. Her eyes communicated total involvement. Her face conveyed the impression that she always knew more than anyone else. Everyone who was acquainted with Hazel felt that she was in touch with a reality greater than the physically obvious. We sensed that she was somehow attuned to some spiritual reality.

My last visit with Hazel was evidence of both her spiritual dimension and her uncanny ability to evoke a conversation. I entered her room at the nursing home and pulled up a chair by her bed. As I reached out and held her hand I relayed greetings from various friends and acquaintances. Hazel's watchful, knowing eyes were turned toward me the whole time I spoke. After about five minutes I stopped chatting and simply held her hand as I looked around her room. I noticed the televison set, greeting cards, flowers, the institutional beige walls. When I turned back toward Hazel, her eyes were still trained on me. I gave her a little smile and resumed glancing around her room silently. I somehow felt that her eyes were saying something to me, something about the room itself.

"This room is kind of silly, isn't it? A really silly space," I blurted out, puzzled by my own words.

Although it is difficult for me to describe how Hazel's expression changed (if it changed at all), I somehow felt that her expression was saying she was in agreement with my words. I nodded with a half smile. Her gaze continued. A few minutes of silent reflection slipped by as I continued to hold her hand. I looked into her eyes again and added, "My words are kind of silly, too, aren't they? Words are kind of silly."

Her eyes were still locked on my face. I felt my thoughts somehow confirmed. With a grin I again reflected in silence, my eyes slightly downcast. When I looked up once more, I said, "And I am kind of silly, too. I'm very silly. We're all very silly people, aren't we?"

I waited a few moments, looked into Hazel's eyes again, and said good-bye with a big, foolish grin.

After leaving her I got in my car and drove around. What had I done? Was I going crazy? Had I done anything other than make a complete fool of myself? I wondered all of that as I drove aimlessly. I felt embarrassed and frustrated. Yet I also sensed something else as I recalled Hazel's eyes. I perceived something was going on inside her that was far beyond my comprehension. It seemed that she was in touch with something very powerful, something very spiritual – something that was flowing from her watchful, knowing eyes.

I officiated at Hazel's funeral service a week later. Over two hundred people attended. At the end of the service, for some unexplainable reason, I asked everyone to rise and give Hazel a standing ovation. An unusual request, certainly, but no one hesitated. Everyone stood and applauded for several minutes. Many people beamed smiles, others sobbed, and some wore dumbfounded looks.

What had happened? I wondered. Was everyone crazy? What was going on? Were people projecting something spiritual onto Hazel? Or was she transporting something spiritual into others? To this day I can still see Hazel's watchful, knowing eyes.

ANDREW

Andrew was the type of guy who always needed to be in control. For him: if he said something was true, it was true. If he told you black was white and white was black, you were not to contradict him. If he told you to do something, you were supposed to do it, and do it exactly the way he wanted it done.

Practically every time his hospice nurse visited him in his home, Andrew would say to her, "As soon as I can breathe okay, everything's going to be just fine." But his nurse knew that Andrew's lungs were not going to clear up; his breathing had been getting progressively worse, and there was no possibility, from her perspective, of it getting any better. Yet, Andrew still kept saying, "As soon as I can breathe okay, everything's going to be just fine." (The nurse knew not to contradict him; everyone around Andrew knew not to contradict him.)

The nurse wrote in her care notes that Andrew was in denial. Also, she would occasionally, very carefully, try to get Andrew to be more "realistic" with what was going on with him. However, he would still keep saying, "As soon as I can breathe okay, everything's going to be just fine."

Andrew's breathing worsened just as the nurse predicted; each day Andrew had more and more difficulty in breathing. Then, early one afternoon, Andrew was taken by ambulance to the hospital because of his terrible breathing. His lungs were treated with some powerful pharmaceuticals. By evening his lungs had cleared up.

At eight o'clock the following morning, Andrew's family came to visit him and were quite surprised to see how much better Andrew was breathing because of that pharmaceutical treatment. Andrew immediately started directing his family to straighten up his hospital room. He directed them to move some of the furniture, telling them he had a "ten o'clock appointment with someone very special, someone who would want him to have his room as nice as possible." He also insisted that he have a clean shave and look the best he could for that appointment.

His family knew not to contradict him; they knew that it was best for everyone involved to just do exactly as Andrew told them to do. So they straightened up his room even though they knew his mind was just not functioning at its best. They gave him a shave and helped him put on a clean pair of pajamas. They took a little more than an hour to follow all of his detailed instructions.

At ten o'clock, the time he said he would have a special appointment, Andrew died. Andrew's death should not have been a surprise to anyone. He had always told his nurse as well as everyone else, "As soon as I can breathe okay, everything's going to be just fine."

JEAN

Jean had many prejudices towards black people. She had grown up in Atlanta during the twenties and thirties when discrimination was taken for granted. Jean was dying.

The last four days of her life she was "hallucinating" all the time. She'd claim that many of her dead relatives were in the room with her. She'd often see her husband who had died over ten years ago. She saw some of her friends who had also died. She even talked to many of these people when she saw them.

The day before she died she told her children that there were about twenty black people around her bed, singing and dancing. She said, "They told me I'm invited to a special party. They said they'll teach me how to sing and dance. And gracious me, do they know how to sing and dance! . . . And you know something else: they also told me that God loves them just as much as me. Can you believe that? . . . You know, I think I believe them! I was totally convinced!"

Her children were convinced that she was hallucinating. I'm not so sure.

TANYA

Although only a teenager, Tanya knew that she would be dying soon and did not want to resist it. But Tanya's mother wanted her to fight, Tanya's mother saying that it "was not God's will that she go so soon." Tanya reluctantly followed her mother's suggestions and tried various aggressive treatments at the hospital where she was staying. But Tanya would still periodically, as best she could, try to tell her mother that she really wanted to die and thought that it was the right time to do it.

Then one day Tanya told her mother that one of the hospital employees, a man she thought was a very caring person, was telling her that it was really okay for her to die. Tanya said that this caring man would often enter Tanya's room as soon as her mother finished her visit.

Tanya's mother, needless to say, was furious; she wanted to track down this hospital employee to confront him for contradicting her wishes. So she asked Tanya what the man's name was. Tanya said she didn't know. So Tanya's mother asked for a description of this man, this man who had the audacity to sneak into the room immediately after her visits and tell her daughter that it was okay to die.

Tanya's description was very detailed. She said the man was about six feet tall, had a white goatee, had a twitch in his right eye, spoke in a loud whisper, and always wore a black shirt and black boots. As Tanya was describing the man, her mother started crying. Tanya had just described her mother's father who had died three years before Tanya was even born.

Tanya's mother then knew it was indeed "God's will" that Tanya go soon.

GUIDED IMAGERY: FAMILY REUNION

The following guided imagery could be read to the care recipient or recorded for the care recipient's use.

      Close your eyes. Picture yourself standing alone. . . . Imagine your mother walking up to you. . . . Picture her standing in front of you. . . . Listen to your mother as she says, "I love you for all that you have been." . . . "I love you for all that you have been." . . . Listen to your mother saying to you, "I love you for all that you are." . . . "I love you for all that you are." . . . Hear her saying, "I love you for all that you will be." . . . "I love you for all that you will be." . . . Listen to your mother's request: "Forgive me for anything I have done to hurt you." . . . "Forgive me for anything I have done to hurt you." . . . Hear your mother saying, "I forgive you for anything that you have done to hurt me." . . . "I forgive you for anything that you have done to hurt me." . . . Listen to her say, "I love you; I always have; I always will." . . . "I love you; I always have; I always will." . . . Notice how it feels when your mother wraps her arms around you and holds you. . . . Feel her holding you now. . . . Know she will always hold you. . . . Know she will always hold you because she loves you. Know she really does love you. . . .

      Picture yourself standing completely alone again. . . . Imagine your father walking up to you. . . . Picture your father standing in front of you. . . . Listen to your father say, "I love you for all that you have been." . . . "I love you for all that you have been." . . . Listen to your father saying to you, "I love you for all that you are." . . . "I love you for all that you are." . . . Hear your father saying "I love you for all that you will be." . . . "I love your for all that you will be." . . . Listen to your father's request: "Forgive me for anything I have done to hurt you." . . . "Forgive me for anything I have done to hurt you." . . . Listen to your father saying, "I forgive you for anything you have done to hurt me." . . . "I forgive you for anything you have done to hurt me." . . . Hear your father saying, "I love you; I always have; I always will." . . . "I love you; I always have; I always will." . . . Notice how it feels when your father wraps his arms around you and holds you. . . . Feel him holding you now. . . . Know he will always hold you. . . . Know he will always hold you because he loves you. Know he really does love you. . . .

      Now open your eyes knowing that your mother loves you and your father loves you. . . .

A CONSIDERATION: Prayer can cause some transformations which neither surgeons nor psychotherapists are capable of producing.

"Prayer is not flight; prayer is power. Prayer does not deliver a man [a woman] from some terrible situation; prayer enables a man [a woman] to face and to master a situation." - William Barkley.

PRAYERS

The following are some prayers that can be used by the terminally ill. The prayers can be used as they are written, or a person can place an invocation before the prayer and a concluding statement after the prayer that are congruent with his/her belief system.

PERCEIVING THE WONDERFUL

I give thanks for perceiving the wonderful.

I look up into the heavens and see a vast array of planets and stars, and I know the
    world is wonderfully made and the subject of Your wonderful love.
I see the intricacies of a single snowflake and hear of the intricacies of a single cell, and
    I know the world is wonderfully made and the subject of Your wonderful love.

Though my heart is weak,
    I perceive that I am wonderfully made and the subject of Your wonderful love.
Though my lungs are tired,
    I perceive that I am wonderfully made and the subject of Your wonderful love.
Though my muscles are sore,
    I perceive that I am wonderfully made and the subject of Your wonderful love.
Though my bones ache,
    I perceive that I am wonderfully made and the subject of Your wonderful love.
Though my emotions are drained,
    I perceive that I am wonderfully made and the subject of Your wonderful love.

I give thanks for perceiving the wonderful.

FOR PEACE, COMFORT, STRENGTH, AND COURAGE

May my mind think of peace.
May my lungs breathe in comfort.
May my heart beat with strength.
May my blood flow with courage.

Peace, comfort, strength, courage:
May they be mine.
May I get them.
May I give them.
May I live them.

MAY MY LAST BE MY BEST

May my final chapter be my best chapter.
May my last season be my best season.
May my last act be my best act.
May my last breath be my best breath.

PRAYER OF SURRENDER

Lead me from individuality to mutuality.
Lead me from despair to hope, from fear to trust.
Lead me from death to Life.
Lead me from myself to You.

MY DYING PRAYER

All that is precious in my life is fading away.
The heart that I have been given is tired.
The mind that I have been given is clouded.
The body that I have been given is weak.

I look back and have regrets and wish forgiveness.
May I be forgiven for the people I have hurt.
May I be forgiven for the time I have spent unwisely.
May I be forgiven for the love I have failed to express.

In the life that I have left, may I be determined to not hurt anyone else.
In the life that I have left, may I be determined to spend my time wisely.
In the life that I have left, may I be determined to express all my love.

PRAYER FOR COURAGE

I pray for a peaceful death, but if there be no peace, please let me have courage.
I pray for a death without pain, but if there be pain, please let me have courage.
I pray for a death where there is no disfigurement, but if there be disfiguring, please let
    me have courage.
I pray for a good death, but if it be not good, please let me have courage.

I GIVE THANKS

I give thanks.
I give thanks.
In the midst of my suffering, I give thanks for all gifts of comfort.
In the midst of my despair, I give thanks for all gifts of hope.
In the midst of my darkness, I give thanks for all gifts of light.
In the midst of the bitter taste of my dying, I give thanks for every sweet taste of life.
I give thanks.
I give thanks.

PRAYER IN THE MIDST OF LONELINESS

I long for a kind word.
I long for a listening ear.
I long for a comforting hand.
I long for a warm embrace.
I long for a gentle kiss.
Help me in my longings.
Help me in my loneliness.
Let me not feel so lonely anymore.
Help me.

I believe there is some help available to me and that is why I pray.
I believe there is some strength available to me and that is why I pray.
I believe there is some comfort available to me and that is why I pray.
Let it be.
Let it be.
Let it be.

PRAYER IN THE MIDST OF FEAR

Things are happening to my body and mind that have never before happened and I am afraid.
I am facing things that are uncertain and unknown and I am afraid.
People are saying that I might die soon and I am afraid.
I am afraid.
Help me with my fear.
I am afraid.
Help me.

I believe there is some help available to me and that is why I pray.
I believe there is some strength available to me and that is why I pray.
I believe there is some comfort available to me and that is why I pray.
Let me have help.
Let me have strength.
Let me have comfort.

PRAYER IN THE MIDST OF PAIN

Help me when I feel there can be no help.
When medicine is inadequate, help me.
When technology fails, help me.
When nothing people say or do brings comfort, help me.
Help me.
Help me to bear what often seems unbearable.
Help me.
Help me when I feel there can be no help.
Help me.

I believe there is some help available to me and that is why I pray.
I believe there is some strength available to me and that is why I pray.
I believe there is some comfort available to me and that is why I pray.
Let me have help.
Let me have strength.
Let me have comfort.

WHEN ALL IS DONE

Because a meal is over, is the nourishment that it gave nullified?
Because we have finished reading a book, has the skill of the author been erased?
Because a day has ended, are its bountiful gifts any less?

Why then should I, at the conclusion of my life, question its value?

Help me to discover what nourishment I have bestowed upon others.
Help me to see the skills I have offered this world.
Help me to realize the gifts I have given.

Chapter Seven

Addressing The Spiritual/Religious Concerns Of The Grieving

"Ritual is a way for us to consciously take a small sample of our chaos, our grief, and to process that sample in our own time. By doing this, we get to know our grief and our chaos. . . . If we don't get to know it in some way, the chances are that the pressure of the chaos will build and the grief will spew forth at whatever time in whatever manner it desires. Doing the sampling work will not stop the grief from coming forth unpredictably, but it will dissipate the pressure, much as a release valve in a steam engine does." - Thomas Golden.

"Ritual gives us a container in which to experience safely the chaos of grief. When grieving, we look for containers much like those in the amusement park – something with sides on it and a handle to grab if we need." - Thomas Golden.

PRIVATE SERVICE OF REMEMBRANCE

In addition to the public funeral service, the mourner might want to have a special service at his or her home the same day as the public service or the following weekend or at the one month anniversary. This service would just be for the family and/or really close friends. Some possible suggestions:

    A. The service could be centered around a particular theme: celebratory, meditative, humorous, solemn.
    B. The service could be preceded or followed by a meal.
    C. Each person attending could give a short presentation: eulogy, reading, poem, musical piece.
    D. Pictures and mementos could be placed all around the room where the service is held.

WHEN NOT BEING PRESENT AT A FUNERAL

The following suggestions are being presented as things people can do if they are, for whatever reason, unable to be present at a funeral service.

>A. You could say a prayer or read through a funeral service liturgy at the same time that the actual funeral service is in progress.
>B. You could light a candle in your home or at a place of worship during the day of the funeral.
>C. You could get a photograph of the person who has died and talk to the photograph, saying everything you always wanted to say but never did.
>D. You could write a long letter to the person who has died, writing everything you always wanted to say but never did.
>E. You could plant a tree, shrub, or flower in a special place you shared with the person who has died.

ANNIVERSARY SERVICE OF REMEMBRANCE

At the one year anniversary of the death, a minister (or other special person) could lead a special memorial service. Some suggestions:

>A. Appropriate readings, prayers and/or music, might be chosen by the bereaved person.
>B. The bereaved person might want to personally choose some people to have certain parts in the service: a way of enhancing service and honoring some of those attending.
>C. The service might somehow be structured so as to portray some kind of transition in mood or resolve, some indication that things are different, and need to be different, from what they were immediately after the death.
>D. The service might end with some kind of activity that emphasizes saying goodbye to the past and hello to the future.

THE ANCIENT STONE CEREMONY

1. The participant would go to a place where there are many stones. The participant would then draw a six foot wide circle in the dirt.

2. The participant would then stand in the center of the circle and invoke the person who has died to come into the circle and stand beside him or her. Then some time is spent feeling the departed person in the circle.

3. The participant would then go out of the circle and find four stones. Each stone would be placed on the edge of the circle, each stone being placed in one of the four directions: south, west, north, and east.

4. From the center of the circle, the participant would face the stone on the south edge of the circle. While facing that stone, the participant would bring to mind the childhood of the person who has died and the childlike qualities of that person. Then the participant would go over to the stone, touch it, and verbalize appreciation for the child in the person.

5. From the center of the circle, the participant would then face the stone on the west edge of the circle. While facing that stone, the participant would bring to mind the brave and courageous qualities of the person who has died. Then the participant would go over to the stone, touch it, and verbalize appreciation for the bravery and courage in the person.

6. From the center of the circle, the participant would then face the stone on the north edge of the circle. While facing that stone, the participant would bring to mind the skills and talents of the person who has died. Then the participant would go over to the stone, touch it, and verbalize appreciation for the skills and talents of the person.

7. From the center of the circle, the participant would then face the stone on the east edge of the circle. While facing that stone, the participant would bring to mind the vision and dreams of the person who has died. The participant would then go over to the stone, touch it, and verbalize appreciation for the vision and dreams of the person.

8. The participant would then sit down in the center of the circle and thank the person who has died for all the contributions the person has made to the participant's life. The participant would then meditate for awhile upon all the gifts that have been received from this person who has died.

9. When the participant is ready to leave this place, he or she would return the rocks to their original places, erase the circle, and leave that place the way it was found. In doing this final step, he or she meditates upon two important realities:

    A. From one point of view, we cannot change time or place. What has happened has happened. Reality is what reality is. When someone has died they are no longer here and will not return.
    B. From another point of view, no thing or no person is completely confined to a particular time or a particular place. I can carry that person with me now wherever I go. That person can now be embodied in me and in everything I witness and experience.

ALTAR OF REMEMBRANCE

The bereaved person could designate a place in his/her home (coffee table, end table, top of a dresser) to be an "Altar of Remembrance." This could be a place of periodic reflection or simply an ever-present reminder of the ongoing presence and influence of the loved one. On the altar, there could be several items:

    A. An altar cloth could be made from some of the person's clothing (a scarf, a cloth cut from a favorite outfit).
    B. Photographs of person (different periods in person's life).
    C. A ring, watch, or other piece of jewelry.
    D. A reminder of a favorite hobby (a model train car for a model train enthusiast, a kitchen utensil for a cook, a golf ball for a golfer, a favorite book for a reader).
    E. A framed birth (or marriage) certificate.
    F. Favorite passages from scripture or other favorite quotations.
    G. A laminated obituary notice.
    H. A candle to burn on the loved one's birthdays, on anniversaries, or on holidays.
    I. A flower or plant.

LETTING GO RITUAL

1. Before the ritual begins the bereaved person selects an object which symbolizes the deceased. This object could be a piece of clothing, picture, or any possession of the deceased.

2. Then the object is taken to a special place the deceased and the bereaved enjoyed together.

3. A hole is then dug in the ground or a fire pit prepared for a ritualistic burial or burning of the object.

4. A short meditation is offered before the object is buried or burnt.

5. The object is then buried or burned.

6. The bereaved meditates upon letting the object and the deceased go.

RIVER OF LIFE

1. Locate a quiet stream or a meandering river.

2. Create, or take with you, an object which symbolizes your relationship with the departed loved one.

3. Hold the object in your hand while you meditate upon the stream and your relationship.

4. When you are ready, drop the object into the stream or river.

5. Watch the object's movement along with the river's current.

6. Notice the obstacles it encounters as it passes along the waterway.

7. Notice the beauty of its free flowing movement as it slips further out of sight.

8. Meditate upon the eventual destination of the object as it takes nature's course.

"He did not say: You will not be troubled, you will not be belabored, you will not be afflicted; but he said: You will not be overcome." - Mother Julian of Norwich.

"When we become aware that we do not have to escape our pains, but that we can mobilize them into a common search for life, those very pains are transformed from expressions of despair into signs of hope." - Henri Nouwen.

A CONSIDERATION: Medicine aims at eliminating pain and suffering. Spirituality aims at helping people find meaning and value in the midst of pain and suffering, even if that pain and suffering cannot be eliminated. As caregivers we might not be able to eliminate people's woundedness, but we can always try to give them meaning and value in the midst of that woundedness.

A BEREAVED PERSON'S SPIRITUAL AFFIRMATIONS

A caregiver could recommend that a care recipient repeat each day, verbally or internally, one or a couple of the following affirmations.

> A. I receive strength through the comfort of God. I receive comfort through the strength of God.
> B. Although clouds of loss and despair might enter my world, I know that the light of God can never disappear.
> C. I will take a day at a time knowing that God is with me when the sun rises and will not desert me when the sun sets.
> D. God was with me yesterday. God is with me today. God will be with me tomorrow.
> E. God's love is behind me. God's love is before me. God's love is in me.

The word "God" is used in these affirmations, but you can substitute "Jesus," "Krishna," "the Revered Buddha," "Allah," "the Goddess," "the Divine Spirit," or any other appropriate wording.

A BEREAVED PERSON'S DREAM JOURNAL

As affirmations can provide meaning and value during one's day, dreams can provide meaning and value at night. To explore that meaning and value, the bereaved person could create a journal summarizing all of his/her memorable dreams. Dreams in which the departed person appears may be especially noteworthy. After recording each dream, the participant would address in the journal the following three questions:

> A. Are there any regrets or unfinished business from the past that is apparent in this dream? What do I need to do in regard to those regrets or that unfinished business?
> B. What does this dream say about what I need to be doing now to help me recover from this death?
> C. What does this dream tell me about what I need to be doing with the loved ones that still remain in my life?

A CONSIDERATION: Oftentimes the greatest spiritual issue for the grieving is the issue of forgiveness. Not necessarily God's forgiveness, but people forgiving one another. Sometimes it's forgiving the person who has died. Sometimes it's the griever needing to feel forgiveness.

"To err is human, to forgive, divine." - Alexander Pope.

"It is by forgiving that one is forgiven." - Mother Teresa.

"There is so much for us all to forgive that we shall never get it done without putting in a lot of practice." - J. Neville Ward.

FORGIVING THE PERSON WHO HAS DIED

1. The participant would acquire three pieces of colored paper: a yellow one, a red one, and a green one. On one side of the yellow piece of paper, the participant would write all the things the person who has died did or said that caused sadness for the participant. On one side of the red piece of paper, the participant would write all the things that person did or said that caused him/her to be angry. On one side of the green one, the participant would write all the other things that person did or said that caused any other kind of hurt.

2. Placing his/her hands on the three pieces of paper, the participant would read the following: "_____, I forgive you for all the times you have made me sad. _____, I forgive you for all the times you have made me angry. _____, I forgive you for all the times you have hurt me. _____, I forgive you. I too have been less than perfect. I too probably caused you sadness, anger, and hurt. I love you and I want to remember you for all the good you have done and all the love that you have shown to me. Life will always have sadness, anger, and hurt. I need to learn from it and grow from it, and I must somehow come to an understanding of how I need to go on learning and growing. I forgive you. I forgive you. I forgive you. I love you. I love you. I love you. And I must go on, somehow learning and growing from any sadness, anger, and hurt."

3. The participant would then turn the three pieces of paper over and cut the paper so as to form a flower. The yellow piece of paper would be cut in the shape of a circle for the center of a flower. The red piece of paper would be cut in the shape of flower petals. A stem and leaves would be made from the green piece of paper.

4. The participant would then paste the pieces of paper on a large sheet of white paper, pasting the written sides down.

5. Finally, the flower is mounted on a refrigerator door or other prominent place as a reminder to the participant of his/her forgiveness of the person who has died: the flower of forgiveness can cover what has been done and said.

GRAHAM'S STEPFATHER

Graham felt very hurt and angry after his parents divorced. When his mother remarried, Graham did not hide his hate for his stepfather. Often Graham even prayed that his stepfather would die. When his stepfather did die, Graham was plagued with guilt, even imagining that he had actually caused his stepfather's death.

RITUAL OF SELF-FORGIVENESS

1. Get three pieces of colored paper: a yellow one, a red one, and a green one. On one side of the yellow one, write all the things that you did or said that might have made the departed person sad. On one side of the red one, write all the things you did or said that might have made the loved one angry. On one side of the green one, write all the other things that you did or said that might have hurt the loved one.

2. Placing your hands on the three pieces of paper, read the following: "I am just human and I have made mistakes. We all do. Yet, I have tried hard to do my best. And I must try to remember the good things that I did and not be overly troubled by my mistakes. I forgive myself for my mistakes. I forgive myself. I forgive myself. I forgive myself. I have intended good. And I have done much good. And I am good."

3. You would then turn the three pieces of paper over and cut the paper so as to form a flower, the flower's center made of yellow, petals of red, stem and leaves of green.

4. You would then paste the pieces of paper on a large sheet of white paper, pasting the written side down.

5. Finally, the flower is mounted on a refrigerator door or other prominent place as a reminder of the forgiveness: the flower of forgiveness can cover what has been done and said.

"Learn to forgive yourself again and again and again." - Sheldon Kopp.

RESOLVING GUILT

Every grief has within it some guilt. This exercise helps the griever explore that guilt.

1. Reflect upon your feelings of guilt.

    A. What do you wish you had done but didn't do?
    B. What do you wish you had said but didn't say?
    C. What do you wish you could do over?
    D. What do you regret that feels like it can never be undone?

2. Meditate upon your penance for your behavior.

    A. What can you now do for yourself or someone else?
    B. What can you now say loud and clear?
    C. What can you now do over for someone else?
    D. What can you do now to make up for your deepest regret?

3. Commit yourself to some specific action(s).

4. As you commence the action(s), meditate upon the fulfillment of your penance.

5. Thank the deceased person for the opportunity to learn from the guilt you felt with him or her.

A CONSIDERATION: Sometimes forgiveness cannot be given, and we, as caregivers, might just need to accept that fact – not forcing our clients/patients to go where they don't want to go. Once again, the caregiver's duty might just involve being present with clients/patients, accepting *who* they are and *where* they are.

DARCEY

Darcey: "I had to be his caregiver as he was dying; there was no one else. . . . Four years earlier he had even held a gun to my head. . . . I don't know how many times he had left me with bruises, cuts, black eyes. . . . And the names he had called me, the things he had said to me. . . . And then when he was dying. That one evening he crawled up to me, begging me to forgive him, asking me to hold him in my bed. Hold him in my bed! I couldn't. How could I? . . . It was painful enough having to care for him, fix his meals, change his bandages, wash him. . . . How could I have done more? I hated myself for even what I was doing. And my children hated me for it too."

TREENA

Treena's alcoholic stepfather had died five months earlier. He had been physically and sexually abusive towards her from age eight to age seventeen. She always felt that she would be greatly relieved and happy when he finally did die. However, since his death, her anger, her rage, had *increased* towards him. That anger, that rage, had been complicated by the fact (and in many ways generated by the fact) that the object of her anger was no longer present to receive it; he had somehow escaped receiving all the retribution she felt he should have received.

A CONSIDERATION: Sometimes we need to just step back and realize that there are some situations where we can give little, if any, help.

A CONSIDERATION: The initial holidays after a death can be quite difficult – especially those spiritual holidays. The holidays can sometimes feel as though they have lost some of their meaning. A caregiver might need to help the care recipient add some meaning back into those holidays.

ALTERNATIVE HOLIDAY RITUALS

On holidays or special anniversaries, instead of trying to duplicate the traditional routines (which carry with them memories that might only produce sadness), a person could start a new ritual. Here are some possibilities:

> A. Take a day to watch videos, watching 2-4 movies staring a favorite actress or actor.
> B. Go on a day trip with a friend. The friend could have also recently lost someone.
> C. Serve a holiday meal in a soup kitchen.
> D. Start a redecorating project in the home.
> E. Plant a tree, some flowers, or some vegetables.
> F. A favorite book could be reread each year, beginning on the day of this holiday.

THE FIRST CHRISTMAS AFTER A DEATH

1. Each surviving family member would think of one of the favorite gifts he/she has received from the departed person. The gift could be tangible or intangible.

2. Each family member would then write the name of that gift on a piece of paper, putting it in a box, and then wrapping the box.

3. These special gifts would be either the first or last gifts opened on Christmas morning.

4. Upon opening the gift, each family member would read aloud what they had written, elaborating upon the reasons that gift means so much to him or her.

THE HOLIDAY TABLECLOTH

Every holiday meal, all the members of a family would sign their names on a special tablecloth if they have not done so previously. (The names could later be embroidered on the tablecloth.) So, every time the tablecloth is brought out, it has the signatures not only of those present at the table, but also all those who have previously sat there. Each meal would then begin with a silent meditation to remember those not currently at the table.

GUIDED IMAGERY: RELEASING YOUR LOVED ONE

The following guided imagery could be read to the care recipient or recorded for the care recipient's use.

    Close your eyes and feel the coolness of each breath that you inhale. . . . Feel the coolness in your lungs. . . . Notice the freshness of the air. . . . Feel the freshness as you inhale. . . . Notice how the cool freshness soon turns to warm heaviness. . . . Feel the warmth of the air in your lungs. . . . Feel the heaviness as you exhale. . . . Feel the warmth and heaviness of the air as you exhale. . . . Feel the cool freshness coming in and the warm heaviness going out. . . .
    Picture in your mind the most loving person that you can possibly imagine. Picture this most loving person standing in front of you. . . . Imagine this person's arms stretched out toward you. . . .
    Imagine that there are hundreds of people standing in a line behind this loving person. The line of people extends very far into the distance, and disappears into the glow of a warm and peaceful light. You see this long line of hundreds of people disappear into that warm and peaceful light. . . .
    In your arms, you are carrying someone who has died, someone with whom you have felt great love. The body hardly has any weight at all. . . . You're looking at this person in your arms, this person who has died, this person you have loved. . . . You are reminded of some special moments you had with this person. Picture in your mind a few of those special moments. . . . Look once again at this person in your arms. . . . Remember and say goodbye. . . .
    Now you carry the body you are holding over to the loving person with outstretched arms. Then gently place the dead body into the outstretched arms. . . . Notice how the loving person turns and places the body in the arms of the next person in the line and you watch the body being passed along the line of people from one to another toward the glowing, warm and peaceful light. The body is gently and carefully

passed from one person to another to another to another. . . . The body is finally passed into that glowing light. You see the light become brighter and warmer and more peaceful as the body enters the light. . . . You know that the body is now safe, very safe, very very safe. . . .

You look once again at the loving person across from you. That person shares a warm and accepting smile and says, "Thank you. Your friend is safe now, very safe. So, it is okay for you to go now." . . . You turn around and begin walking away from this special place. As you are leaving, you once again become aware of your breathing. . . .

Feel the coolness and freshness of each breath that you inhale. . . . Feel the warmth and heaviness of each breath that you exhale. . . . Feel the freshness come in and the heaviness go out. . . . Your friend is safe. . . . You are experiencing great relief. . . . Your friend is safe. . . . You feel peaceful. . . . Your friend is safe. . . . You are relieved. . . .

JENNIFER

Dr. Miller was a pediatric cardiologist. She had performed two open-heart surgeries on Jennifer, one when Jennifer was five years old and one when she was eight.

Jennifer was in the hospital again with some serious complications, and a third surgery seemed necessary, even though the last surgery had occurred just ten months earlier. This third surgery would surely be life threatening. Jennifer was only nine years old.

Dr. Miller was very emotionally attached to Jennifer. Jennifer could tell.

Dr. Miller had just finished meeting with Jennifer's father and mother, and the three of them entered Jennifer's room to talk to her about what was going to happen. Jennifer decided to speak first. She said, "Mom, dad, Dr. Miller, I know you've been talking. Can I say something first?"

Jennifer's mother and father looked at Dr. Miller. Dr. Miller was puzzled, but said, "Sure, Jennifer. What is it you want to say?"

"I know what you've been talking about. . . . I want you to know that I'm ready to die. Really. . . . But I don't feel the three of you are ready to let me go. . . . It's okay, mom and dad. It's okay, Dr. Miller. Everything will be okay. Really. I'm going to be alright. . . . Maybe the three of you can help each other after I'm gone."

DONALD

I met Donald when he was thirty-eight years old, immediately after he had been diagnosed as having a brain tumor. His doctor said he had 2-4 months to live. Except for occasional periods of confusion and mild pain, Donald's mind functioned fairly well. He lived with Liz, his thirty-two year old wife, and their two children, ages two and four. A third child was due in a couple months.

Donald's doctor introduced me to Donald as someone who was familiar with brain tumors and had a strong religious background, something that was very important to Donald. We became friends quickly over the next two months.

Donald and Liz believed that his brain tumor would go away because they had faith in God's healing powers, they lived a moral life, and they were praying that the tumor would disappear. As Donald's pain increased, he and Liz felt that was a sure sign that God was in fact healing the tumor; they felt the pain was coming from the tumor being broken up and destroyed.

I fully accepted Donald and Liz's choice of faith that he would get better. I never talked about his illness unless he raised the subject. I never once implied that anything would happen to him other than what he expected. When he and Liz talked about Donald's saving money for their children's college education, I even joined in the conversation with no hint that the planning might be useless.

I was with Donald when he received the news of the birth of his third child. I had never seen a man more happy.

Donald died three days later.

Some people might label Donald, Liz, and I "irresponsible" because we did not explore the implications of a man's dying and leaving a wife and three young children. Some people might label us "irrational" because we did not acknowledge that no faith or positive thinking was going to postpone or stop Donald's brain tumor. Some people might label us "impractical" because we did not try to squeeze out every possible benefit that can come from anticipatory grief and preparing for the inevitable.

Yet, I saw a man die happy, and I do not believe that Liz and the children were any more grieved because of our supposed "irresponsible," "irrational," and "impractical" behavior. Also, who knows whether or not Donald actually got exactly what he was praying for, some "healing," perhaps even more healing than what any of us can even imagine? Who knows?

PRAYERS

The following are some prayers that can be used by grieving care recipients. The prayers can be used as they are written, or the care recipient can place an invocation before the prayer and a concluding statement after the prayer that are congruent with his/her belief system.

PRAYER OF MOURNING

I pray for all of us who mourn.
May we face each day with courage, strength, and hope.
May nothing destroy what we have been given.
May nothing erase our memories of joy.
May all the good of the past overpower the fear of the future.
May our current laments of grief eventually change into prayers of thanksgiving.
I pray for all of us who mourn.

PRAYER OF LAMENT

A hand I used to hold, I hold no more.
A voice I used to hear, I hear no more.
A fragrance I used to smell, I smell no more.
A smile I used to see, I see no more.

The love I used to know, I know no more.
My senses are deprived.
I am empty.
May my emptiness somehow be filled.

May my emptiness somehow be filled.
Please fill my emptiness.

I WILL ALWAYS REMEMBER
THE BEAUTY OF OUR LOVE

Just as all seasons have beauty,
So it has been in the seasons of our love.

I will always remember the beauty in the spring of our love.
I will always remember the beauty in the summer of our love.
I will always remember the beauty in the fall of our love.
I will always remember the beauty in the winter of our love.

We have been together in love.
We are together in love.
We will always be together in love.

I give thanks for your love.
I give thanks for God's love.

I give thanks for love.
I will always remember the beauty of our love.

"They shall grow not old, as we that are left grow old:
Age shall not weary them, nor the years condemn.
At the going down of the sun and in the morning
We will remember them." - Laurence Binyon.

Chapter Eight

Spiritual/Religious Tools For Use With Either The Terminally Ill Or Grieving

"Physical things depend on spiritual things and not the opposite." - The Cloud of Unknowing.

"The spirit is the true self, not that physical figure which can be pointed out by your finger." - Cicero.

"It is good if man can bring about that God sings within him. - Rabbi Elimelekh of Lizhensk.

A CONSIDERATION: As caregivers we might want to discover someone's spiritual vocabulary. We might want to assess a care recipient's spiritually in our quest to uncover and feed his/her strengths.

A CONSIDERATION: The typical spiritual assessment in a health care institution goes something like this: "Tell me the name of your faith community. What's their address? Telephone number? Name of your minister?" End of assessment. – What has that told me? Nothing. The labels we often use to describe people's belief and values (and the labels they use) are not very descriptive. (Both Jesse Helms and Bill Clinton have claimed to be faithful Southern Baptists. What does that tell me? Nothing.)

A SPIRITUAL ASSESSMENT: WORD ASSOCIATION

All of the previously mentioned assessments could elicit someone's spiritual strengths as well as their non-spiritual strengths. This assessment focuses more specifically on that area of spirituality. Here the person could be asked to write down or verbalize the first word that comes to mind after hearing each of the following words:

    A. God
    B. Clergy
    C. Evil
    D. Scripture
    E. Prayer
    F. Death
    G. Nature
    H. Worship
    I. Afterlife
    J. Love

After completing the above, a discussion between the person assessing and the person being assessed would follow. The person assessing would not interpret responses; only the person being assessed.

A SPIRITUAL ASSESSMENT: EXPLORATORY QUESTIONS

In this spiritual assessment the person would be asked to write down or verbalize his or her answers to some or all of the following questions:

    A. How would you describe your basic philosophy or belief system? In other words, what is the "glue" that holds your world together?
    B. How would you describe your purpose in living? In other words, what do you believe is the best thing that you can do with your life?
    C. Do you believe that there is a force or a being responsible for the creating and sustaining of our existence? If so, why? If not, why not?
    D. What is responsible for the pain and suffering that exists in this world?
    E. How would you describe who or what you were before you were born?
    F. How would you describe who or what you will be after you die?

A SPIRITUAL ASSESSMENT: PRESIDENT OF THE BOARD

Sometimes we might want to make a subtle assessment of someone's spirituality. (It is so easy to offend people on the subject of spirituality/religion.) In this subtle assessment the care recipient would be given the following scenario: Imagine that you are the president of the board of directors of the largest religious building in your community. You can direct how that building is used and what the staff do.

    A. How would that building be used if it were promoting your values/theology? What activities would occur there on a regular basis?
    B. How would that staff be best employed? What would that staff be doing on a regular basis?

The answers to these questions tell us more about the person being assessed than they tell us about buildings.

A SPIRITUAL ASSESSMENT: DEAN OF THE SEMINARY

Here is another subtle spiritual assessment. The person could be given the following scenario: Imagine that you are the dean of a seminary. You get to determine four required courses for every seminarian. What would those four required courses be?

A CONSIDERATION: In assessing a care recipient's spirituality, we need to be quite open-minded. The spiritual language/vocabulary can sometimes be quite unique. We need to be receptive and respectful of that uniqueness.

"Do we not all have a right, not only to have our bodies treated with respect, but also, and perhaps even more important, our spirits? Spiritual care is not a luxury for a few; it is <u>the</u> essential right of every human being, as essential as political liberty, medical assistance, and equality of opportunity." - Sogyal Rinpoche.

JIM

I was making an initial visit at Jim's home. I knocked on the front door. Jim's wife Barbara greeted me at the door. Before I had even walked into the house, she requested that I make my visit brief because Jim had had a rough night.

She then escorted me into the kitchen, where seated at the kitchen table was Jim. His physical presence communicated to me the exact opposite of what Barbara had told me at the front door. Jim was wearing a three-piece suit. That three-piece suit said to me: "Look, Doug, I went through a lot of effort to get ready for your visit here. I'm not treating this lightly. So I don't want you to treat it lightly either."

There appeared to be two different agendas: Barbara's and Jim's. I decided to compromise somewhere in between the two. So, what would have normally been about a forty minute visit, I decided to make about twenty minutes. Normally on an initial visit, I would like to assess people in physical, psychological, and spiritual terms. In the twenty minutes I only covered physical and psychological stuff; I didn't get into anything spiritual. In my haste to leave (I think it was accidental), I left my overcoat in Jim's home.

When I got back to the office I received a telephone call from Jim reminding me that my overcoat was in his home. I asked when would be a good time for me to come by and get that overcoat. Jim said, "Five o'clock." I said, "I'd like to end my day around five. Is there any possibility of me coming a little bit earlier?" "No!" said Jim. "Okay, I'll come at five." (There appeared to be some mysterious things happening in that household. But I knew I better show up exactly at five.)

I showed up at five and knocked on the door. This time Jim came to the door. Now he was wearing blue jeans. Also, apparently he had had a wig on in the morning which he did not have on in the afternoon. Before I was even completely in the home, Jim said, "It's okay, Doug. Barbara's in the basement under a hair dryer. She'll be there for at least another twenty minutes, and we can talk. Come on in."

As I entered the home he asked, "Would you like to have a beer?" "No thanks." "Would you mind if I had one?" "No. Go ahead." He got a beer. As he was sitting down, he said, "You know what I miss the most?" "No, Jim. What do you miss?" "I miss Stormy's Bar." "Why do you miss Stormy's Bar?" "That bar was run just the way a church ought to be run."

I don't know how we got there, but we were there: about to explore the spiritual. "What do you mean, Jim?"

"There's several things my church could learn from Stormy's. Several.

"First of all, I can go to Stormy's with these blue jeans on, or I could go to Stormy's in that three-piece suit that I had on this morning, and I know that no matter what I'm wearing, people aren't going to look at me funny because of what I might happen to have on. But if I went to my church in these blue jeans, people would look at me kind of funny. To tell you the truth: sometimes I just feel like wearing blue jeans, and that doesn't mean I don't feel like church. I'd like to go to my church dressed however I feel and know I can be comfortable there and not be judged, no matter what I'm wearing.

"Second, I go to Stormy's and I sit down next to someone or someone sits down next to me, and we get in a conversation. Sometimes that conversation might even end up being an argument. At the end of that interaction I would have learned something about who that other person is, and that other person would have learned something about me. I go to my church and I sit down next to someone or someone sits down next to me: I not only have to say the same thing as that other person, I have to say it in unison. How am I ever going to learn anything about that other person, or that other person learn anything about me?

"And another thing: I go to Stormy's and they have a few rules – not a lot, just a few. But if you break one of those rules, you get kicked out of the bar. I go to my church, and you wouldn't believe how many rules they have there. I know nobody ever follows all those rules. Everyone pretends as though they do. But nobody gets kicked out. What kind of rules are those? How can you call those rules?"

Jim had just given me his spiritual assessment. He was saying, "Look, Doug. If you want to talk about religion, you need to know that I'm a down-to-earth kind of guy. I'll be shooting from the hip. I expect you to do the same. It's alright if we argue. But let's go to it. Let's quit messing around." He had just given me his spiritual language.

A CONSIDERATION: During the process of dying or grieving, a care recipient's faith can go several different directions. We need to be ready for whatever direction it might take.

A WITHERING FAITH

Bernie was angry with God. God had betrayed him. In Bernie's thinking God had given him the woman of his dreams, had allowed the two of them to marry, and then took her away before they could even celebrate their first anniversary. For Bernie, such a God was too cruel to ever pray to, too cruel to ever worship.

A GOD WHO IS IN THE PAIN

An entry from B.J.'s journal:

"I went to my first and last counseling session with Pastor Hanson today. He quoted a passage of scripture to me: 'All things work together for good for those who love God.' How dare he quote that to me! How dare he belittle my pain! How dare he belittle my faith!

"I need someone to acknowledge my pain, to legitimize my suffering. Things do not always work together for good; there are some pains that never go away. The God I believe in is not just a God of peace and happiness. My God has to also be with me when I'm angry, when I'm scared, when I'm depressed, when I just don't give a damn.

"I do not live in a fairy tale world! And God doesn't either!"

"When sufferings come, utter thanks to God, for suffering draws you near the Holy One." - The Talmud.

A BLOSSOMING FAITH

For Ginny, her faith blossomed after the death of her husband; her faith took on a maturity it had never before had. She told me, "Before I would only mouth the words. I participated in the worship service simply because everyone else was doing it – no other reason. But now I know what the words mean. Now I know that God is truly with us wherever we are, wherever we go: the heights and the depths."

"Life offers us innumerable opportunities. . . . The lesson we have to learn is not how we can get better opportunities, but how we may make the best use of those we have." - Swami Paramananda.

"Our life's work is to use what we have been given to wake up. . . . It doesn't matter what you're given, whether it's physical deformity or enormous wealth or poverty, beauty or ugliness, mental stability or mental instability, life in the middle of a madhouse or life in the middle of a peaceful, silent desert." - Pema Chodron.

"When we become aware that we do not have to escape our pains, but that we can mobilize them into a common search for life, those very pains are transformed from expressions of despair into signs of hope." - Henri Nouwen.

HOW CAN I USE THIS

1. What is now causing you the most amount of sadness?

    A. How can you use this to become a better person?
    B. How can you use this to help others improve their well-being?

2. What is now causing you the most amount of pain?

    A. How can you use this to become a better person?
    B. How can you use this to help others improve their well-being?

3. What is now causing you the most amount of anger?

    A. How can you use this to become a better person?
    B. How can you use this to help others improve their well-being?

4. What is now causing you the most amount of depression?

    A. How can you use this to become a better person?
    B. How can you use this to help others improve their well-being?

"During the times that we feel most vulnerable, that which is invulnerable within us becomes uncovered, becomes more apparent." - Dean Ornish.

"When the soul is making most progress, it is traveling in darkness and unknowing." - St. John of the Cross.

"The greatest treasure comes out of the most despised and secret places. . . . This place of greatest vulnerability is also a holy place, a place of healing." - Albert Kreinheder.

THE WOUNDED HEALER RESUME

The following activity involves constructing a resume based upon your past and present wounds: problems, pain and suffering, disabilities, imperfections, shortcomings. Our wounds can often make us better persons. This activity helps to show how those wounds do make us better.

1. First list your major past and present wounds: problems, pain and suffering, disabilities, imperfections, shortcomings.

2. Then, after each of the above items, write how that item makes you a better person. Questions that could help:

> A. How does that item equip you to better handle your future wounds?
> B. How does that item help you to better understand, and address, the wounds of others?
> C. How does that item improve you in qualities like strength, courage, endurance, faithfulness, and hope?
> D. How has that item brought forth qualities you did not know you had?

3. Finally, organizing all of the above material, write the resume in a formal form, just like a regular resume.

"In our attempt to banish illnesses from the world, we banish the knowledge that can save us. . . . We have to learn from our illnesses and the sacred spaces we inhabit in pain." - Kat Duff.

"All the juicy, smelly, negative thoughts and feelings we have are the rich compost that lets our hearts mature." - Karen Kissel Wegela.

"Our brilliance, our juiciness, our spiciness, is all mixed up with our craziness and our confusion, and therefore it doesn't do any good to try to get rid of our so-called negative aspects, because in that process we also get rid of our basic wonderfulness." - Pema Chodron.

JOYS AND CONCERNS ALTAR

"Every cloud has a silver lining." "Every coin has two sides." No matter how negative things might be, there is always something positive in the same vicinity. This activity helps people realize that truth.

1. The care recipient would designate a place in his or her home (coffee table, end table, top of a dresser) to be a "Joys And Concerns Altar." The care recipient would then place two candles on the altar: a candle for concerns and a candle for joys. At regular intervals (every evening, every Sunday evening) the two candles would be lit with a dedication and a meditation.

2. The "candle for concerns" is lit first with the care recipient dedicating it to a particular worry, pain, or trouble that he or she has had during the day or week. The care recipient then prays or meditates for 3-5 minutes on that worry, pain, or trouble.

3. The "candle for joys" is then lit with the care recipient dedicating it to a particular peace of mind, happiness, or pleasure that was had during the day or week. The care recipient then prays or meditates for 3-5 minutes on that peace of mind, happiness, or pleasure.

"Is not the cup that holds your wine the very cup that was burned in the potter's oven? And is not the lute that soothes your spirit, the very wood that was hollowed with knives?" - Kahlil Gibran.

"When the sun rises each morning, it comes out of the darkness. You can too." - Sydney Barbara Metrick.

SHOWING SOME SPIRITUAL MUSCLE

Often spiritual practice can be perceived as a way of having the invisible affect the visible. This exercise is a clear example of that truth.

1. Choose a muscle group that you would like to improve (stomach muscles, buttocks, or leg muscles).

2. As soon as some person or some thing comes into your presence with negative energy (energy that you are receiving in a negative way), internally thank that person or thing for coming into your presence. You are being given a potential positive gift.

3. While you are receiving all that negative energy, use that energy to tighten and loosen, tighten and loosen, tighten and loosen your chosen muscle group.

4. When you no longer feel any more negative energy, internally thank the person or thing for coming into your presence and hope that he/she/it might soon return to give you more gifts of energy so that you can further improve yourself.

"For truly I say to you, if you have faith as a mustard seed, you shall say to this mountain, 'Move from here to there,' and it shall move; and nothing shall be impossible to you." - Jesus.

"Faith heals, faith creates, faith works wonders, faith moves mountains." - Sivananda.

"By faith you can move mountains; but the important thing is not to move mountains, but to have faith." - Arthur Clutton-Brock.

SPIRITUAL EXPLORATIONS
BASED ON TAOIST THOUGHT

1. A person would rewrite the following quotations using his or her own words rather than the words of the text, trying to duplicate the text's meaning but in different words. This rewriting will help the participant explore and understand the meaning of the quotations.

2. Although the following quotations come from a Taoist tradition (from the book <u>The Way of Lao Tzu</u>), the person doing the rewriting does not have to be a Taoist:

> A. "Manifest plainness,
>   Embrace simplicity,
>   Reduce selfishness,
>   Have few desires."
> B. "The softest things in the world overcome the hardest things in the world."
> C. "I treat those who are good with goodness,
>   And I also treat those who are not good with goodness.
>   Thus goodness is attained."
> D. "He who knows the eternal is all-embracing."

3. The rewritten statements could then be discussed with a friend, family member, counselor, or caregiver, having some of the conversation center around how these rewritten statements might relate to the person's current circumstances.

SPIRITUAL EXPLORATIONS
BASED ON CHRISTIAN THOUGHT

1. A person would rewrite the following quotations, using his or her own words rather than the words of the text, trying to duplicate the text's meaning but in different words. This rewriting will help the participant explore and understand the meaning of the quotations.

2. Although the following quotations come from a Christian tradition (from the New American Standard Bible), the person doing the rewriting does not have to be a Christian:

> A. "Whoever exalts himself shall be humbled; and whoever humbles himself shall be exalted."
> B. "Draw near to God and He will draw near to you."
> C. "Whether we are awake or asleep, we may live together with Him."
> D. "Rejoice always."

3. The rewritten statements could then be discussed with a friend, family member, counselor, or caregiver, having some of the conversation center around how these rewritten statements might relate to the person's current circumstances.

SPIRITUAL EXPLORATIONS
BASED ON HINDU THOUGHT

1. A person would rewrite the following quotations using his or her own words rather than the words of the text, trying to duplicate the text's meaning but in different words. This rewriting will help the participant explore and understand the meaning of the quotations.

2. Although the following quotations come from a Hindu tradition (from the book <u>The Ten Principal Upanishads</u>), the person doing the rewriting does not have to be Hindu:

> A. "He who gives with purity, gets purity in return; he who gives with passion, gets passion in return; he who gives with ignorance, gets ignorance in return."
> B. "The man who can see all creatures in himself, himself in all creatures, knows no sorrow."
> C. "Spirit is everywhere, upon the right, upon the left, above, below, behind, in front. What is the world but Spirit?"
> D. "From joy all things are born, by joy they live, toward joy they move, into joy they return."

3. The rewritten statements could then be discussed with a friend, family member, counselor, or caregiver, having some of the conversation center around how these rewritten statements might relate to the person's current circumstances.

SPIRITUAL EXPLORATIONS
BASED ON BUDDHIST THOUGHT

1. A person would rewrite the following quotations using his or her own words rather than the words of the text, trying to duplicate the text's meaning but in different words.

2. Although the following quotations come from a Buddhist tradition (from the book The Teaching Of Buddha), the person doing the rewriting does not have to be a Buddhist.

>   A. "Human beings tend to move in the direction of their thoughts. If they harbor greedy thoughts, they become more greedy; if they think angry thoughts, they become more angry; if they hold foolish thoughts, their feet move in that direction."
>   B. "Each man has a different view of things according to the state of his mind. Some people see the city where they live as fine and beautiful, others see it as dirty and dilapidated. It all depends on the state of their minds."
>   C. "Buddha does not always appear as a Buddha. Sometimes He appears as an incarnation of evil, sometimes as a woman, a god, a king, or a statesman; sometimes He appears in a brothel or in a gambling house."
>   D. "Buddhahood fills everything."

3. The rewritten statements could then be discussed with a friend, family member, counselor, or caregiver, having some of the conversation center around how these rewritten statements might relate to the person's current circumstances.

SPIRITUAL EXPLORATIONS BASED ON JEWISH THOUGHT

1. A person would rewrite the following quotations using his or her own words rather than the words of the text, trying to duplicate the text's meaning but in different words.

2. Although the following quotations come from a Jewish tradition (from the <u>Tanakh</u>), the person doing the rewriting does not have to be Jewish:

> A. "When you call Me, and come and pray to Me, I will give heed to you. You will search for Me and find Me, if only you seek Me wholeheartedly."
> B. "Cast your burden on the Lord and He will sustain you."
> C. "The Lord is my light and my help; whom should I fear?
>   The Lord is the stronghold of my life, whom should I dread?"
> D. "Though I walk through a valley of deepest darkness,
>   I fear no harm, for You are with me;
>   Your rod and Your staff – they comfort me."

3. The rewritten statements could then be discussed with a friend, family member, counselor, or caregiver, having some of the conversation center around how these rewritten statements might relate to the person's current circumstances.

"The path is always right beneath your feet." - Issan Dorsey.

CELEBRATING LIFE

The existence of beauty and miracles can often be perceived all around us. We merely need to open up our senses.

1. The person spends 5 minutes just being mindful of his/her breathing.

2. Then 5 minutes are spent viewing, feeling, and smelling a flower.

3. Then 5 minutes are spent viewing, feeling, smelling, and slowly chewing a piece of bread.

4. Then 20 minutes are spent slowly making a cup of coffee or tea, smelling it, sipping it, and feeling it flow throughout the body.

5. Then 10 minutes are spent doing a creative dance that expresses the feelings felt after doing all the above activities

6. Finally, 5 minutes are spent looking in a mirror. The next to last minute is spent frowning and the last minute smiling.

"If the only prayer you say in your whole life is 'Thank you,' that would suffice." - *Meister Eckhart.*

GIVING THANKS

1. Find a quiet place where you have never been, a place away from potential interruptions. Sitting comfortably in this space, focus for a couple minutes on your breathing.

2. Silently give thanks for your lungs, for all the work they have done for you with little, if any, effort from you. Give thanks that they have kept you alive since the day you were born. Pause in thanksgiving for your lungs.

3. Silently give thanks for your heart, for all the work it has done for you with little, if any, effort from you. Give thanks that it has kept you alive since the day you were born. Pause in thanksgiving for your heart.

4. Silently give thanks for your ability to see, hear, taste, touch, feel, and think. Give thanks for all the wondrous experiences you have had through your senses. Pause in thanksgiving for your ability to see, hear, taste, touch, feel, and think.

5. Silently give thanks for all the people who have supported you throughout your life. Give thanks for your family. Give thanks for all those who supported you without even knowing you, growing your food, making your clothes, building your house, providing you with everything you have needed. Pause in thanksgiving for all those who have supported you throughout your life, those you know and those you do not know.

6. Silently give thanks for this universe and all that it contains. Give thanks for the earth beneath your feet. Give thanks to the animals and plants that have given you sustenance. Give thanks for the water and the sunshine. Give thanks for the day and the night. Pause in thanksgiving for this universe and all that it contains.

7. Slowly stand. Smile and bow to that which is in front of you. Smile and bow to that which is behind you. Look up and smile. Look down and smile. Look within and smile. Pause as you just close your eyes and smile.

8. Return back to where you came from before you began this exercise and continue your day, giving thanks for all that you have been given.

"The world is as you are." - Maharishi Mahesh Yogi.

DEDICATING ONESELF TO LIVING A SACRED LIFE

1. The person would take a candle, a bowl of water, and some incense to a quiet, isolated place.

2. After lighting the candle and the incense, the participant would take 10 minutes to fully examine his or her surroundings: being conscious of breathing in the quietness of the place, breathing in the light of the candle, and breathing in the fragrance of the incense.

3. The participant would then dip some fingers in the bowl of water and touch the wetness to his or her forehead, saying, "I bless my mind and my understanding. May my thoughts be focused on all that is good and pure in this life."

4. The participant would then dip some fingers in the bowl of water and touch the wetness to his or her ears, saying, "I bless my ears and my hearing. May I strive to hear all that is good and pure in this life."

5. The participant would then dip some fingers in the bowl of water and touch the wetness to his or her eye lids, saying, "I bless my eyes and my seeing. May I strive to see all that is good and pure in this life."

6. The participant would then dip some fingers in the bowl of water and touch the wetness to his or her lips, saying, "I bless my lips and my speaking. May I strive to say only what is good and pure, only that which can be for the benefit of others."

7. The participant would then wash his or her hands in the bowl of water, saying, "I bless my hands and my doing. May I strive to do only what is good and pure, only that which can be for the benefit of others."

8. The participant would then reflect for 10 minutes on the words that were spoken.

CHANGING PHILOSOPHY

1. With the help of family members, friends, and caregivers identify and write down a philosophical position that you have that can produce psychological disturbances for you or others. Distress-producing philosophical positions that are sometimes found among people in their final years are: a) "I am old and therefore I am useless." b) "All the personnel in the nursing home do not care about me." c) "God must not love me if I'm allowed to become old and infirm."

2. The caregiver and the care recipient then discuss ways in which the care recipient, consciously and subconsciously, expresses this philosophy in words and actions.

3. The caregiver would then help the care recipient to formulate, with paper and pencil, an alternative philosophical position that does not produce as many disturbances. Whatever the new philosophy might be, it will likely produce little disturbances if it makes logical sense, is practical, and allows for flexibility. [Example: The old philosophy: "I am old and therefore I am useless." The new philosophy: "I am old, but that oldness does not have to have bearing on whether I am useful or useless. There have been many older people who have been quite useful to society and there have been others who have not been so useful. I have a choice."]

4. The caregiver then assists the care recipient in looking at ways of manifesting this new philosophical position. A written report might be made showing how the new philosophical position would improve the person's environment. Each of the following areas could be examined:
    A. relations with spouse or partner,
    B. relations with children,
    C. relations with friends,
    D. a person's physical health,
    E. attitudes toward change,
    F. attitudes toward religious/spiritual issues,
    G. responses to criticisms and rejection from others,
    H. responses to progressive physical dissolution,
    I. responses to the imminence of death.

5. The caregiver needs to tell the care recipient, and reinforce the fact, that simply examining a new philosophy is not as beneficial as believing in a new philosophy, which is not as beneficial as manifesting a new philosophy. A step-by-step plan of manifesting the new philosophy would then be spelled out through the cooperative efforts of the caregiver and the care recipient.

GUIDED IMAGERY: MY LOVING COMPANION

The following guided imagery could be read to the participant or recorded for the participant's use.

Close your eyes and concentrate on your breathing. . . . Breathe in and breathe out. . . . Breathe in and breathe out. . . . Imagine yourself standing in an open field, standing there in all of your vulnerability. You are standing as a wounded person, a person without any armor, standing there with all of your hurt, with all of your pain, with all of your disappointment, with all of your sadness. Imagine yourself standing in such a state, standing in the middle of an open field. . . .

As you are standing there, you see in the distance a person coming towards you. This is the most loving person that you can imagine, walking towards you. Imagine the most loving person imaginable walking towards you. . . . You see love pouring out from this person, pouring out towards you. . . . As the person comes up to you and stands before you, you hear these words come from the person's mouth: "I accept you with all of your wounds. . . . I accept you with all of your pain. . . . I accept you with all of your anger. . . . I accept you with all of your sadness. . . . I accept you for everything that you are." . . .

Now picture this loving person say to you: "I too am wounded. . . . I too am in pain. . . . Let us hold one another so that we are one." . . .

The two of you come together with arms wrapped around one another. Your arms are softly, very softly, wrapped around one another. . . . Relax in those arms. . . . Your woundedness is accepted. . . . You are loved, . . . even with all of your pain, . . . even with all your anger, . . . even with all of your sadness. . . . You are loved. . . .

Slowly unwrap your arms from one another, and, holding each other's hands, begin slowly walking out of that field. . . . I want you to imagine that you are now walking together into this very room where you find yourself right now, walking over to two chairs that are placed side by side. . . . The two of you sit down, next to one another. . . . This person is seated next to you right now. . . . Imagine this loving person sitting next to you right now, . . . this person who loves you. . . .

Slowly open your eyes. . . .

A CONSIDERATION: Your body influences your spirit; your spirit influences your body.

GUIDED IMAGERY: ON PEACE

The following guided imagery could be read or recorded.

    Get as physically comfortable as you possibly can. Concentrate on the word "relax." Relax. . . . Relax. . . . Relax. . . .
    Concentrate on the word "peace." Peace. . . . Peace. . . . Peace. . . .
    Imagine the most peaceful location that you can possibly envision. . . . Imagine a very serene place. . . . What does that place look like? . . . Look in all directions at this peaceful place. . . . Relax in this peaceful place. . . .
    Now, still keeping your eyes closed, imagine the most pleasant smell that you can possibly imagine. . . . Imagine breathing in this serene fragrance. . . . Relax as you breathe in this calming fragrance. . . .
    Now, imagine the most soothing taste that you can possibly imagine. . . . Imagine savoring this pleasant taste. . . . Relax as you experience this peaceful taste. . .
    Now, imagine the most relaxing touch that you can possibly imagine. . . . Imagine being caressed and held with this comforting touch, being peacefully caressed and held by someone you love very dearly. . . . Relax as you are gently touched by this person whom you love. . . .
    Relax as you see your peaceful scene. . . . Relax as you smell that soothing fragrance. . . . Relax as you taste that pleasing taste. . . . Relax as you are caressed and held with peaceful touch. . . . Relax. . . . You are at peace. . . . You can relax. . . . Peace. . . . Peace. . . . Peace. . . .

GUIDED IMAGERY: THE HOLY WOMAN

The following guided imagery could be read to the participant or recorded for the participant's use.

Close your eyes. . . . Relax. . . . Relax. . . . Relax. . . .

You have just been granted a special audience with a holy woman named "Rose Of Sharon." Rose Of Sharon is a very famous holy woman, known throughout her homeland of Southern Africa. She is a very knowledgeable woman, said to know things that no other person knows; what others do not know, Rose Of Sharon knows, and she has had this knowledge for a long, long time. . . .

Rose Of Sharon is a very large woman. Her skin is as black and as beautiful as the most precious ebony. Her hair is so thick and full that it is said that there is as many hairs on her head as there are animals on the continent of Africa. Her clothes are said to contain all the colors of the rainbow: every single color of the rainbow. . . . Picture Rose Of Sharon. . . . See how large she is. See her black and beautiful skin. . . . See her great head of hair: more hair than animals in Africa. . . . See her robes with all the colors of the rainbow. . . . Look into her eyes and see all her knowledge, great knowledge, very special knowledge, knowledge which nobody else has. . . . This is a holy woman. This is a special woman. This is a great woman. This is a knowledgeable woman. . . . Holy, special, great, and ever-so knowledgeable is Rose Of Sharon. . . .

Try in your mind to hear the sounds of the African home of Rose Of Sharon. Try to imagine the sounds of Africa. . . . These are sounds that reach back to the beginning of time. You feel like you are back in some very, very distant time. . . . Hear the sounds of the bird. . . . Hear the sounds of the elephant. . . . Hear the sounds of the lion. . . . Hear the sounds of the water. . . . Hear the sounds of the wind. . . . These are sounds that go back to the beginning of time. These are the sounds that surround this holy woman named Rose Of Sharon. . . .

Try to imagine the smells of the African home of Rose Of Sharon. Try to breathe in the smells of Africa. . . . These smells, like the sounds, take you back to the beginning of time. You feel like you are back in some very, very distant time. . . . Breathe in the musky scent of Africa. . . . Breathe in the animals. . . . Breathe in the plants and the trees. . . . Breathe in the earth and the people. . . . Breathe in the forests and the deserts. . . . Breathe in all the ancient history of this place. This is a very, very old place. . . .

Now, in your imagination, visualize Rose Of Sharon sitting across a fire from you. . . . The flames of the fire penetrate the evening sky. Sparks are flying. Flames are dancing. . . . Look across the fire into the eyes of Rose Of Sharon. Look into her all-knowing eyes. . . . As she looks across at you she tells you that you have three questions that you may ask her, three questions that she will answer from the knowledge that she has that no one else has. . . . She will answer three of your questions. . . . She is here just for you: to answer your questions. . . .

Think. What one question do you want answered more than any other question. . . . What is the very first question you want to ask Rose Of Sharon. . . . What one thing do you most want to know right now? . . . In your imagination, ask this one question to Rose Of Sharon as she sits across from you. Ask this holy woman that question. . . .

Imagine the all-knowing Rose Of Sharon pondering your question. . . . Imagine Rose Of Sharon now answering your question with all of her knowledge. . . . Listen to her response. Feel her message. . . .

You now have another question. What is your second, and next to last, question that you wish to ask the all-knowing Rose Of Sharon? In your imagination, ask her that question. . . .

Imagine the all-knowing Rose Of Sharon pondering this question. . . . What answer does Rose Of Sharon give to your second question? . . . Listen to her response. Feel her message. . . .

Now for your last question. This question needs to be special because it is the last question that you will be able to ask the all-knowing Rose Of Sharon. Ask Rose Of Sharon your last question. . . .

Imagine the all-knowing Rose Of Sharon pondering this question. . . . What answer does Rose Of Sharon give to your last question? . . . Listen to her response. Feel her message. . .

Now thank Rose Of Sharon. . . .

Now, before leaving you feel that you want to give something to Rose Of Sharon, something that shows your appreciation for her answering all of your questions. What do you have to offer as a gift of thanksgiving? What do you want to give Rose Of Sharon? . . . Imagine yourself giving this gift to her, . . . once again thanking her, . . . and turning to leave this place, . . . leaving with your new knowledge. . . .

You are saying goodbye. . . . You are leaving Rose Of Sharon, leaving with your new knowledge. . . .

Now picture where you are right now. Picture the room where you are right now. . . . What can you recall about the room with your eyes closed? . . . Visualize this room. . . .

Now slowly open your eyes. . . .

GUIDED IMAGERY: MY SACRED TEMPLE

The following guided imagery could be read to the participant or recorded for the participant's use.

While in a comfortable position, close your eyes and center all of your attention upon your feelings. . . . Sense the particular feelings that you have when I say the following words: "peace," . . . "contentment," . . . "freedom," . . . "safety." . . . Now, with those feelings in your consciousness, imagine a special place of retreat made just for you. This is your private, sacred temple. Imagine this place that is characterized by peace, contentment, freedom, and safety. . . . Whatever place comes into your consciousness, stay there in your mind. . . . Do not let other places or thoughts intrude. If they do, keep returning to that place of peace, . . . contentment, . . . freedom, . . . and safety. . . .

Become completely absorbed in this place. . . . Imagine the soothing feelings that permeate your entire body. . . . Imagine the relaxing sounds that you hear in this place of peace. . . . Try to sense the soothing aromas that are present in this place. . . . Examine what is around you. . . . Examine what is below you. . . . Examine what is above you. . . . Examine what you see in the distance. . . . Examine what is close to you. . . . Examine everything that is contributing to your peace, . . . contentment, . . . freedom, . . . and safety. . . .

This is your special place. . . . This place belongs completely to you, and you may come here whenever you want to come. . . . Whenever you are anxious, you may close your eyes and go to this place of peace, . . . contentment, . . . freedom, . . . and safety. . . . This is your special place. . . . Once again, examine this place with all of your senses: the sights, . . . the sounds, . . . the aromas. . . .

You are about to leave this place. . . . But you may return whenever you wish. All you need to do is just close your eyes and travel in your imagination back to this place. . . . For now, say goodbye to the soothing aromas. . . . For now, say goodbye to all the pleasant sights. . . . For now, say goodbye to the peace, . . . contentment, . . . freedom, . . . and safety. . . . Whenever you are ready, knowing that you can always return, slowly open your eyes. . . .

GUIDED IMAGERY: THE GIFT OF HOLINESS

The following guided imagery could be read to the care recipient or recorded for the care recipient's use.

     Close your eyes and imagine that you are walking across a vast desert. . . . The desert is hot. . . . The desert is dry. . . . The desert is barren. . . The desert is lonely. . . . You are now in a hot, dry, barren, lonely place. . . .
     You are lost, without any direction, without any purpose. . . . You feel discontented. . . . You feel uncomfortable. . . . You are alone, without friend. You are alone. . . .
     You realize that there have been many times in your life when you have experienced similar feelings. You realize that there have been many moments when your life felt just like this hot, dry, lonely desert. . . . Perhaps you are now in one of those times. . . . Perhaps you are now feeling very little purpose, very little contentment, very little companionship. . . .
     Be aware of these feelings as you imagine yourself walking across this desert. . . . You feel the hot sun. . . . You trudge through the dry sand. . . . You see the empty horizon. . . . As you are looking at that lonely horizon, you see some gathering clouds way off in the distance. . . . Clouds are gathering: mighty, billowing, glorious clouds. . . . The clouds are at once gentle and powerful. You know that these clouds are being sent by a loving God. . . . As the clouds come closer, you grow more and more aware that they are God-given clouds, intended just for you. . . . These are clouds that are being sent to bring you some refreshing rain, refreshing rain that will wash away all of your troubles. . . .
     These mighty, billowing clouds are now directly over your head, blocking the hot rays of the sun. . . . From the clouds, a gentle, cleansing rain begins to fall. . . . You turn your face to the sky and feel these cleansing raindrops wash your face. . . . The rain washes away all your shortcomings. . . . Every shortcoming that you have ever had is being washed away by this gentle rain. . . . All of your mistakes are being washed away. . . . Every mistake you have ever made is being washed away by this gentle, cleansing rain. . . .
     As the rain falls, you look around and see that the desert is gradually turning into a luxuriant garden. . . . Trees are sprouting up before your eyes and are reaching for the sky. Trees are sprouting up all around you. . . . Green grass is growing out of the sand, creating a lush carpet beneath your feet. Green grass is all around you. . . . Flowers, red, yellow, pink, are blossoming around the tree trunks and blooming throughout the green grass. Flowers are blossoming all around you. . . .

As the rain gradually stops, you notice the rainwater slowly evaporate from your skin. . . . The clouds are drifting away and revealing a new sun, a pleasantly warm, a welcoming sun. A relaxing sun. A God-given sun. . . . You see a rainbow in the sky, a beautifully colored rainbow. . . . You hear birds singing. . . . You see butterflies fluttering among the flowers. . . .

As you breathe in the fresh air, the God-given air, you feel all your burdens being taken away. . . . As you breathe in the fresh, God-given air, you feel your body straightening, your chin rising. . . . You feel proud of who you are. . . . You feel loved just as you are. . . . You feel content just as you are. . . .

The pleasant warmth of the sun cradles you. . . . The fresh air permeates your body with its freshness. . . . You are surrounded with warmth. You are saturated in freshness. . . .Breathe in the pleasant warmth. . . . Breathe in the freshness. . . . You are softened with love. . . . You are saturated with love. . . . You are relaxed with contentment. . . . You are softened with contentment. . . . You are at peace. . . . God is fully with you. . . . God will never leave you. . . .

REWARD YOURSELF

Often care recipients need to reward themselves for the progress they have made. Rewards can encourage further progress.

1. Remind yourself that you could be functioning a lot worse than is currently the case.

2. Then choose a reward to acknowledge your good job at coping.

    A. A massage.
    B. A new outfit or pair of shoes.
    C. An uplifting play, musical, or concert.
    D. An out-of-town retreat.
    E. A course at a local community college, YMCA, or YWCA.
    F. A trip to visit a friend.
    G. A mindful book to read.

3. Periodically reward yourself if you continue to cope well.

PRAYERS

Sometimes caregivers can feel awkward when approached to say prayers by their care recipients. How might caregivers respectfully respond to such prayer requests?

One way not to respond is to say, "Let me go get someone who is professionally trained in that area." That is a disrespectful response. That is disrespectful because *you* were asked to pray for them. Finding someone else to do the job is avoiding their request, not respecting it.

So, how can caregivers respectfully respond to such a request? Here are six possible respectful responses. (One particular response might be most comfortable for you. Or a particular situation might make one of these responses more appropriate than another.)

1. One way of responding respectfully is very direct. First ask, "What would you like me to pray for, and how would you like me to pray?" Then adjust your prayer to what they say. That's a respectful response.

2. Another way is to first say, "I appreciate your request. However, before I begin, do you mind if I pray in the way that I'm accustomed to?" By saying that first before you begin your prayer, you are alerting this person that maybe their expectations of what you deliver might be very different from what you actually deliver. (They're Southern Baptist and you're Roman Catholic, and they think you're Southern Baptist. Or, they're Christian and you're Jewish, and they might think you're Christian.) That's a respectful response: before praying, get permission to pray in your accustomed way.

3. A third way to respond respectfully is to give a generic prayer. The only thing that divides faith communities on the issue of prayer is simply how we begin and how we end our prayers. The middle is always the same. I know what that middle is by analyzing the question: I know three things about anyone who asks the question "Will you pray for me?" even if I do not know that person's faith. (1) I know that person obviously believes that there is some kind of power in praying. That person would not be asking for something that didn't do anything. (2) That person is not asking me to give a meditation on the spring time; that person wants a prayer that directs that power specifically towards him/her. (3) That person has a particular need driving him/her to ask for that prayer. All I need to know is the need (I do not need to know the faith) in order to pray with that person. For I can internally begin and internally conclude and externally share the common center. [Example: Willard grabs my arm and says, "Will you pray for me?" I do not know Willard's faith, but I do know he's experiencing a lot of anxiety. So I internally begin (saying what I normally say). Then I verbally

share the common center: "I am asking that Willard might find comfort and peace. And as I am praying for Willard, I sense that he has available to him, both within and around him, comfort and peace. And as I am praying, I sense that Willard has that awareness as well. May that awareness grow this day and in the days ahead, so that tomorrow and the next day Willard might have more comfort and more peace. And as I am praying, I know that it will be so. And I give thanks that it is." Then internally I can conclude (whether I say "in the name of the Father, the Son, and the Holy Spirit" or "praise be to Jesus" or "praise be to Allah" or "praise be to the Goddess."). I have thus respectfully responded to Willard's request by sharing the common center to prayer that I know he shares with me.]

4. A fourth way to respond respectfully is to say, "Let's pray together. You begin and I'll follow." Then you can adjust your contribution depending upon how he/she begins.

5. A fifth way: "Let's pray together in silence. I will be praying for you. I would appreciate you praying for me." That's respectful.

6. "I have you now, and I will keep you, in my thoughts and in my prayers."

Any of these above responses are respectful, much more respectful than saying, "Let me go get someone else."

The following prayers can be used with people of various spiritual traditions. They can also be altered to fit specific traditions.

PRAYER IN THE MIDST OF DOUBT

Am I talking to myself?
Who could I be speaking to if not myself?
I think I am asking if there might be something more than what I can touch, see, or measure.
I want there to somehow be some principle or force of caring at the center of this universe.
I want there to be something more.
Something more!
Please!
Listen!
Speak!
Care!

PLEA FOR INTERVENTION

That which is Light, please shine in my darkness.
That which is Goodness, please deliver me from my evil.
That which is Wisdom, please educate me in my ignorance.
That which is Power, please lift me out of my weakness.

PRAYER FOR ONENESS WITH GOD

God's thoughts must be filtered through a human brain.
God's love must flow through a human heart.
God's will must be portrayed through a human spirit.
God's pain must be felt in a human body.

Let my brain know the thoughts of God.
Let my heart beat with the love of God.
Let my spirit be driven by the will of God.
And, even though my body might feel some of the pain of God, let me believe that
        God's thoughts are always with me, God's love is always for me, and God's will
        always seeks my greatest good.

THE PRAYER OF NO FEAR

In the beginning, there was God.
Today, there is God.
Tomorrow, there will be God.

Before today, God was with me.
During this day, God is with me.
If I am here tomorrow, God will be with me then as well.

If this is in fact so, and I do believe it, how can I have any fear?
Why would I ever be afraid of anything?
What worries could I ever have?

PRAYER FOR GUIDANCE

Creator of light, please give me guidance.
Creator of mountains, please give me strength.
Creator of lakes, please give me serenity.

Creator of me, please open me up to receive You,
With all of Your guidance,
With all of Your strength,
With all of Your serenity.

REMIND ME THAT I AM IMMERSED IN LOVE

Flowers and candy are strange expressions of love.
Love expresses itself best in the midst of pain and suffering.
Love expresses itself best in the midst of doubt, depression, and sadness.
Love expresses itself best in the midst of anger and chaos.
Love expresses itself best in the midst of open sores and human waste.
Perhaps I get no flowers or candy, but that does not mean that I am not immersed in
    love.

Remind me that I am immersed in love.
Remind me that I am immersed in love.
Remind me that I am immersed in love.

HELP ME TO LEARN THAT HOLINESS IS EVERYWHERE

Help me to learn that this is a holy moment.
Help me to learn that this is a holy place.
Help me to learn that holy people are all around me.
Help me to learn that I am also holy.

Help me to learn that holiness is everywhere.
Holiness is everywhere.
Holiness is everywhere.

LOVE IS EVERYWHERE

Love has been with me.
Love will be with me.
Love is over me.
Love is under me.
Love is to the right of me.
Love is to the left of me.
Love is within me.
Love surrounds me.

HELP ME RECEIVE HELP

Help me receive help from others.

Help me, in my sorrow, to receive the joy of others.
Help me, in my weakness, to receive the strength of others.
Help me, in my pain, to receive the comfort of others.
Help me, in my anxiety, to receive the peace of others.
Help me, in my loneliness, to receive the love of others.

Help me receive help from others.

BLESSED ARE THOSE

Blessed are those who come into my presence.
Blessed are those who listen to my truth.
Blessed are those who hear my doubts.
Blessed are those who see my anger.
Blessed are those who sense my pain.
Blessed are those who witness my tears.
Blessed are those who hold my body.
Blessed are those who will not turn away.

HELP ME CONVINCE MYSELF

Help me convince myself that I am worth loving.
Help me convince myself that these hands are worth holding.
Help me convince myself that others want to look into my eyes.
Help me convince myself that I am worth loving.

Chapter Nine

Additional Tools To Increase A Caregiver's Effectiveness

"There is no higher religion than human service. To work for the common good is the greatest creed." - Albert Schweitzer.

"Life is best spent in alleviating pain, assuaging distress, and promoting peace and joy. The service of man is more valuable than what you call 'service of God.' God has no need of your service. Please man, you please God." - Sathya Sai Baba.

"The most satisfactory thing in life is to have been able to give a large part of oneself to others." - Pierre Teilhard de Chardin.

"Give, and it shall be given unto you; good measure, pressed down, and shaken together, and running over." - Jesus.

"Service of God consists in what we do to our neighbor." - Leo Baeck.

"They serve God well, who serve his creations." - Caroline Norton.

THE IDEAL COUNSELOR

The counselor might want to have the client/patient describe the ideal counselor. That way the counselor can have some idea as to what the client/patient is expecting, and can adjust the caregiving to address those ideal expectations. The client/patient would answer the following questions.

1. What three adjectives would best describe your ideal counselor?

2. Would this ideal counselor do more speaking or more listening?

3. Would you prefer this ideal counselor to be more directive or more non-directive?

4. Would this ideal counselor be a man or woman?

5. How would this ideal counselor rank in importance the following subjects: (A) your past, (B) your future, (C) your present, (D) your internal well-being, (E) your social well-being.

THE IDEAL NURSE

The nurse might want to have the client/patient describe the ideal nurse so that the nurse can be in alignment with the client's/patient's needs, concerns, expectations, and priorities. The client/patient would answer the following questions.

1. What three adjectives would best describe your ideal nurse?

2. Would this ideal nurse do more speaking or more listening?

3. Would you prefer this nurse to be provide more aggressive treatments than the typical nurse or less aggressive?

4. Would this ideal nurse be a woman or a man?

5. How would this ideal nurse rank in importance the following subjects: (A) keeping you informed of your medical situation, (B) giving you choice and control, (C) pain control and symptom management, (D) being a communication link with your physician, (E) being a communication link with your family.

THE IDEAL CHAPLAIN

The chaplain might want to have the client/patient describe the ideal chaplain so that the chaplain can be in alignment with the client's/patient's needs, concerns, expectations, and priorities. The client/patient would answer the following questions.

1. What three adjectives would best describe your ideal chaplain?

2. Would this ideal chaplain do more speaking or more listening?

3. Would you describe this ideal chaplain as primarily liberal or primarily conservative?

4. Would this ideal chaplain be a man or a woman?

5. How would this ideal chaplain rank in importance the following subjects: (A) prayer/meditation, (B) counseling, (C) scripture, (D) preaching, (E) theology/philosophy.

The above activity can be rewritten to address other expectations for other roles. There can be activities entitled "The Ideal Physician," "The Ideal Massage Therapist," "The Ideal Bereavement Counselor," "The Ideal Volunteer," "The Ideal Family Member," "The Ideal Friend," etc.

"It is one of the beautiful compensations of this life that no one can sincerely try to help another without helping himself (herself)." - Charles Dudley Warner.

A CONSIDERATION: A key to good caregiving is not labeling care recipients as somehow less than us. They are of equal value, equal worth. Their opinions are equally valuable. Their ideas are of equal worth.

"Pathologizing dichotomizes; dichotomizing pathologizes." - Abraham Maslow.

"Learn your theories as well as you can, but put them aside when you touch the miracle of the living soul." - Carl Jung.

"Binary or dualistic logic sees the world in either/or terms: good or bad, strong or weak. . . . When binary thinking places the differences between people within a paradigm for human relations of supremacy and subordination, the result is alienation and violence." - K. Louise Schmidt.

CAREGIVER EXERCISE:
PERCEIVING THE HOLY INCARNATE

1. The task of caregiving is made easier when it is perceived as spiritual work.

2. As a caregiver, consider the person in your care as an incarnation of the holy. View your work as spending time with the Christ; you are caring for Jesus. View your work as spending time with the Buddha; you are caring for Buddha. As a caregiver, you are working with the Tao, Krishna, Allah, the Goddess, all that is holy.

3. When considering the care recipient as Jesus, you would need to consider this person as fully human and fully divine. When considering this person as the Buddha, you would need to consider this person as being made of the same stuff as the Buddha, the Buddha's human nature and the Buddha's enlightened nature. This person is not *like* Jesus; this person *is* Jesus. This person is not *like* the Buddha; this person *is* Buddha. All that is holy is in this person.

4. You also might want to perceive yourself as the incarnation of the holy. In caring, you are walking with the feet of Jesus. You are reaching out with the arms of the Buddha. You are touching with the hands of Allah. You are speaking with the voice of Krishna. You are showing the love of the Goddess. You are representing the presence of the Tao. In giving care, you are doing holy stuff with holy people.

"If you have done it onto one of the least of these, you have done it unto me." - Jesus.

"The Buddha has 10,000 faces. Will you just look around you?" - Anonymous.

"The Lord abides in the heart of all beings." - The Bhagavad-Gita.

"Every direction you turn, there is the face of Allah." - Muhammad.

"Let a man (woman) always consider himself (herself) as if the Holy One dwells within him (her)." - The Talmud.

"There is no separation from God, not even the slightest! It is impossible to be separated from God, absolutely impossible. We exist in eternal unity with God. It is totally impossible to be divorced from the Great One. It is an obscene suggestion that we could ever, even in a fraction of our being, be removed from the Room of the great Lord. It is absolutely impossible." - Da Free John.

A CONSIDERATION: Ironic but true: though good caregiving involves recognizing that we, as caregivers, are doing a godly task, that godliness most often comes from recognizing our humanness, our imperfections, our shortcomings.

"The man who claims that he knows, knows nothing; but he who claims nothing, knows." - The Upanishads.

"Before honor comes humility." - The Book of Proverbs.

"Everyone who exalts himself (herself) shall be humbled, and he (she) who humbles himself (herself) shall be exalted." - Jesus.

"Unfathom yourself if you can. If you find out your own limits, it will be the takeoff point to the limitless." - Jalal ud-Din Rumi.

"In the beginner's mind there are many possibilities, in the expert's mind there are few." - Shunryu Suzuki.

"When we admit our vulnerability, we include others; if we deny it, we shut them out." - May Sarton.

"At the heart of any real intimacy is a certain vulnerability. It is hard to trust someone with your vulnerability unless you can see in them a matching vulnerability and know that you will not be judged. In some basic way it is our imperfections and even our pain that draws others close to us." - Rachel Naomi Remen.

"It's our woundedness that allows us to trust each other. I can trust another person only if I can sense that they, too, have woundedness, have pain, have fear. Out of that trust we can begin to pay attention to our own wounds and to each other's wounds – and to heal and be healed." - Rachel Naomi Remen.

A CONSIDERATION: Often good caregiving involves dropping our armor – physical armor, social armor, and psychological armor.

DROPPING OUR ARMOR

During my first staff meeting as director of a hospice, I made a rather foolish announcement. I said, "Just because I'm not in patient care anymore, doesn't mean you can't call on me for a patient need." I had no idea what I was inviting people to do. Because of that announcement, I had to give a man a bath and I had to remove catheters from two people who had died. My education in counseling had certainly not trained me for such activities.

Then one morning the hospice receptionist buzzed me on the intercom to say that one of our patients, a man named Alex, who had ALS, had just had diarrhea all over himself, his wheelchair, and the carpet. She said there was not a home health aide available to go over to his home, but she remembered my invitation. "Doug, there's a need."

With great nervousness I drove over to Alex's house wondering how I was going to ever be able to do what I was being asked to do. However, as soon as I walked into Alex's home, I found it relatively easy to do what I was being asked to do. That was because the armor I was being asked to release was nothing like the armor that Alex had to release to even have me come into that home. As difficult as it is to clean diarrhea off of someone, it is much more difficult to have to ask someone to clean diarrhea off of us. Because Alex first released that serious armor of dignity, I could certainly release my silly armor of administrative respectability.

Alex helped me grow that day.

"People want their helpers to be both skilled and human, professional and vulnerable, competent and caring." - Dale Larson.

KRISTEN AND DR. ALBERS

Kristin was my first child: a premature child, being born about seven weeks premature. She came into this world with several internal malformations: four kidneys rather than two, a defective heart, probably brain damage, and several other problems. She also had some very unusual external traits: extremely pale skin, very long black hair, and eyes that were almost jet black in color, eyes that often rolled up into her head, leaving only the whites of her eyes behind. Her cry was unusual also, very high-pitched and eerie sounding, sometimes sounding as if it was not coming from her, but from some distant place behind her or above her.

Immediately after being delivered, Kristin was flown from the hospital of her birth to another hospital fifty miles away, a hospital with an intensive care unit for newborns. Before Kristin was taken from my wife and I, we literally baptized her with our own tears. More tears came as we left the hospital, my wife being taken out of the hospital in a wheelchair, carrying flowers instead of a child.

What followed was a grueling seven weeks of one hope being dashed after another: excitement every time Kristin gained an ounce, despair when that one ounce gain was followed by a two ounce loss. During those seven weeks our suffering was shared by many people: other parents of newborns, our own parents, friends, co-workers, ministers, even strangers who somehow heard of our plight. As we waited, we received cards, telephone calls, visits: people not knowing exactly what to say, but all offering their support in whatever way they could.

One person who was especially supportive was Dr. Albers, a cardiologist. He talked with us, occasionally held our hands, occasionally gave us hugs. Dr. Albers was the one who arranged for us to touch Kristin – something no one else would let us do – something that was very important for us. He was also the person who informed us that Kristin needed to have open heart surgery, telling us that the operation would have only a five percent chance of being successful, but without the operation Kristin would soon die. Also, after the operation, when Kristin did die, it was Dr. Albers who said, "We have just lost *our* daughter." Then he cried with us.

Dr. Albers was a great human being. He was a great physician.

DROPPING THE CLINICAL DISTANCE

Once when I was an assistant minister at a church I was approached in my office by five members of the same family. They had just come from the hospital where they had been told that a relative of theirs named Anna was only going to live for a couple more hours at the most. They insisted that I go immediately to the hospital to say a prayer at her bedside. I knew only one of those five people in my office, and I had never met Anna.

As they were making that request of me, I was having some rather disturbing thoughts. In ten minutes I had an important appointment with the president of my board. Yet it was a ten minute drive to the hospital and ten minutes back, and I couldn't just say the prayer, I would need to talk to Anna as well. That visit could make me an hour late for my appointment, and I knew the president of my board would not wait for an hour. But I needed to meet with him that day. I was having many disturbing thoughts.

Then the family said something that caused my thinking to make a radical shift. They said that Anna had been unresponsive for the last couple weeks. When they said that my thinking made a shift: not a very noble one. I thought that if she's unresponsive, it's now just ten minutes there, ten minutes back, and a minute for the prayer. I don't have to talk to Anna: she doesn't talk. I'm now eleven minutes late rather than an hour. The president of my board might wait eleven minutes.

I said, "Yes, I will go immediately to the hospital."

I got in my car, rushed to the hospital, rushed into Anna's room. As soon as I entered the room I noticed she had that heavy labored breathing that often precedes death. I get uncomfortable around that so I was reconfirmed in my intent to be brief.

I had a little bit of decency in me. I noticed that one of Anna's arms had fallen down beside the bed. I thought: I'll pick up the arm, place it beside her, say the prayer, then I'll leave – that was the decency. I reached down and took Anna's hand. Although Anna might have been unresponsive in many ways, she was not unresponsive in her hand: she took a tight grip on my hand. I was stuck: I either had to wait until she let go or drag her with me to that appointment.

As I was stuck there I was forced to look at Anna, this woman I had never met. I noticed some things. Anna had beautiful hair. I thought to myself: that's nice looking hair. Then I wondered about things I didn't see: what did her eyes look like, what did her smile look like, did she have a good life. Then the realization came to my mind that I was standing in front of a person, and I almost treated her as if she were not. That was not a nice thought to have.

Tears started welling up in my eyes; they were not coming down, but they were welling up.

After a few moments I had a second realization: this touch is somehow important for Anna, and I remember when touch was so important for me with my daughter Kristin when she was dying. That was enough to make the tears come down.

Then I had a third realization that caused my knees to buckle. I realized that in my busyness I had literally gotten "out of touch." I needed to get "back in touch;" I needed to drop my clinical distance.

MORE DROPPING OF CLINICAL DISTANCE

Eric volunteered for Meals-On-Wheels. On his first day of delivering meals, he went to Rinaldo's house. Rinaldo was an elderly blind man who lived alone in a shack just on the outskirts of Eric's town.

Eric drove up to the shack, knocked on the door, opened the door, and walked inside with the meal. He noticed that inside the shack everything was in disarray, dust and dirt and garbage everywhere, and there was a terrible odor. He saw Rinaldo sitting in a dark corner and then he simply said, "Meals-On-Wheels." Rinaldo said, "You must be new." "How do you know?" responded Eric. "Everyone else just knocks on my door and leaves the meal outside. You're the first person to ever come in."

"Whatever you wish that men would do to you, do so to them." - Jesus.

"Do not do to others what you do not want them to do to you." - Confucius.

"One going to take a pointed stick to pinch a baby bird should first try it on himself to feel how it hurts." - Nigerian Proverb.

A CONSIDERATION: Sometimes good caregiving might involve simply recognizing that some people don't need us and don't want us – the importance of letting patients be themselves and be by themselves.

SOMETIMES WE'RE JUST NOT NEEDED

A social worker named Wilma was making her initial assessment visit with her hospice patient. After about ten minutes into the visit, the man said, "Wilma. I don't know what it is, but I don't think we're a good match. I think it would be best if you just leave." He then escorted her to the door.

The man then called me, Wilma's supervisor, and reiterated the statement he had made to Wilma. "I'm not sure what it is, but I don't think Wilma and I belong together. I'd appreciate it if Wilma not come back to my house again." I assured him that I would speak to Wilma and that she would not return.

In spite of the man's request and my review of that request with her, Wilma did not hear the message. She felt the man simply did not give her a chance. She felt she could have offered the man much, but that he had just not giver her any opportunity to do that. So, she returned to the man's home. He would not let her through the screen door, once again telling her he did not want to interact with her. He then shut the door.

Wilma still did not hear the message. She still felt that the only problem was that the man had not given her a chance to offer all she could offer. So, Wilma went around to the man's bedroom window and tried to talk to him there.

When Wilma came back to the office, I had to inform her that that man was not the only person who did not need her anymore. I relieved Wilma of her duties.

CHARLIE

At age seventy, Charlie was struggling with lung cancer and chronic obstructive pulmonary disease. In his youth he had helped his father raise tobacco in Kentucky. He began smoking at age six and learned to make moonshine at age eight. By age fifteen Charlie decided to hit the road for Chicago. He worked as a cook, bus driver, and self-ordained minister over the years.

In his treatment regimen for lung cancer, Charlie had been receiving pain pills and duragesic patches to address his pain. He often just pretended to swallow the pills, and he secretly took off the patches. When discovered, he said he preferred to follow his own regimen of pain control – smoking heavily, praying often, and strongly believing in a reunion in heaven with his beloved wife.

Although there was no question that pain medication brought him some comfort, Charlie liked being able to choose his own form of care. If he had been allowed complete control, he said, he would toss out all the prescribed medications "as quick as I used to hide the moonshine from the revenuers."

GIVER/RECEIVER DIALOGUE

Whenever family members, friends, nurses, home health aids, or social workers find themselves disagreeing with chosen actions or attitudes of the recipients of their care, they might find some emotional assistance in doing imaginary dialogues with those care recipients. For example, a caregiver might object to a care recipient's choice to not aggressively treat an illness. The caregiver would then imagine the care recipient sitting in a chair while the caregiver asks why this person is making that choice. Then the caregiver would imagine the person giving a response, a likely response that the person might make. An imaginary dialogue would ensue, hopefully resulting in a better understanding of the care recipient by the caregiver.

Even if the caregiver comes to no better understanding of the care recipient through this exercise, the effort of doing the exercise is good in and of itself. The process of going through the exercise communicates a desire to understand and accept the care recipient, a major goal of good caregiving. This participating in the effort of understanding and accepting gives the caregiver a good mind set for the task of caring, preparing the caregiver to allow the care recipient to have the right to be in control.

"Our own pulse beats in every stranger's throat." - Barbara Deming.

BECOMING THE CLIENT/PATIENT

A caregiver might want to periodically imagine himself/herself as the client/patient. It always helps caregivers to know what is in the mind of the care recipient. The caregiver could go through the following.

1. Find a comfortable, quiet place.

2. Make yourself comfortable, and quiet your mind. Close your eyes.

3. Recall a specific interaction between you and the client/patient when there was some friction between the two of you, when the interaction was far from being the best it could be.

4. Review that interaction from your perspective: (A) how you perceived the setting, (B) how you perceived the way you greeted each other, (C) how things evolved, (D) when the friction was at its greatest from your perspective, (E) what three adjectives you would use to describe your client/patient at that moment, (F) how you perceived the way you departed from one another.

5. With a creative leap in imagination, review that interaction from the client's/patient's perspective: (A) how the client/patient perceived the setting, (B) how the client/patient perceived the way you greeted each other, (C) how things evolved, (D) when the friction was at its greatest from the client's/patient's perspective, (E) what three adjectives you would use to describe your caregiver at that moment, (F) how the client/patient perceived the way you departed from one another.

6. What did you learn from this activity?

A CONSIDERATION: Caregivers and care recipients are often brought together through touch. However, we must always remember to *assess* before we *express*; we must be careful to not administer touch unless we know that it is wanted.

NOURISHING TOUCH

As caregivers, we can sometimes create a new sense of connectedness and intimacy with our care recipients just by changing our normal touching patterns.

A. If our typical greeting or farewell is a three-second handshake with cursory eye contact, we could try lengthening the handshake ten seconds and making direct eye contact. Or we might hold the hand without shaking it, or grasp the hand with both of ours, or follow the handshake with a quick hug.
B. If our normal greeting or farewell is a firm bear hug, we might try softening it, or place our hands on the person's shoulders as we give a gentle massage. We might ask to receive a hug rather than always initiating one, or we might substitute a kiss on the cheek.

By altering our usual greeting or farewell, we force ourselves to think about what we are doing. This brings more sincerity to gestures that often become routine. The receiver of our new greeting or farewell will feel our sincerity, and a new sense of connectedness can flourish.

SENSUAL BACK RUB

First create a sensual, relaxing environment for your care recipient. A quiet time in the evening might be best. Ideally, the room should be slightly warmer than normal. Soft music could be playing in the background. The room might be lit only by candles – scented candles for added ambiance.

The care recipient should lie face down on the bed with no clothing on the back. Gently, slowly clean the back with a damp, warm, soft washcloth. Pat it dry with a soft towel. Gently rub body oil onto the back until the entire back has a thin coating. Your hands might need to be immersed in oil again periodically and rubbed together as you apply enough oil to cover the back completely.

Awaken the back's sensory capacity by patting it with your palms or gently chopping with the edge of your hands. Tap all over the back with your fingertips. Use one or two fingers and your thumbs as if they are legs walking up and down and all around the back.

Stroke, rub, and knead the back. Imagine that you are sending loving energy from the center of your being out through your fingertips. This step would involve the most amount of time of all the steps.

Again, tap all over the back with your fingertips. With a thumb or index finger, print messages of caring on the back. Ask your care recipient to guess what you are writing. Sample messages: "We have had some good times together." "You are so beautiful." "I care so much for you." "You are such a good wife (husband, father, mother, partner, or friend)."

Finally, gently and slowly clean the back again with a slightly damp, warm, soft washcloth and pat it dry with a soft towel.

FOOT WASHING

The caregiver would bring into one place a comfortable chair, a large basin of warm water, some pleasantly scented soap, soft washcloth, soft towel, and skin lotion or oil. The caregiver would then proceed through the following steps:

1. Invite your care recipient to sit in the comfortable chair.

2. Soak your care recipient's feet in warm water for several minutes.

3. Slowly cleanse his or her feet with the soap, warm water, and washcloth.

4. Pat your care recipient's feet dry with the towel.

5. With the skin lotion or oil on your palms, caress and massage his or her feet.

6. You may want to repeat the washing to remove the lotion or oil, though some may not need to be washed away.

7. Put soft slippers or socks on your care recipient's feet to keep them warm.

SHARING THE SILENCE

Sometimes the best thing we can do is simply share time together in silence, supporting a person simply through our presence. A caregiver should not be quick to end these times. A caregiver should relax, knowing that his/her simple presence can sometimes change a profane world into a holy one.

"Silence is unceasing Eloquence. It is the best language." - Ramana Maharshi

"There are hurts so deep that one cannot reach them or heal them with words." - Kate Seredy.

"Be still and know that I am God." - The Hebrew Psalmist

"The first stage of worship is silence." - Muhammad

"When you close your lips, God begins to speak." - Hazrat Inayat Khan

"I suspect that the most basic and powerful way to connect to another person is to listen. Just listen. Perhaps the most important thing we ever give each other is our attention." - Rachel Naomi Remen.

TONGLEN

1. In the presence of a care recipient, the caregiver, with each in-breath, would breathe in this person's pain and suffering, taking into the lungs, heart, and soul all of this person's troubles.

2. With each out-breath the caregiver would breathe out all of his/her own joy and happiness, directing all of that joy and happiness toward the care recipient.

3. This practice would last for as many breaths as it takes for the caregiver to perceive some changes in himself/herself or in the care recipient.

BURNOUT

The typical burnout theory states that if a caregiver is *too* focused on another, especially another in much pain and suffering, that the caregiver will experience burnout. The typical burnout theory states that if a caregiver does not maintain a *clinical distance* from the care recipient, the caregiver will experience burnout.

In working with the terminally ill and the grieving caregivers are often asked questions like: "Don't you experience burnout in that work?" "How can you do that kind of work and not be totally exhausted, totally spent?" Many of the people working with the terminally ill and grieving would answer those questions by saying: "I don't get depressed or depleted from my work; I get energized and nourished."

Certainly there are some people who are "toxic," people who just take energy away from others: if caregivers just work with toxic people they will experience burnout. If caregivers only know how to give and do not know how to receive, they will experience burnout. Also, if caregivers have some kind of conflictual message (the caregiver's heart wants to do one thing and the head another, or the caregiver wants to do one thing and the caregiver's supervisor another) there can be burnout. However, when caregivers are giving to most people in pain and suffering, opening themselves up to receive from those they serve, and not having any internal conflictual message, they come away *full-filled*, not emptied; energized, not burned out.

A CONSIDERATION: Making every day count for a care recipient means not only giving each and every *today* significance, but also giving significance to *tomorrow*.

LOOKING FORWARD TO TOMORROW

Positive anticipation of tomorrow can enliven today. Caregivers can foster that feeling in small but significant ways, such as bringing something new for care recipients to enjoy at regular intervals. These efforts need not be costly or time-consuming, but they will let care recipients know that they have a place on our agenda, and that is something to look forward to. Here are some suggestions for things we could do regularly:

    A. Give them a different greeting card each Monday;
    B. Read a chapter of a book to them each day;
    C. Treat them to a surprise flavor of ice cream every Friday;
    D. Bring a different video to watch every Wednesday.

APPRECIATION AWARD

Social workers, nurses, and other caregivers are honored annually for their specific contributions: Social Worker Month, Nursing Week, Volunteer Appreciation Day. Why not have a time set aside to show appreciation to patients? Most caregivers readily acknowledge that they receive immense benefits from their patients, but there is not an officially recognized month, week, or even day for them.

Caregiving teams could correct this oversight by presenting a plaque, or a bouquet, or a single rose to a care recipient. Every care recipient could have a special day when everyone on the caregiving team would somehow show extra appreciation for that person: Bertha's Day, Andrew's Day, Shirley's Day. Such recognition would acknowledge the gifts that have been received from that individual. This gesture not only honors the recipient, but it also reminds us that we are helped by those we help. Both caregivers and care recipients benefit in the act of caring.

"At a certain point 'helper' and 'helped' simply begin to dissolve. What's real is the helping — the process in which we're all blessed, according to our needs and our place at the moment. How much we can get back in giving! How much we can offer in the way we receive!" - Ram Dass.

"In a true healing relationship, both heal and both are healed." - Rachel Naomi Remen.

"Those whom we support hold us up in life." - Marie Ebner von Eshenbach.

A CONSIDERATION: We can benefit by lessening our imposing of "musts" upon ourselves. Our self-imposing of "musts" lessens our effectiveness, creating an artificial barrier between ourselves and the recipients of our care. It could also adversely affect our sense of self-worth. We would benefit ourselves and others by challenging our "musts" and substituting rationality. [Example: Changing "I *must* have a positive attitude around my care recipients" to "I will try to have a positive attitude if that helps them. Yet, if I am unable to do it all the time, I am not a totally awful person."]

A CONSIDERATION: A subtle way in we try to control people is when we do the imposing of "shoulds" and "oughts" upon our care recipients. [Examples: "Dying people should conserve their energy." "Dying people ought to experience and express anger." "People who are in the final phases of their lives should want to talk about spiritual issues." "Grieving people ought to finish the grieving process within a year." "Grieving people ought to seek either individual or group therapy." "My patient ought to not use the word 'ought.'" "My patient should not use the word 'should.'"] By eliminating our demands on our care recipients, we can save ourselves and them a lot of unnecessary trouble.

CHANGING THE CAREGIVER'S "I NEED" TO "I WANT"

A subtle way that we often control our care recipients, without allowing them any control, is when we impose our supposed needs upon them, whether we do this consciously or unconsciously. [Examples: "I need to have my patients appreciate everything that I do." "I need to have this person be just as cooperative with me as he or she is with that other caregiver." "I need to have my father control his bowels whenever I am around him." "I need to have my mother agree with whatever I recommend for her."]

Whenever we catch ourselves imposing our supposed needs, we can lessen our own tension, and the tension of the care recipient, when we think of these supposed "needs" as "wants," realizing the full implications of this need-to-want switch in our consciousness. [Examples: "I *want* my patient to appreciate everything that I do, but my world will certainly not end if that does not occur." "I *want* to have my father control his bowels whenever I am around him. However, I am certainly capable of cleaning up anything that needs to be cleaned up." "I *want* my mother to agree with everything that I recommend for her, but I will certainly survive without her compliance to my wishes. Besides, except in very rare cases, if there are any exceptions at all, my mother really knows what is best for her, and always has known."]

CAREGIVER'S REPORT CARD

The dying and grieving can often feel as though they are the ones being inspected, judged, or graded. This activity turns the tables a bit. Caregivers might occasionally need to be graded (once a week or once a month) by the care recipient to see if needs, concerns, expectations, and priorities are being met.

Subject	Grade
Allowing me to make my own decisions	_____
Listening skills	_____
Knowing or finding answers to my questions	_____
Ability to address my physical needs	_____
Ability to address my emotional needs	_____
Ability to address my spiritual needs	_____
Appropriate touch	_____
Appropriate humor	_____

General comments about how my caregiver might improve: _____
_____
_____

A DAY'S REWARD

Since the person who is caregiving wants to allow the recipient of care to do, think, or be whatever the person wishes, the caregiver might want a reward for accomplishing that facilitation, a sort of positive reinforcement for good behavior. If the caregiver goes a full day without telling the care recipient what to do, think, or be, the caregiver could receive a predetermined reward. [Examples of rewards: a special desert for dinner, an hour's reading time with a good book, an hour's worth of time completely alone, etc.]

"For so much of my life I was run by this nagging voice in the back of my head that kept insisting, 'You're not doing enough! You're not doing enough!' But now I'm starting to listen to my body a lot more. It needs tender loving care and I'm the only one who can provide that. Even though I always feared that if I took better care of myself it would mean I'd become selfish or self-indulgent, I've discovered that's not the case." - Leonard Felder.

"Nothing may be more important than being gentle with ourselves. . . . We learn the value of recognizing our limits, forgiving ourselves our bouts of impatience or guilt, acknowledging our own needs. We see that to have compassion for others we must have compassion for ourselves." - Ram Dass.

WHO AM I?

Self-reflection is often important in clarifying who we are, what we are doing, and why we are doing it. A caregiver might want to answer the following questions and periodically revisit them.

1. When do I do the greatest good to myself?

2. When do I do the greatest good to others?

3. When do I feel that what I am doing is effortless?

4. When do I feel that what I am doing is full of effort?

5. Who is most important to me?

6. What is most important to me?

7. When did I do or say something that was not at all like myself? Who was I being? Why was I trying to be like that person?

8. When do I like myself the best? What do I look like? What am I doing? How do others perceive me?

9. When and how do I express my "real" self best?

10. When and how do I inadequately express my "real" self?

11. What is my ultimate goal in life?

12. Is what I am doing now compatible with my ultimate goal in life? How can I make it more compatible?

"When you make choices for your own growth, . . . you also make opportunities for others to grow as well." - Carmen Renee Berry.

A CONSIDERATION: Often the whole work of caregiving can be easily summarized as merely showing kindness. That is often the ultimate goal of caregiving.

"My religion is kindness." - The Dalai Lama.

"Be the living expression of God's kindness – kindness in your face, kindness in your eyes, kindness in your smile, kindness in your warm greeting." - Mother Teresa.

"There are three rules of dealing with those who come to us: (1) Kindness, (2) Kindness, (3) Kindness." - Fulton J. Sheen.

PRAYERS

DEDICATION PRAYER

May this prayer be Your prayer.
May my deliberations be Your deliberations.
May my feelings be Your feelings.
May my intentions be Your intentions.
May my resolutions be Your resolutions.
May my actions be Your actions.

A CAREGIVER'S MORNING PRAYER

As I begin this new day, let me have the courage and strength to face what lies ahead.
Let me practice tolerance and patience.
Let me reveal empathy and love.
Let me offer sustenance and hope.
And, let me have the wisdom to know when I need to step forward and when I need to step back.

I ask all of this so that when I come to the end of this day, I might rest having known that my time and energy have been wanted and needed.
Yes, I am asking all of this for my own sake, but I am also asking for the sake of another.

A CAREGIVER'S EVENING PRAYER

I give thanks for the courage and strength that has carried me through this day.
I give thanks for whatever tolerance and patience I have been able to practice.
I give thanks for whatever empathy and love I have been able to reveal.
I give thanks for whatever sustenance and hope I have been able to offer.

I give thanks at the conclusion of this day and into this night for having been needed and wanted.
Let me rest with a thankful body, mind, and spirit.
Let me rest so that I might greet tomorrow with renewed courage and strength.
I give thanks for rest.

SEEING THE HOLY

Let me see all that is Holy in this person who is before me.
In holding this person's hand, may I realize that I am holding Your hand.
In feeding this person, may I realize that I am feeding You.
In washing this person, may I realize that I am washing You.
In giving this person my love, may I realize that I am giving my love to You.

PRAYER FOR JOY

May we remember only joy.
May we seek only joy.

May we receive only joy.
May we give only joy.

May joy be within us.
May joy be around us.

May our next moment be filled with joy.
May our last moment be filled with joy.

May joy be always with me.
May joy be always with you.

RECEIVING THROUGH GIVING

May my self-esteem grow through providing others with self-esteem.
May my strength be founded upon building the strength of others.
May my fulfillment come in bringing fulfillment to whoever is in my care.
May whatever I receive be based upon whatever I give.

RECEIVING MORE THROUGH GIVING MORE

In giving strength, I receive strength.
In giving comfort, I receive comfort.
In giving peace, I receive peace.

In touching another, I am touched.
In holding another, I am held.
In loving another, I am loved.

SHARING THE BOUNTY

Giver of peace, may I be a giver of Your bounty.
Contributor of comfort, may I be a contributor of Your bounty.
Provider of strength, may I be a provider of Your bounty.
Guarantor of hope, may I be a guarantor of Your bounty.

WHATEVER I HAVE

Although I may not have the strongest of hands, I offer whatever I have for Your service.
Although my feet might not be the most steady, I offer whatever I have for Your service.
Although I may not have the most loving of hearts, I offer whatever I have for Your service.
Although my mind might not be the most astute, I offer whatever I have for Your service.
Although I may not have abundant energy, I offer whatever I have for Your service.
Although my soul might not be the most peaceful, I offer whatever I have for Your service.
Although I may not have the most determined of wills, I offer whatever I have for Your service.
Please receive whatever I have.
I am in Your service.

MAY IT BE ENOUGH

May the strength that I have be enough so that I might give strength to another.
May the comfort that comes to me be enough so that I might give comfort to another.
May the love that I have found be enough so that I might give love to another.
May the hope that I discover be enough so that I might give hope to another.

PROPER PERSPECTIVE

Help me to not have any false self-importance
So that I might always know what truly is important.

Help me to laugh at myself
So that I might always be amused.

Help me to see all my foibles
So that I might always be entertained.

Help me to not have any false self-importance
So that I might always know what truly is important.

HELP ME TO REMEMBER

Help me to remember that there is little I need to say and a lot I need to hear.
Help me to remember that I have little to teach and a lot to learn.
Help me to remember that sometimes the most important thing I can give is simply my
      presence, and sometimes nothing more is even wanted.
Help me to remember that all my education, all my training, and all my experience
      must always be secondary to my simple presence.
Help me to remember that I must accept and reaccept and reaccept and reaccept the
      uniqueness of the individual before me.

Help me to remember that I am not here for me: I am here for another.

BEFORE AN OPERATION: A PRAYER FOR MY PATIENT

Strengthen _____ to do what he (she) has to do and bear what he (she) has to bear; that, accepting the skills and gifts of surgeons and nurses, he (she) may be restored to health with a spirit of thanksgiving. Grant this strength. Grant this acceptance. Grant this restoration. Grant this thanksgiving. Confidently I pray.

FOR RELIEF FROM PAIN: A PRAYER FOR MY PATIENT

I am praying for the relief of pain. I ask that the pain which _____ feels might be lightened. Lighten the pain. Soften the hard feelings. Ease the suffering. Bring comfort. Bring respite. Bring relief. As I pray, the pain is being soothed. Comfort is coming. Respite is coming. Relief is coming. _____ is feeling the comfort as it comes. _____ is feeling the relief as it comes. A lightening. A softening. An easing. Comfort. Respite. Relief. It is happening as I pray.

FOR STRENGTH, JOY, AND COMFORT: A PRAYER FOR MY PATIENT

I ask that in the midst of weakness, strength might be found. I pray that in the midst of sorrow, joy might be found. I pray that in the midst of pain, comfort might be found. Give _____ strength. Give _____ joy. Give _____ comfort. As I pray for _____, I sense the welling up of strength. I sense the welling up of joy. I sense the welling up of comfort. May this strength, joy, and comfort continue to build. Let it be.

FOR SANCTIFICATION: A PRAYER FOR MY PATIENT

I pray that _____ may become fully aware of the presence of all holy powers. May those powers continue to grow in him (her). _____, you are being touched by the Holy. _____, you are being held by the Divine. _____, you are being fully surrounded by all powers of sanctification. As I pray, this is all coming into being. Let it be now and always.

PRAYER OF DEDICATION

Open sores and human waste,
Sadness and anger,
Frustration and depression,
Physical pain and emotional suffering:
The compost for the planting of my beautiful garden.
My work.
My mission.
My calling.

MY LIMITS AND MY HEALTH

Help me to learn that there is knowledge I cannot have.
Help me to understand that there are things I cannot do.
Help me to know that there are burdens I cannot bear.
For in discovering my limits, I keep my health.
And, in keeping my health, I can be of service to others.

GIVING THANKS FOR MY HARD WORK

I give thanks for the gift of my tears.
I give thanks for my muscle aches.
I give thanks for the gift of my sweat.
I give thanks for my anger.
I give thanks for the gift of my doubts.
I give thanks for my despair.

These are the confirmations of my hard work.
Without these my growth is limited.
Without these my service is suspect.
These are the confirmations of my hard work.

FOR YOU AND FOR ME

To hold another is to hold ourselves.
To heal another is to heal ourselves.
To love another is to love ourselves.
To forgive another is to forgive ourselves.
To abandon another is to abandon ourselves.

THE QUIET AND THE LOUD

May my feet walk gently in your world.
May my hands touch softly on your skin.
May my voice speak sweetly to your ears.
And may my love rattle your bones, blow your mind, and cause your spirit to soar.

ONLY THE GOOD

May my will want only the good.
May my mind think only the good.
May my eyes see only the good.
May my ears hear only the good.
May my mouth speak only the good.
May my hands do only the good.

"Helping is tough work – it is inevitably stressful, conflicted, and exhausting at times. Yet when you make a difference, when you see the real impact of your caring, any doubts about the value of your efforts disappear." - Dale Larson.

Bibliography

Adams, R. (1999). <u>When Parents Die</u>. Routledge.
    A book for counselors drawing upon some recent research on coping with parental loss.

Anderson, M. (2001). <u>Sacred Dying</u>. Prima Publishing.
    With sensitivity, a down-to-earth realism, and some healthy skepticism, Megory Anderson presents a counseling approach that values rituals in helping people make death into a spiritual experience, a spiritual experience for both the caregiver and the care recipient.

Aries, P. (1974). <u>Western Attitudes Toward Death: From The Middle Ages To The Present</u>. Johns Hopkins University Press.
    The author traces our attitudes towards death throughout history, defining what a 'good death' is. He emphasizes how some of our former ways of viewing death were more healthy than some of our current attitudes.

Attig, T. (1996). <u>How We Grieve: Relearning The World</u>. Oxford University Press.
    Thomas Attig tells real-life tales to illustrate the poignant disruption of life and suffering that loss entails. He shows how through grieving we meet daunting challenges, make critical choices, and reshape our lives. The grieving process is seen as a process of "relearning" our world.

Bernard, J.S., & Schneider, M. (1996). <u>The True Work Of Dying</u>. Avon Books.
    Two nurses have written this book comparing their background in midwifery with their hospice work: showing how the process of dying mirrors that of childbirth. Many patient stories.

Boerstler, R.W., & Kornfeld, H.S. (1995). <u>Life To Death</u>. Healing Arts Press.
    The authors present a technique called 'comeditation,' an ancient yet timeless holistic technique for giving comfort and clarity to the dying. If you're afraid that you might say or do the wrong thing, you can never go wrong doing comeditation, a way of simply being present with someone.

Borysenko, J. (1987). <u>Minding The Body, Mending The Mind</u>. Bantam Books.
    Joan Borysenko teaches us how to elicit the mind's powerful relaxation response to boost our immune system, overcome chronic pain and alleviate the symptoms of stress-related illness.

Brussat, F., & Brussat, M.A. (2000). <u>Spiritual Rx: Prescriptions For Living A Meaningful Life</u>. Hyperion.

The Brussats identify the best ways to explore 37 essential practices (e.g. hope, forgiveness, gratitude, meaning, etc.). They suggest fiction, poetry, audiotapes, art, and music selections for inspiration and contemplation. They suggest insightful first steps for individuals — journal and imagery exercises, household and community projects.

Buckman, R. (1992). How To Break Bad News: A Guide For Health Care Professionals. Johns Hopkins University Press.

The book's title describes the content. Robert Buckman, a medical oncologist, assisted by Yvonne Kason, a family psychotherapist, gives many examples on the 'wrong' way and the 'right' way to break bad news, showing why particular strategies and responses are better than others. This is an excellent book on basic communication skills for all health care employees.

Byock, I. (1997). Dying Well. Riverhead Books.

A hospice physician's perspective on how to die with dignity, with little pain. Ira Byock is someone who 'walks the talk,' helping families deal with doctors, helping them make the end of life as meaningful and precious as the beginning. A good book for physicians as well as other medical professionals.

Callanan, M., & Kelley, P. (1992). Final Gifts. Bantam Books.

The authors present an approach to working with the dying that emphasizes jumping into the terminally ill person's world, honoring their experiences and their language, experiences and language that might seem quite foreign to us, but very meaningful.

Cassidy, S. (1991). Sharing The Darkness. Orbis Books.

Warm, honest, and highly personal, Christian physician Sheila Cassidy meditates upon the mystery of our wounded humanity, trying to bring forth meaning and a spirituality of caring out of the reality of suffering.

Chogyam Trungpa. (1991). Orderly Chaos. Shambhala.

Through meditative practices the opposites of experience – confusion and enlightenment, chaos and order, pain and pleasure – are revealed as inseparable parts of a total vision of reality.

Corey, G. (1996). Theory And Practice Of Counseling And Psychotherapy. Brooks/Cole.

A great text on basic counseling techniques.

Diamant, A. (1998). Saying Kaddish: How To Comfort The Dying, Bury The Dead & Mourn As A Jew. Schocken Books.

Diamant shows how to make Judaism's time-honored rituals into personal, meaningful sources of comfort.

Doka, K.J. (Ed.). (2002). Disenfranchised Grief. Research Press.

Doka looks at all those grief situations that do not follow the 'typical' pattern of grieving: suicide, sudden death, murder, etc.

Doka, K.J. (Ed.). (1993). <u>Death And Spirituality</u>. Baywood Publishing.
> *The book presents a series of chapters aimed at addressing the various religious/spiritual needs of a dying person and a dying person's family.*

Epstein, M. (1998). <u>Going To Pieces Without Falling Apart</u>. Broadway Books.
> *Mark Epstein, a Buddhist psychiatrist, encourages us to relax the ever-vigilant mind in order to experience the freedom that comes only from relinquishing control. He teaches us that only by letting go can we start on the path to a more peaceful and spiritually satisfying life, showing us ways of having peace in the midst of chaos.*

Fine, C. (1999). <u>No Time To Say Goodbye: Surviving The Suicide Of A Loved One</u>. Main Street Books.
> *Using her own experiences from the suicidal death of her husband, the experiences of other survivors, and the advice of mental health professionals, the author provides a guide for dealing with the guilt, anger, and confusion connected to suicide.*

Fitzgerald, H. (1994). <u>The Mourning Handbook</u>. Fireside Book.
> *This book is written as a companion to those mourners in need of practical and emotional assistance during the trying times before and after the death of a loved one. With many subchapters and cross references, it can be consulted for a specific problem or read at length.*

Ford, D. (1998). <u>The Dark Side Of The Light Chasers</u>. Riverhead.
> *Debbie Ford shows how we hide and deny our dark sides, rejecting these aspects of our true natures rather than giving ourselves the freedom to live authentically, then provides some guidelines for living authentically.*

Frankl, V.E. (1959). <u>Man's Search For Meaning</u>. Washington Square Press.
> *A book on how to survive suffering by someone who has been there, someone who has walked the talk.*

Furman, J., & McNabb, D. (1997). <u>The Dying Time</u>. Bell Tower.
> *The book provides details on how to make a dying person's environment conducive to peace and tranquility, give personal care, and understand and respond to the emotional and spiritual crises that naturally occur. It also addresses how caregivers can remain healthy in the process.*

George, M. (2000). <u>Discover Inner Peace: A Guide to Spiritual Well-Being</u>. Chronicle Books.
> *Drawing from Buddhism, Taoism, and Western meditation traditions, the author presents insights and step-by-step exercises for controlling emotions, achieving mental clarity, and maintaining positive thinking.*

Golden, T. (2000). <u>Swallowed By A Snake: The Gift Of The Masculine Side Of Healing</u>. Golden Healing Publishing.
> *Tom Golden's skillful blend of folklore, cross-cultural analysis, and*

clinical advice will help both men and women understand the specific context and needs of grieving men.

Grollman, E. (1995). <u>Living When A Loved One Has Died</u>. Beacon Press.

Rabbi Earl Grollman has not written this book as a self-help book. There are no tools and techniques. The emphasis is merely on letting people know it's alright to feel the way they do: anger, sadness, etc. A comforting book to give those who are grieving to let them know that they are not alone in their struggles.

Hazrat Inayat Khan. (1979). <u>The Unity Of Religious Ideals</u>. Sufi Order Publications.

In this book a Muslim mystic presents the common messages contained in all faiths, how to transform our lives from the mundane to the spiritual.

Hick, J.H. (1976). <u>Death & Eternal Life</u>. Harper & Row.

This book examines the beliefs of various cultures and faiths about what occurs after death.

Hinton, C. (1997). <u>Silent Grief</u>. New Leaf Press.

Writing of her own grief from a miscarriage and interviewing many women and men who have struggled with miscarriage, this author draws comfort from Christian scripture and the fact that grievers need not feel alone in their grief.

Hollis, J. (1996). <u>Swamplands Of The Soul: New Life In Dismal Places</u>. Inner City Books.

The author, a Jungian psychotherapist, shows ways of discovering meaning and the seeds of growth in the midst of our reactions of guilt, grief, loss, betrayal, doubt, loneliness, depression, despair, obsessions, addictions, anger, fear, angst, and anxiety. There is a chapter on each one of these reactions.

Huxley, L. (1963). <u>You Are Not The Target</u>. Farrar, Straus and Giroux.

A book of "recipes" on how to convert negative energy into positive energy, ways of breaking out of downward spirals of depression and suffering.

James, J., & Friedman, R. (1998). <u>The Grief Recovery Handbook</u>. HarperCollins.

Drawing upon their own histories, as well as from others, the authors illustrate what grief is and how it is possible to recover and regain energy and spontaneity. They offer some specific tools and actions needed to go through the grieving process from beginning to end.

James, J., & Friedman, R. (2001). <u>When Children Grieve: For Adults To Help Children Deal With Death, Divorce, Pet Loss, Moving, And Other Losses</u>. Harper Collins.

Although the title promises to help children get through many types of losses, the focus is primarily on loss due to death. Although the book is good, it would be better if both the title and text were shortened.

Johanson, G., & Kurtz, R. (1991). <u>Grace Unfolding</u>. Bell Tower.

A sensible and compassionate book for counselors that relates the principles of the Tao Te Ching to the practice of contemporary psychotherapy.

Johnson, C.J., & McGee, M.G. (Eds.) (1991). How Different Religions View Death And Afterlife. Charles Press.

Each chapter of this book examines a different faith, each chapter is written by someone who actually practices that faith.

Kabit-Zinn, J. (1994). Wherever You Go There You Are. Hyperion.

Jon Kabat-Zinn maps out a simple path for cultivating mindfulness in one's own life. He speaks both to those coming to meditation for the first time and to longtime practitioners.

Kapleau, P. (1989). The Wheel Of Life And Death. Doubleday.

Combining the writings of both Eastern and Western religions on death and dying, and interweaving his own experiences as a Zen Buddhist teacher, the author emphasizes how to be at peace with dying, how to die serenely. The book is easily understood by people from all spiritual traditions.

Klein, A. (1998). The Courage To Laugh. Penguin Putnam.

Allen Klein shows readers how to face the end of life with dignity and compassion. The book is filled with heartwarming stories and anecdotes from patients, doctors, nurses, children, and comedians.

Kornfield, J. (2000). After The Ecstasy, The Laundry. Bantam Books.

Drawing on the insights of practitioners within Buddhist, Christian, Jewish, Hindu and Sufi traditions, this book offers a uniquely intimate and honest understanding of how the modern spiritual journey unfolds, finding meaning in the ordinary.

Kramer, K.P. (1988). The Sacred Art Of Dying. Paulist Press.

The book presents various perspectives on death in a comparative religious context.

Kramer, K.P. (1993). Death Dreams. Paulist Press.

The author examines death dreams from multiple vantage points, investigating unconscious imagery of death. He relies much on cross-cultural traditions, myths, and stories, exploring how we can grow through our death dreams.

Kurtz, E., & Ketcham, K. (1992). The Spirituality Of Imperfection. Bantam Books.

Coming from a 12-Step philosophy the authors look at how to find meaning within suffering.

Kushner, H. (2001). When Bad Things Happen To Good People. Schocken Books.

After examining the inadequacies of the traditional answers to the problem of evil, the author presents a rational, practical, and compassionate answer.

Lao-tzu. Trans. Mitchell, S. (1988). Tao Te Ching. Harper Collins.

> *A primer on living, a primer on interacting with others, a primer on counseling, the Tao Te Ching offers timeless advice.*

LaGrand, L.E. (1998). <u>After Death Communication</u>. Llewellyn Publications.
> *Louis LaGrand takes a well-researched approach to examining a griever's interactions (visual and verbal) with the deceased.*

Lamm, M. (1969). <u>The Jewish Way In Death And Mourning</u>. Jonathan David Publishers.
> *Maurice Lamm presents a comprehensive look at Jewish practices related to death and mourning.*

Larson, D.G. (1993). <u>The Helper's Journey</u>. Research Press.
> *This is a good book on caregiving that spends equal time on caring for the caregiver as the care recipient.*

Levang, E. (1998). <u>When Men Grieve: Why Men Grieve Differently & How You Can Help</u>. Fairview Press.
> *Elizabeth Levang offers illuminating insights and strategies for partners, friends, and relatives who want to help grieving men. This book will help women understand men in grief and help men to understand themselves.*

Levine, S. (1982). <u>Who Dies?</u>. Anchor Books.
> *Stephen Levine advocates a process called 'conscious dying.' Some of his chapter headings give hints to his highly spiritual approach to dying: 'Opening To Death,' 'Getting Born,' 'Letting Go Of Control,' 'Healing/Dying – The Great Balancing Act.'*

Lewis, C.S. (2001). <u>A Grief Observed</u>. Harper.
> *This book explores the struggles of a famous Christian theologian after the death of his wife. It is a beautiful and terribly honest portrayal of the journey through despair in search of meaning.*

Longaker, C. (1997). <u>Facing Death And Finding Hope</u>. Doubleday.
> *Drawing upon her experiences of losing a husband in her twenties and her work in hospice, the author, from her Tibetan Buddhist perspective, shows how we can all grow emotionally and spiritually in light of death, the death of others and our own death.*

Lynn, J., & Harrold, J. (1999). <u>Handbook For Mortals</u>. Oxford.
> *Written by two physicians, this book covers all the essential medical topics in caring for the dying (making it understandable for the non-medical person): managing symptoms and controlling pain, what to expect as terminal illness progresses, getting the most out of conversations with your doctor, etc.*

Magida, A.J., & Matlins, S.M. (1999). <u>How To Be A Perfect Stranger</u>. (2 Vols.). Skylight Paths.
> *This is a book on how to adjust to the religious services of faiths that are different from our own.*

Martin, P. (1999). The Zen Path Through Depression. Harper Collins.
Philip Martin offers gentle guidance and sensitivity that come from his own personal experiences in using Zen practices and wisdom to alleviate his own depression. The tools and techniques he offers are easy to follow, basic and practical, and non-confrontational.

Martin, T., & Doka, K. (2000). Men Don't Cry . . . Women Do: Transcending Gender Stereotypes Of Grief. Brunner/Mazel.
This text offers a refreshing change from the popular gender stereotypes of grief, emphasizing that there are many healthy ways to cope with grief. Two patterns of grieving are examined: an intuitive pattern where individuals experience and express grief in an affective way (stereotyped as female); and an instrumental pattern where grief is expressed physically or cognitively (stereotyped as male).

Mayo, P.E. (2001). The Healing Sorrow Workbook. New Harbinger Publications.
Peg Elliot Mayo, a Jungian psychotherapist and storyteller, offers emotional, physical, intellectual, and spiritual pathways out of sorrow and back into the pleasures of life. This is truly a 'work' book; it emphasizes the 'how' of recovery.

McMullin, R.E. (1986). Handbook Of Cognitive Therapy Techniques. W. W. Norton.
This book provides a systematic and comprehensive look at cognitive therapy techniques, providing many specific tools for the therapist.

Metrick, S.B. (1994). Crossing The Bridge. Celestial Arts.
This book guides the reader into creating rituals that can help in the grieving process, showing how to create rituals through intention, planning, preparation, manifestation, and incorporation. Sample rituals are presented as models.

Mitchell, K., & Anderson, H. (1983). All Our Losses, All Our Griefs: Resources For Pastoral Care. Westminster John Knox Press.
The authors explore the multiple dimensions of the problem of grief, including origins of grief, loss throughout life, dynamics of grief, care for those who grieve, and the theology of grieving. Coming from a Christian perspective, the authors show how grieving can be addressed through both personal counseling and public worship.

New American Standard Bible. (1973). Lockman Foundation.
Christian scripture.

Pema Chodron. (1991). The Wisdom Of No Escape. Shambhala.
Pema Chodron, an American Buddhist nun, talks about saying yes to life, about making friends with ourselves and our world, about accepting the delightful and painful situation of "no exit." She exhorts us to wake up wholeheartedly to everything and to use the abundant, richly textured fabric of

everyday life as our primary spiritual teacher and guide.

Pema Chodron. (1997). <u>When Things Fall Apart: Heart Advice For Difficult Times</u>. Shambhala.

The author teaches that there is only one approach to suffering that is of lasting benefit, and that approach involves moving 'toward' painful situations to the best of our ability with friendliness and curiosity, relaxing into the essential groundlessness of our entire situation. It is there, in the midst of chaos, that we discover the truth and love that are indestructible.

Ram Dass & Gorman, P. (1985). <u>How Can I Help?</u>. Alfred A. Knopf.

A good, basic counseling manual for the would-be helper, a manual that emphasizes patient-centeredness and the joy that comes from serving others.

Rando, T. (1991). <u>How To Go On Living When Someone You Love Dies</u>. Bantam Books.

Recognizing that there's no right way or wrong way to grieve, Therese Rando presents a compassionate and comprehensive guide on how we can discover our own personal way of traveling through the grieving process. Although the author comes from an academic setting and is thoroughly research-based, this book is intended for the general reader.

Remen, R.N. (1996). <u>Kitchen Table Wisdom</u>. Riverhead Books.

Rachel Naomi Remen shares 'stories that heal.' She talks about how we can help people heal, showing how true healing is a two-way street: we heal as we are healing. A good basic text for counseling skills.

Ring, K. (1998). <u>Lessons From The Light</u>. Insight Books.

This book examines the whole phenomenon of 'near-death experiences.' It is well-researched, presenting many references, stories, and resource suggestions.

Rosen, M.I. (1998). <u>Thank You For Being Such A Pain</u>. Three Rivers Press.

This book reveals gentle and compassionate guidance for understanding and healing relationships with difficult people: theory and tools.

Rosenberg, L. (2000). <u>Living In The Light Of Death</u>. Shambhala.

Larry Rosenberg shows us simple ways to wake up to our lives with chapters like 'Aging Is Unavoidable,' 'Illness Is Unavoidable,' and 'Death Is Unavoidable.'

Rosof, B.D. (1995). <u>The Worst Loss: How Families Heal From The Death Of A Child</u>. Henry Holt.

In this book a child psychologist combines anecdotal case histories and the latest research to help bereaved parents cope with the loss of a child.

Sanford, J.A. (1970). <u>The Kingdom Within</u>. Paulist Press.

John Sanford explores the inner meaning of the teachings of Jesus, offering guidance toward a more conscious, creative life.

Singh, K.D. (1998). <u>The Grace In Dying</u>. Harper Collins.
Kathleen Dowling Singh illuminates the profound psychological and spiritual transformations experienced by the dying as the natural process of death reconnects them with the source of their being. The book offers a fresh, deeply comforting message of hope and courage as we contemplate the meaning of our mortality.

Smith, D. (1994). <u>The Tao Of Dying</u>. Caring Publishing.
The book goes through each of the chapters of the Tao Te Ching, rephrasing it to apply to care of the dying, emphasizing the natural process of dying and our need to naturally accept it, emphasizing the importance of non-interference.

Smith, D. (1997). <u>Caregiving: Hospice-Proven Techniques For Healing Body And Soul</u>. Macmillan.
Included in this book are easy-to-follow techniques and practical tools for improving care: how to give people a sense of control and a sense of purpose. Suggestions are given for promoting spiritual growth, encouraging life review, facilitating touch, and honoring laughter, anger, sadness, and denial among the dying.

Smith, D. (1999). <u>Being A Wounded Healer: How To Heal Ourselves While We Are Healing Others</u>. Psycho-Spiritual Publications.
In this book Doug Smith presents a 'Spiritual Model of Care' to complement the 'Medical Model of Care.' The Medical Model wants to eliminate pain and suffering, the Spiritual Model wants to help people find meaning and value in the midst of pain and suffering. The book shows how we grow through our pain and suffering and how we can grow through the pain and suffering of others.

Smith, D., & Chapin, T. (2000). <u>Spiritual Healing</u>. Psycho-Spiritual Publications.
This is a handbook of activities, guided imagery, meditations, and prayers for exploring and enhancing our own spirituality and the spirituality of others. All the tools and techniques offered can be applied to people of diverse beliefs and values.

Sogyal Rinpoche. (1992). <u>The Tibetan Book Of Living And Dying</u>. Harper Collins.
Sogyal Rinpoche gives us practical instruction and spiritual guidance on how to live in light of the greatest of all teachers – death. He presents a lucid, inspiring, and complete introduction to the practice of meditation and to the trials and rewards of the spiritual path.

Starhawk. (1997). <u>The Pagan Book Of Living And Dying</u>. HarperCollins.
Beautifully crafted and deeply spiritual, this guidebook acknowledges the cycle of birth, growth, death, and rebirth as the underlying order of the universe. The book offers very practical tools, techniques, and rituals for those

experiencing loss and grief.

Staudacher, C. (1987). <u>Beyond Grief: A Guide For Recovering From The Death Of A Loved One</u>. New Harbinger.

A good basic text on grief recovery addressing in separate chapters loss of a spouse, loss of a parent, loss of a child, accidental death, suicide, and murder.

<u>Tanakh</u>. (1988). Jewish Publication Society.

Jewish scripture.

<u>Teaching Of Buddha, The</u>. (1966). Toppan Printing.

Buddhist scripture.

<u>Ten Principal Upanishads, The</u>. (1937). Shree Purohit Swami and W. B. Yeats (Trans.). Collier Books.

Hindu scripture.

Wegela, K.K. (1996). <u>How To Be A Help Instead Of A Nuisance</u>. Shambhala.

A promoter of 'contemplative psychotherapy,' Karen Wegela shows helpers how to exude 'maitri,' loving-kindness, tenderness and gentleness toward our own experience and the experience of others, whatever those experiences might be.

Westberg, G. (1986). <u>Good Grief: A Constructive Approach To The Problem Of Loss</u>. Fortress Press.

This short book describes what happens to us whenever we lose someone or something important, the small griefs and the larger grief experiences. It presents the stages of grief in an easily understood manner. A good book to give the average client or patient.

Wicks, R. (1986). <u>Availability: The Spiritual Joy Of Helping Others</u>. Crossroad Publishing.

The author shows how the Christian calling to serve is a calling requiring humility, self-knowledge, awareness of our own limitations, and a determination to carry on despite challenges.

Worden, J.W. (1991). <u>Grief Counseling & Grief Therapy: A Handbook For The Mental Health Practitioner</u>. Springer Publishing.

William Worden, a former professor of psychology at the Harvard Medical School, provides mental health professionals with a guide describing specific counseling principles and procedures that may be helpful in working with bereaved clients undergoing normal and abnormal grief reactions. This is a practical book centered around some sound, well-researched principles.

Yancey, P. (2001). <u>Where Is God When It Hurts?</u> Zondervan Publishing.

This is a good book to give people of the Christian faith. It shows how Christians, though mostly good-intentioned, often respond to other people's pain in very unhelpful ways. The book goes on to show how to best comfort someone in pain and suffering, especially someone of the Christian faith.

Zerah, A. (2001). As You Grieve: Consoling Words From Around The World. Sorin Books.

Aaron Zerah, a leading minister of the interfaith movement, brings together some of the most profound words written and spoken over the centuries from traditions as diverse as those of Native Americans, Africans, Buddhists, Moslems, Hindus, Jews, and Christians. Many of the passages are suitable as prayers or meditations for people of many faiths.

Doug Smith's Workshops

If you wish to have Doug do a workshop in your community or at your institution as an education event or a fund raising activity, please contact Doug directly: (608) 231-1541 or dougcsmith@juno.com.

Final Rights: Caring for People in the Final Phases of Life (3-6 hrs)

This workshop looks at the way we care for the needs of the dying, the "rights" of the dying. Topics covered: The Right To Be In Control, The Right To Have A Sense Of Purpose, The Right To Touch And Be Touched, The Right To Have Our Beliefs And Values Respected, The Right To Hear The Truth, The Right To Be In Denial, The Right To Reminisce, The Right To Laugh.

Putting The 'Care' Back Into Health Care (3-6 hrs)

This workshop follows the same format and subjects as the above workshop, but applies the principles to a more generic audience, exploring how we can use some of the things learned in hospice with all patients and clients: physical sicknesses of all types, emotional and psychological problems, addiction issues, mental retardation, etc.

Exploring and Enhancing Spirituality: How to Care for the Spiritual Needs of the Sick, Dying, and Bereaved (3-6 hrs)

This workshop looks at a "spiritual model of care" to complement the medical model. The medical model seeks to cure people of pain and suffering; the spiritual model seeks to help people find value in the midst of pain and suffering. This workshop looks at various tools and techniques for assessing and addressing spiritual needs. It also looks at several faith traditions and their attitudes towards sickness, dying, and grieving.

Different Ways Of Grieving, Different Ways Of Healing: Practical Counseling Tools And Techniques (3-6 hrs)

This workshop looks at the differences between "Intuitive Grievers" (feeling oriented people) and "Instrumental Grievers" (cognitive/action oriented people), examining gender differences and similarities. The emphasis in the workshop is clearly on practical tools and techniques for addressing the varied psycho-social and psycho-spiritual needs of people experiencing loss and grief.

Being A Wounded Healer (1-2 hrs)

This workshop presents the "spiritual model of care" that can complement the "medical model of care." The workshop centers around a model of care that helps us grow in the midst of our own pain and suffering as we are helping others grow in the midst of their pain and suffering. It has been given in various locations, including an international gathering of Alcoholics Anonymous.

Workshop Comments

"This needs to be mandatory for all health care workers." - Cherie Doolin, nurse, Indianapolis, IN.

"Beyond any doubt, this was the most inspiring workshop I have ever attended in over forty years as a professional nurse." - Marilyn Kopriva, nurse, Londonderry, NH.

"Doug's seminar offered greater depth and intensity of content than any seminar I've attended in thirty years of professional practice." - Phillip Dalton, social worker, San Antonio, TX.

"Not only was it helpful professionally, it also challenged me emotionally and spiritually. I have come away a better person and a better priest." - Douglas Freer, minister, Rahway, NJ.

"This is the ONLY seminar I've ever attended where 100% of my attention was on the speaker 100% of the time." - Jessie Wrinn, health care administrator, Greenville, SC.

The whole seminar: phenomenal! Doug is such a life-affirming speaker. He inspires, motivates, made me laugh — brought me a quiet joy! Made me question myself without guilt or blame. Yippee!" - Kathy Rindock, social worker, Allentown, PA.

"Doug not only walks the talk but challenges each person to do the same." - Sr. Anthony Marie Valdez, chaplain, Columbus, OH.

"I feel inspired, supported, energized, empowered and humbled by this day. Only seminar I've ever attended where I never looked at my watch." - Judith Ingram, psychologist, Minneapolis, MN.

"I have never been so moved. . . . This speaker is a master when it comes to touching hearts." - Eileen Wrzesniewski, nurse, Philadelphia, PA.

" I laughed. I cried. I learned." - Peggy Faye Benson, nurse, Hagerstown, MD.

"Can't say enough." - Natalie Lloyd, nurse, San Francisco, CA.

Ordering Doug Smith's Books

THE TAO OF DYING Caring Publishing (1997) IBSN 0-962836-39-7
    This book contains a group of meditations for caregivers of the dying. The meditations are accompanied by photographs by Marilu Pittman. This book is out of print. It can, however, be found in many book stores and ordered through the Internet.

CAREGIVING Macmillan Publishing (1997) ISBN 0-02-861663-4
    This book contains a collection of tools and techniques centered around addressing the rights of the terminally ill (the right to be in control, the right to have a sense of purpose, the right to laugh, etc.). The book also has many stories. It can be ordered through bookstores, on the Internet, or directly through the author (see below).

BEING A WOUNDED HEALER Psycho-Spiritual Publications (1999) ISBN 0-9672870-0-6
    This book is about the author's struggles with several wounds in his life (death of his daughter, being a patient in a mental hospital, losing his priesthood, etc.). The book presents a "spiritual model" of care to complement the "medical model." The medical model seeks to eliminate wounds; the spiritual model seeks to find meaning and value in the midst of wounds. This book can be ordered through www.amazon.com or directly through the author.

SPIRITUAL HEALING Psycho-Spiritual Publications (2000) ISBN 0-9672870-1-4
    This book is a handbook of activities, guided imagery, meditations, and prayers for exploring and enhancing spirituality. The material (addressing the needs of the sick, dying, grieving, and general public) is designed to be used by people of any spiritual or religious tradition. This book can be ordered through www.amazon.com or directly through the author.

THE COMPLETE BOOK OF COUNSELING THE DYING AND THE GRIEVING Psycho-Spiritual Publications (2003) ISBN 0-9672870-3-0
    This book has all the tools, techniques, patient stories, and quotations from the author's various workshops: close to 300 8½ x 11 pages of helpful material. The book can be easily used as a training manual for professional caregivers as well as volunteers, a textbook, and a valuable resource manual.

BOOKS CAN BE ORDERED DIRECTLY THROUGH DOUG SMITH

CAREGIVING $15
BEING A WOUNDED HEALER $20
SPIRITUAL HEALING $20
THE COMPLETE BOOK OF COUNSELING $40

Make check payable to "Doug Smith." Add $1.50 per book for shipping and handling. All books sent via "Priority Mail" within 3 days after receiving payment. Send check to:

Doug Smith
601 N. Segoe Rd. #305
Madison, WI
53705